"Oakman brokers for us many conversations. He hears and responds to the conversations of his professional peers, who are often monochromatic in focus: only agriculture, numismatics, pottery, taxes, etc. Taking them honorably into account, he advances the conversation by drawing their data together by means of overarching social science models, thus making their data say much more. . . . Oakman never fails to engage my settled opinions with fresh data and unavoidable invitations to think again, to fill out the picture, and to take seriously scholarship speaking a different language. But Oakman is a gracious, enlightened, fair, trustworthy, and competent conversational partner, well worthy of our close reading. For traditional scholarship, this opens a new dimension."

— JEROME H. NEYREY, SJ, Professor Emeritus of New Testament Studies, University of Notre Dame

"Doug Oakman is highly respected for his social-science studies of Jesus as a radical critic with a vision of economic justice. With this book, Oakman takes his studies of Jesus from the historical past to the political present. A strong critic of parochial and literalist Bible readings, Oakman engages in a fruitful dialogue with contemporary philosophy and politics to make the Bible speak to the essentially human in today's world."

— HALVOR MOXNES, Professor Emeritus in Theology, University of Oslo

"*The Radical Jesus* distills the profound wisdom of Doug Oakman's career-long engagement with the Bible, the Jesus tradition in particular. It integrates his unique grasp of the material, especially economic, dimensions of the biblical context, his penetrating social-scientific insights, his meticulous engagement with textual detail, and the overall framework of Lutheran Christianity that he embodies to an exemplary degree. For understanding what Jesus meant and what he still means, this book merits our closest attention."

— PHILIP F. ESLER, Portland Chair in New Testament Studies, University of Gloucestershire

"A powerful demonstration of why the estrangement of the Bible and its world from modern America cannot be overcome by unconsciously reading ourselves into its pages . . . or by removing it from the real world of the struggling 95 percent in its own time whose voices are never heard."

— RICHARD L. ROHRBAUGH, Paul S. Wright Professor of Religious Studies Emeritus, Lewis & Clark College, Portland. Oregon

"For more than three decades Douglas Oakman has taught us how to read the Bible using the social sciences as our guide. Always creative and sometimes provocative, this current collection continues in that endeavor. Both the academic guild and the faith communities need to hear this voice."
—David A. Fiensy, author of *The Archaeology of Daily Life: Ordinary Persons in Late Second Temple Israel*

"Oakman's sharp analysis of Jesus and Paul's views on the economic issues of their days is a breath of fresh air in a world dominated by greed and profit. This book will show believers and non-believers alike that there is a more humane way to manage the economy."
—Santiago Guijarro, Theology Faculty Member, Pontifical University of Salamanca, Spain

"Douglas E. Oakman's decades-long research on Jesus traditions in their original Galilean social, economic, and political setting comes to mature expression in this engaging collection of essays. The essays represent rigorous historically oriented social-scientific study combined with perceptive discussion of the present relevance of biblical traditions. The author's interest in the meaning of Scriptures is rooted in his Lutheran background but grows to break all doctrinal and confessional boundaries by challenging readers, regardless of their confession or lack of it, to ponder 'what does it mean' to take seriously the economic implications of biblical traditions and especially of the original message of Jesus."
—Petri Luomanen, Professor of New Testament and Early Christian Culture and Literature, University of Helsinki

"No one better articulates the economic and cultural impact of the Roman imperium on ancient Palestine, and no one makes a stronger case for understanding Jesus's message as a response to it. As he has done in the past, Oakman once again displays mastery of both interpretive theory and the literary and material records of first-century Palestine. He also shows the contemporary relevance of Jesus's message in the building of a more just and humane world."
—Richard E. DeMaris, Senior Research Professor, Valparaiso University

"This is an essential guide for anyone who is interested in the politics of the historical Jesus and wonders how to adapt the biblical message to times of great inequality and strife. The clarity of his sociological method and critical attention to textual and archaeological detail encourage readers to pursue their own questions and discover for themselves what the Bible and Christian tradition, including Paul and others, might mean for us today."

— GILDAS HAMEL, Senior Lecturer Emeritus in History, University of California, Santa Cruz

"This important new collection of articles from Doug Oakman makes accessible his provocative and stimulating insights into Jesus's aims and how Jesus's kingdom message was appropriated subsequently. For some it may come as a shock. The first-century challenge to social, economic, and political life presented by Jesus of Nazareth is set out sharply and with scholarly skill. The implications for modern values that Oakman draws may well prove unsettling rather than comforting!"

— RONALD A. PIPER, Professor Emeritus of Christian Origins, University of St Andrews

"This book is strongly commended. *The Radical Jesus* is an appeal for transformation in the past and present, densely and clearly articulated. It is a book about a call for a 'new kind of leadership.' It is about Jesus, killed by imperial power long before his crucifixion. Nowhere else have I learned more in such a condensed way than in this book about the economic and political context of Jesus . . . Douglas Oakman records Jesus's transformative ethos of radical grace, words 'that might still be taken seriously.'"

— ANDRIES VAN AARDE, Emeritus Professor, University of Pretoria

"*The Radical Jesus*, a follow-up to *Jesus and the Peasants*, again showcases the immense contribution Oakman has made to understand the social meanings of the historical Jesus in his Galilean context. Topics such as Galilee as an advanced agrarian society, Jesus and politics, peasant values, debt and taxes in Roman Palestine, the ancient political economy in the time of Jesus, and many more, have become synonymous to the work and legacy of Oakman. *The Radical Jesus* yet again provides essential information to understand the world of Jesus, but also addresses the question whether Christianity and the Bible has something to say to a society embedded within a market capitalist economy that is detrimental to social relations and is driven by greed. *The Radical Jesus*, yet again, is Oakman at his best."

— ERNEST VAN ECK, Head of Department of New Testament and Related Literature, University of Pretoria

The Radical Jesus, the Bible,
and the Great Transformation

MATRIX
The Bible in Mediterranean Context

PREVIOUSLY PUBLISHED VOLUMES

Richard L. Rohrbaugh
The New Testament and Social-Science Criticism

Markus Cromhout
Jesus and Identity

Pieter F. Craffert
The Life of a Galilean Shaman

Douglas E. Oakman
Jesus and the Peasants

Stuart L. Love
Jesus and the Marginal Women

Eric C. Stewart
Gathered around Jesus

Dennis C. Duling
A Marginal Scribe

Jason T. Lamoreaux
Ritual, Women, and Philippi

Ernst Van Eck
Parables of Jesus the Galilean

John J. Pilch and Bruce J. Malina, eds.
Handbook of Biblical Social Values, 3rd ed.

K. C. Richardson
Early Christian Care for the Poor

The Radical Jesus, the Bible, and the Great Transformation

DOUGLAS E. OAKMAN

CASCADE *Books* · Eugene, Oregon

THE RADICAL JESUS, THE BIBLE, AND THE GREAT TRANSFORMATION
Matrix: The Bible in Mediterranean Context 12

Cascade Books
An Imprint of Wipf and Stock Publishers
199 W. 8th Ave., Suite 3
Eugene, OR 97401

www.wipfandstock.com

PAPERBACK ISBN: 978-1-7252-8664-1
HARDCOVER ISBN: 978-1-7252-8665-8
EBOOK ISBN: 978-1-7252-8666-5

Cataloguing-in-Publication data:

Names: Oakman, Douglas E., author.
Title: The radical Jesus, the Bible, and the great transformation / Douglas E. Oakman.
Description: Eugene, OR: Cascade Books, 2021. | Matrix: The Bible in Mediterranean Context 12. | Includes bibliographical references and indexes.
Identifiers: ISBN: 978-1-7252-8664-1 (paperback). | ISBN: 978-1-7252-8665-8 (hardcover). | ISBN: 978-1-7252-8666-5 (ebook).
Subjects: LCSH: Jesus Christ. | Gospels. | Paul. | Hermeneutics. | Social scientific criticism. | Galilee.
Classification: BS2417.E3 O3444 2021 (print). | BS2417 (ebook).

Manufactured in the U.S.A.   JANUARY 15, 2021

Dedicated with deep gratitude
to John H. Elliott (1935–2020)
and
K. C. Hanson
encouraging *Gesprächspartnern* over many years

And with profound indebtedness to
Karl Polanyi, pioneer in the study
both of the ancient substantivist economy
and the Great Transformation

Contents

CONTENTS

Tables and Figures

Acknowledgments

The following essays are reprinted with permission of the respective original publishers.

Chapter 1: "The Radical Jesus: You Cannot Serve God and Mammon." *BTB* 34 (2004) 122–29.

Chapter 2: "The Biblical World of Limited Good in Social, Cultural, and Technological Perspective." *BTB* 48 (2018) 97–105.

Chapter 3: "Debate: Was the Galilean Economy Oppressive or Prosperous? A. Late Second Temple Galilee: Socio-Archaeology and Dimensions of Exploitation in First-Century Palestine." In *Galilee in the Late Second Temple and Mishnaic Periods*, Vol. 1, *Life, Culture, and Society*, edited by David A. Fiensy and James Riley Strange, 346–56. Minneapolis: Fortress, 2014.

Chapter 4: "Execrating? or Execrable Peasants!" In *The Galilean Economy in the Time of Jesus*, edited by David A. Fiensy and Ralph K. Hawkins, 139–64. Early Christianity and Its Literature 11. Atlanta: Society of Biblical Literature, 2013.

Chapter 5: "The Galilean World of Jesus." In *The Early Christian World*, edited by Philip F. Esler, 97–120. London: Routledge, 2017.

Chapter 7: "Culture, Society, and Embedded Religion in Antiquity." *BTB* 35 (2005) 4–12.

Chapter 8: "Biblical Economics in an Age of Greed." In *Market and Margins: Lutheran Perspectives*, edited by Wanda Deifelt, 82–97. Minneapolis: Lutheran University Press, 2014.

Chapter 9: "Biblical Hermeneutics: Marcion's Truth and a Developmental Perspective." In *Ancient Israel: The Old Testament in its Social Context*, edited by Philip F. Esler, 267–82. Minneapolis: Fortress, 2006.

Chapter 10: "The Perennial Relevance of St. Paul." *BTB* 39 (2009) 4–14.

Chapter 11: "The Promise of Lutheran Biblical Studies." *Currents in Theology and Mission* 31 (2004) 40–52.

Abbreviations

/	A virgule between synoptic passages indicates close parallel material
AB	Anchor Bible
ABD	*Anchor Bible Dictionary*. 6 vols. Edited by David Noel Freedman. New York: Doubleday, 1992
'Aboth	*'Aboth* (tractate in Mishnah or Talmud)
Ag. Ap.	Josephus, *Against Apion*
ANRW	*Aufstieg und Niedergang der römischen Welt*
Ant.	Josephus, *Antiquities of the Judeans*
ASOR	American Schools of Oriental Research
b.	Babylonian Talmud (*Babli*)
b.	*ben* ("son of") in Hebrew names
BA	*The Biblical Archaeologist*
BASOR	*Bulletin of the American Schools of Oriental Research*
BAR	*Biblical Archaeology Review*
BDAG	Walter Bauer, Frederick W. Danker, William F. Arndt, and F. Wilbur Gingrich, *A Greek-English Lexicon of the New Testament and Other Early Christian Literature*, 3rd ed. Chicago: University of Chicago Press, 2000
BDB	Francis Brown, S. R. Driver, and Charles A. Briggs, *A Hebrew and English Lexicon of the Old Testament*.

	1906. Reprint with corrections, Oxford: Clarendon, 1957
B. Bathra	*Baba Bathra* (tractate in Mishnah or Talmud)
B. Meṣ.	*Baba Meṣiʿa* (tractate in Mishnah or Talmud)
BETL	Bibliotheca Ephimeridum Theologicarum Lovaniensum
BTB	*Biblical Theology Bulletin*
cf.	confer, compare
CBQ	*Catholic Biblical Quarterly*
CD	Damascus Rule, Dead Sea Scrolls
DJD	Discoveries in the Judaean Desert
Eccl. Hist.	Eusebius, *Ecclesiastical History*
f., ff.	following page, following pages
Giṭ.	*Giṭṭin* (tractate in Mishnah or Talmud)
Gos. Thom.	Gospel of Thomas
Ha	one hectare = 2.47 acres
HTR	*Harvard Theological Review*
HTS	*Hervormde Teologiese Studies*
IDB	*Interpreter's Dictionary of the Bible.* 4 vols. Edited by George Arthur Buttrick. Nashville: Abingdon, 1962
IEJ	*Israel Exploration Journal*
INJ	*Israel Numismatic Journal*
JAAR	*Journal of the American Academy of Religion*
JBL	*Journal of Biblical Literature*
JJS	*Journal of Jewish Studies*
JPS	*Journal of Peasant Studies*
JRA	*Journal of Roman Archaeology*
JRS	*Journal of Roman Studies*
JSJ	*Journal for the Study of Judaism*

JSNT	*Journal for the Study of the New Testament*
L	the unique or special material in the Gospel of Luke
LCL	Loeb Classical Library
Life	Josephus, *The Life*
M	the unique or special material in the Gospel of Matthew
m.	Mishnah
n., nn.	note, notes
NIDB	*New Interpreter's Dictionary of the Bible*. 6 vols. Edited by Katheryn Doob Sakenfeld. Nashville: Abingdon, 2006–2009
NovTSup	Novum Testamentum Supplements
NRSV	New Revised Standard Version of the English Bible
OCD	*Oxford Classical Dictionary*. 3rd ed. Edited by Simon Hornblower and Antony Spawforth. Oxford: Oxford University Press, 2003
OED	*Oxford English Dictionary*
OTP	*The Old Testament Pseudepigrapha*. 2 vols. Edited by James H. Charlesworth. Garden City, NY: Doubleday, 1983, 1985
par.	parallel(s)
Pe'ah	*Pe'ah* (tractate in Mishnah or Talmud)
Pesaḥim	*Pesaḥim* (tractate in Mishnah or Talmud)
PFES	Publications of the Finnish Exegetical Society
PEQ	*Palestine Exploration Quarterly*
Q	the earliest collection of Jesus' sayings, the Sayings Gospel. This source lies behind the double tradition in Matthew and Luke, but apparently was not known to Mark. For a brief description of Q's contents, see Kloppenborg, *Q, The Earliest Gospel*, 41–45, 50–51; for a more detailed review of Q's stratification assumed in this book (earlier Q1 wisdom, later Q2

	deuteronomic materials), Kloppenborg [Verbin], *Excavating Q*, 143–53
qtd.	quoted
RB	*Revue biblique*
RSV	Revised Standard Version of the English Bible
SBL	Society of Biblical Literature
SBLSP	*SBL Seminar Papers*
SEHHW	Michael Rostovtzeff, *Social and Economic History of the Hellenistic World.* 3 vols. Oxford: Clarendon, 1941
SEHRE	Michael Rostovtzeff, *Social and Economic History of the Roman Empire.* 2 vols. 2nd ed. Oxford: Clarendon, 1957
Sheb.	*Shebi'it* (tractate in Mishnah or Talmud)
Sheqal.	*Sheqalim* (tractate in Mishnah or Talmud)
SNTSMS	Society of New Testament Studies Monograph Series
Spec. Laws	Philo, *On the Special Laws*
t.	Tosefta
TJT	*Toronto Journal of Theology*
TDNT	*Theological Dictionary of the New Testament.* Edited by Gerhard Kittel and Gerhard . Translated by Geoffrey W. Bromiley. Grand Rapids: Eerdmans, 1964–1976
v., vv.	verse, verses
War	Josephus, *Jewish War*
WUNT	Wissenschaftliche Untersuchungen zum Neuen Testament
y.	Jerusalem Talmud (*Yerushalmi*)
ZNW	*Zeitschrift für die neutestamentliche Wissenschaft und die Kunde der älteren Kirche*

Prologue

The Radical Jesus, the Bible, and the Great Transformation

"Without . . . theory, it is impossible to know what to look for . . . the relevance of evidence depends upon the theory which is dominating the discussion." —Alfred North Whitehead[1]

[*The Livelihood of Man*] is an economic historian's contribution to world affairs in a period of perilous transformation. Its aim is simple: to enlarge our freedom of creative adjustment, and thereby improve our chances of survival. —Karl Polanyi[2]

THE PRESENT COLLECTION OF essays represents something of an interdependent companion to my *Jesus and the Peasants* (2008). The contents of this volume focus more persistently than did that previous collection upon the perduring social meanings of the historical Jesus and the Bible. The eleven chapters as a consequence do not present the original articles in chronological order but divide them into two major parts, largely along thematic lines. Part One focuses on the radical Jesus and ancient political economy. Part Two aims to tie historical and sociological investigations of Jesus, Paul, and the Bible to issues raised by Polanyi's *Great Transformation*. These essays gather my efforts to answer this central question: What do those meanings continue to mean in the twenty-first century? The hermeneutical task is brought centrally to the fore.[3]

1. LeClerc, *Whitehead's Metaphysics*, 45.
2. Polanyi, *The Livelihood of Man*, xliii.
3. Given the sixteen-year time span of the original articles, there are bound to be some inconsistencies and noticeable modifications of opinion. Cross references identify some

While I am a lifelong Lutheran Christian—and am especially cogni-
zant that a quintessential, perhaps the quintessential Lutheran question is,
What does this mean?—these essays require no particular religious faith or
conviction. Perhaps the ideal reader will be an imaginative person vitally
alive to questions of real-life importance raised by the study of social history. The two central New Testament figures Jesus and Paul are understood
here as figures of world importance, not just confessional points of identity,
and arguably as influential in the world as few have been. Likewise, the
Bible remains a potent force in contemporary cultural life worldwide, both
for good and for ill. If at some points in this book I make particular connections to the Christian tradition or to the peculiar context of the United
States, they are not exclusively the goal, nor are these connections meant to
serve a doctrinal orthodoxy. However, they are very much in the interest
of asking how Christianity and the Bible will continue to speak in a world
after the Great Transformation.

Karl Polanyi's famous post-World War II book *The Great Transformation* (1944) attempted to understand how preindustrial societies had organized life, and especially economic life, and comparatively how society
had changed radically after the Industrial Revolution and the advent of
modern capitalism. Karl Polanyi came from a Hungarian Jewish family;
worked during the interwar period as a journalist writing about economic
affairs for *Der Österreichische Volkswirt*; penned essays about Christian
socialism and witnessed the rise of fascism and National Socialism; and
then, after leaving behind Europe, assumed a professorship at Columbia
University in the United States. Throughout his professional life, Polanyi
wrote searching and critical essays about the social changes that had come
about in modern societies embedded in capitalism. He argued persuasively
that in the preindustrial ages economy was embedded in social relations
and served necessary social purposes, while after the Great Transformation
society became embedded within market capitalist economy to the detriment of social relations. His work influenced and inspired many areas of
academic endeavor, from the work of ancient historians to the researches
of comparative anthropology. His notion of a substantive economy directed

---

repetitions in treatment. Some points are given greater substantiation or subsequently
dropped. Where appropriate, original references have been updated and/or changed to
accord with chapters in *Jesus and the Peasants*. Some of this volume's material has also
been previously incorporated in various ways into my *The Political Aims of Jesus* (2012)
and *Jesus, Debt, and the Lord's Prayer* (2014). Biblical quotations in this book may be
from the RSV, NRSV, or in places my own translations.

toward human need was greatly contested by formalists who insisted that economies had always worked through impersonal laws, rational self-interest, and exchange markets. After his death, Polanyi's daughter, Prof. Kari Polanyi Levitt, along with Prof. Marguerite Mendel, established an institute in Montréal, Canada, at Concordia University that is still vitally alive to continue Karl Polanyi's work and influence.[4]

Readers will perceive in this volume, then, Polanyi's many influences on me as well as my kindred spirit. In Jesus' aphorism "You cannot serve God and Mammon," properly understood, can be found Jesus' shrewd critique of self-service versus other-service. Both Jesus and Polanyi sought a society, a community in which human need was met rather than frustrated, a social order that did not allow selfish Mammon-worship to aggrandize the life-security of some at the expense of the many. Indeed, Jesus' "Mammon-critique," if we can call it that, resounds in a new age when power and wealth are so woefully maldistributed as they are today.

I have had many excellent teachers and conversational partners in biblical studies over many years. Perhaps two of the most important in terms the social study of the Bible have been Drs. John H. Elliott and K. C. Hanson. Personal interactions with both began in the 1980s and continue to this day. Professor Elliott, a member of my doctoral committee, encouraged me to engage social theoretical work—both sociological and anthropological—as an essential tool for the social-scientific study of the Bible. When he assumed leadership of the Context Group in the late 1980s, I continued my collaborations with him for over thirty years. His book *What Is Social-Scientific Criticism?* (1993) is a classic in this academic endeavor. I have also been supported and encouraged throughout my career since graduate study by Drs. Herman Waetjen, Marvin Chaney, the late Robert N. Bellah, and the Rev. Dr. Edward A. Wilson.

In 1988 I had the pleasure of meeting K. C. Hanson at the Catholic Biblical Association annual meeting in Notre Dame, Indiana. A conversation ensued that issued ten years later in publication of *Palestine in the Time of Jesus: Social Structures and Social Conflicts*. We continued our long association especially at meetings of the Context Group, and we have often exchanged ideas on other occasions. It was due to Dr. Hanson's influence that I went on to publish the collected essay volume *Jesus and the Peasants*;

---

4. The Karl Polanyi Institute of Political Economy, https://www.concordia.ca/research/polanyi.html; on Polanyi's importance and achievement, see also Humphreys, "History, Economics, and Anthropology"; McRobbie, *Humanity, Society and Commitment.*

The Political Aims of Jesus; Jesus, Debt, and the Lord's Prayer; and now this collection, *The Radical Jesus, the Bible, and the Great Transformation.* To all my teachers and conversation partners, and especially to Drs. John H. Elliott and K. C. Hanson, I dedicate this volume.[5] It is further my hope that it will continue to inspire the hope and cause of that great social saint, Karl Polanyi.

5. The Rev. Dr. John H. Elliott died on December 13, 2020, as this book was in the final stages of production. *Lux aeterna luceat ei.* For further testimony to Elliott's significant influence within the field of biblical studies, see the Festschrift edited by Stephen K. Black, *To Set at Liberty: Essays on Early Christianity and Its Social World in Honor of John H. Elliott* (Sheffield: Sheffield Phoenix, 2014).

PART ONE

The Radical Jesus, Political Economy, and the Great Transformation

CHAPTER 1

The Radical Jesus

You Cannot Serve God and Mammon

A VERY COMMON INTEREST among U.S. Christians today [2004], espe-cially in the multitudinous "Bible churches," is the guidance offered by Scripture and in particular the biblical example of Jesus Christ. Indeed, the Bible might seem more important in American culture today than the Constitution of the United States. Under such impulses a few years ago, people began wearing bracelets inscribed with the letters WWJD, which stand, as most readers probably know, for "What Would Jesus Do?"[1]

A number of presuppositions are wrapped up with any answers to such a question—for instance, without in any sense attempting to be com-prehensive, the presuppositions that the gospel material recounting Jesus' example or words stems by and large from Jesus himself, or that Jesus' ex-ample or words should somehow be directly relevant to our situation with-out further investigation, or that nothing between Jesus and us has shaped Christian sensibilities and ethics.

All of these deserve more thorough exploration than can be given here. Suffice it for now to say that even scholars have (perhaps more sophis-ticated) versions of this interest and these presuppositions. I need only cite three instances: In 1953, Ernst Käsemann launched the Second Scholarly Quest of the Historical Jesus with his well-stated repudiation of teacher Rudolf Bultmann's position that Jesus was simply the presupposition of

---

1. This chapter was originally delivered in 2003 as a lecture at Pacific Lutheran Uni-versity, Tacoma, Washington, and then in 2004 as an Edgar Goodspeed Lecture at Deni-son University, Granville, Ohio. For more information on this lectureship, see chapter 10 in this volume.

New Testament theology. Käsemann argued that Christianity would be reduced merely to an ideology if there were no critical principle of its meaning in Jesus; conversely, the Second Quest attempted to show the points of continuity especially between Jesus' proclamation and the *kerygma* or proclamation of the early Christian movement. More recently, in 1972, John Howard Yoder's fine study *The Politics of Jesus* assumed that Jesus had a politics and that it is important for Christian reflection on political life. Yoder's treatment, however, lacked refinements of scholarly study of the gospels so that his Jesus turned out essentially to be that of the Gospel of Luke. Finally, the strenuous efforts of the so-called Third Quest for the Historical Jesus, on-going since 1980 and caught between the horns of the dilemma of a socially irrelevant apocalyptic or cynic Jesus and a socially relevant politically-engaged figure, shows the persistence of concern with the Man at the Root of the Christian Tradition, the Radical Jesus.[2]

The portrait of a socially irrelevant Jesus is to some extent the editorial product, based in scriptural and theological interpretation, of the scribes of the first-century Jesus traditions. Critical sifting of the earliest traditions, closer to the Galilean soil, shows that at the core of the concern of Jesus of Nazareth was a politically charged critique of Mammon, carried on under the proclamation of God's ruling power. Let us proceed, then, by way of a careful investigation of the Jesus-saying preserved in the Q tradition, "You cannot serve God and Mammon" (Q 16:13).[3]

Luke's Moralistic Treatment of the Saying

Some years ago, I wrote an essay attempting to "locate" the ideology of Luke, the writer of the Third Gospel of the New Testament, and concluding that he had transformed the social register of Jesus' original message:

> What was originally a radical social critique by Jesus and his followers of the violent and oppressive political-economic order in

2. Herzog, *Jesus, Justice, and the Reign of God*, 23–33.

3. Robinson, Hoffmann, and Kloppenborg, *The Sayings Gospel Q*, 9. Q refers to the collection of Jesus' words in the Sayings Gospel, the earliest material about Jesus that we possess (around 50 CE). This source lies behind the double tradition in Matthew and Luke, but apparently was not known to Mark. For a brief description of Q's contents, see Kloppenborg, *Q, The Earliest Gospel*, 41–45, 50–51; for a more detailed review of Q's stratification assumed in this book (earlier Q1 wisdom, later Q2 deuteronomic materials), Kloppenborg, *Excavating Q*, 143–53. Q passages are cited today by their location in Luke, and that convention will be followed throughout this book.

the countryside under the early empire becomes in Luke's conception a rather innocuous sharing-ethic ambiguous in its import for rural dwellers . . . For Jesus, the kingdom of God was world reconstruction, especially beneficial for a rural populace oppressed by debt and without secure subsistence. For Luke, political expediency demands that the world restructuring be limited to alleviating the harshest aspects of political economy within the local Christian community by benefaction and generalized reciprocity.[4]

This assessment involves the judgment that Luke's gospel represented an "elite-directed moralism." It is likely that Luke–Acts is one of the first in a line of apologetic works for the early Christian movement. Luke dedicates his two volumes to Theophilus, perhaps an elite city councillor somewhere in the late first- or early second-century Roman Empire. Luke–Acts has the general theme that the Jesus movement represents no threat to the Roman order. Luke's propaganda can be styled "moralistic" because Luke glosses over the harsher aspects of Roman relations and expresses a message of heartfelt concern for the poor, which at bottom is an appeal to noblesse oblige.

Luke presents several sayings of Jesus about Mammon in Luke 16, immediately following the parable of the Unjust Steward. The context has long been seen to be an artificial literary construction, since the unjust steward parable, which appears only in Luke, is followed by a series of appended applications that do not belong to the parable proper.[5] Included here is the statement of Jesus to "make friends by means of the Mammon of Injustice." These application statements in turn are followed by the sayings about faithful stewardship and the impossibility of serving two masters or God and Mammon. The sayings about two masters and Mammon are found in identical order in Q (as can be seen from Matt 6:24). From Gos. Thom. 47, however, the saying about two masters had another trajectory in the tradition where it was paired differently with sayings about the impossibility of riding two horses or stretching two bows.

---

4. Oakman, "'All the Surrounding Country,'" 161–62.

5. Jeremias, *Parables*, 46–47.

The Meaning of Mammon

Appreciation of Luke's moralistic applications and this brief tradition analysis give us license to inquire as to the meaning of these statements for Jesus himself, especially the Q-word "You cannot serve God and Mammon."

The term "Mammon" calls for a word study that elicits some fascinating results, of which we can only give the outlines here. The word appears four times in the New Testament, and only in connection with sayings of Jesus: Luke 16:9, Luke 16:11, and of course Q 16:13/Matt 6:24. Though the earliest collection of Jesus' sayings we can reach historically—the Q sayings—are already in Greek, Jesus' mother tongue was Aramaic, the language of the first-century Palestinian village. This shows in numerous places in the early Jesus traditions, for instance, in the Aramaic address to God as 'Abba' ("Father"; Mark 14:36; Rom 8:15; Gal 4:6; Aramaic probably stands behind the Greek of Q 11:2) or nicknames like Cephas ("Rock," as Jesus called Simon) or Semitic idioms such as "son of man" or phrases like *talitha koum* (a Greek transliteration of Aramaic: "little girl, arise," Mark 5:41).[6]

The word Mammon likewise is Semitic. Though the noun *mmōn* does not appear in the Hebrew Bible, it emerges in later Hebrew and Aramaic. "Mammon of injustice"—translated "Mammon of Unrighteousness" in the Authorized and American Standard Versions, "unrighteous Mammon" in the Revised Standard Version, and "dishonest wealth" in the New Revised Standard Version—becomes a stock expression *mmōn dšqr* in the targumic and rabbinic traditions after 70 CE, where Mammon has the standard meaning of wealth, money, or property.[7] The strict either–or choice between God and Mammon in Q 16:13, however, is probably closer to the authentic speech of Jesus in the 20s CE. Mammon is set in stark contrast to "God," without the suggestion at all that there could be a "Mammon of Justice," an acceptable and legitimate Mammon or *mmōn šl 'mth*, as allowed in later targumic and rabbinic traditions.[8]

Without more detailed first-century evidence, etymological considerations are indispensable for apprehending Jesus' meaning. Old Latin translations of the Gospels confused etymological discussion by doubling the middle *m*; this spelling carried over into late Greek manuscripts, early

---

6. Brown, "Jesus' Aramaic," 203–73.

7. BDAG, 614; Black, *Aramaic Approach*, 139.

8. Hauck, "*Mamōnas*," 389.

Protestant translations of the Bible, and modern English. However, the best Greek manuscripts have a single *m*, with the accent on the last syllable of the word, *mamōnas*. This suggests that the Greek transliterates the Aramaic word *mmōn'* in the emphatic state, that is, *The* Mammon.[9] Four roots come into discussion: 1) *mnh* or *mōn*: "to count or apportion"; 2) *hmh* "to roar," hence in noun form, "to represent a crowd or metaphorically abundance"; 3) *ṭmn*, "to conceal, lay up," and 4) *'mn* to confirm, support, or trust. The play on words in Luke 16:11 (faithless with unrighteous mammon, entrusted with righteous mammon) gives a very powerful indication that Jesus' intention and meaning was closest to root 4—*'mn*, to trust.[10] From *'mn*, we get the familiar English transliteration Amen, truly. What is trustworthy is true; what is untrustworthy is false. This attitude comes from an ancient culture where epistemology is rooted in social relations and strong-group perceptions.[11] The meaning of Mammon is bound up with trust and true and false social perceptions of reality.

But what is it that is falsely trusted in the usage of Jesus? The linguistic evidence points to Mammon as signifying wealth collected in the bank or the storehouse or the treasury, wealth that then becomes the object of trust for the powerful-wealthy to the exclusion of God and neighbor. More importantly, Mammon is based in a system that exploits the many for the benefit of the few. To serve Mammon is to be alone in one's self-sufficiency; to serve God is to have concern for others and to practice reciprocity. To trace the further meaning of Jesus' critique of Mammon, we need to investigate and see more clearly his central interests in context.

Jesus' Critique of Mammon

At the time of Jesus' historical activity (late 20s CE), Galilee had stood under Roman provincial arrangements for nearly a century (beginning with Pompey in 63 BCE). Herod the Great wrested the area from bandits and Hasmoneans, and managed to have the Roman Senate declare him king of the Judeans (37–4 BCE). At his death, when Jesus was a small child in Nazareth, a Galilean insurrection resulted in the intervention of the Syrian legate Varus and the destruction of Sepphoris just down the road from Nazareth. Herod Antipas, the son of Herod the Great, subsequently rebuilt

9. Hauck "*Mamōnas*," 388; Nestle, "Mammon," 2913.

10. Nestle, "Mammon," 2914.

11. Malina, *New Testament World* (2001), 58–79.

Sepphoris, making it according to Josephus into the "ornament of all Galilee" (Josephus, *Ant.* 18.27). Families of builders such as the family of Joseph and Jesus perhaps even participated in this work. Around 20 CE, Herod Antipas began construction of his other major Galilean city, Tiberias by the Galilean lake. He did this, I believe, to secure greater control over the tax revenues from fishing.[12] Perhaps Jesus participated in this building work as well; but not long thereafter, Jesus appeared at Capernaum on the north end of the Lake delivering his message about the kingdom of God.

It is increasingly persuasive, based on historical evidence and comparative social science, that Jesus' message held social significance. Exorbitant taxation and debt seems to have been a central concern, as is often the case among peasants.[13] Agrarian tax systems, which have no formal checks and balances to protect the village cultivator, are typically oppressive. Early Roman imperial taxes were fixed and levied in imperial silver. These were exacted from an agricultural base, hence had to be "converted" from agricultural produce into money. Fixed or invariable taxes showed no respect for natural variance in product. When villagers were unable to pay, tax debts were tabulated in written records kept in royal and imperial archives. James C. Scott's comparative political studies of peasantry offer us helpful perspectives on the general issue. For instance, Scott writes in his book *Domination and the Arts of Resistance*:

> in the region in which I have conducted fieldwork [farmers] have resented paying the official Islamic tithe. It is collected inequitably and corruptly, the proceeds are sent to the provincial capital, and not a single poor person in the village has even received any charity back from the religious authorities. Quietly and massively, the Malay peasantry has managed to nearly dismantle the tithe system so that only 15 percent of what is formally due is actually paid. There have been no tithe riots, demonstrations, protests, only a patient and effective nibbling in a multitude of ways: fraudulent declarations of the amount of land farmed, simple failures to declare land, underpayment, and delivery of paddy spoiled by moisture or contaminated with rocks and mud to increase its weight.[14]

Scott's category of "everyday peasant resistance" is helpful for contextualizing Jesus' activity. Traditional peasantries have employed a number

---

12. Hanson and Oakman, *Palestine in the Time of Jesus*, 99–103.

13. Hanson and Oakman, *Palestine in the Time of Jesus*, 105–8.

14. Scott, *Domination*, 89.

of means of day-to-day resistance (Scott's "fraudulent declarations of the amount of land farmed, simple failures to declare land, underpayment, and delivery of paddy spoiled by moisture or contaminated with rocks and mud to increase its weight"), though none of these ever does away with the systemic problem.

Ancient peasant revolts were infrequent because of the perennial localism of peasants and the highly organized means of violence in the hands of elite groups. Not surprisingly, the great Judean Revolt of 66–70 CE was accompanied by tax remedies. The Jerusalem debt archives were burned during the initial phases (Josephus, *War* 2.427), and Simon bar Giora later announced the release of prisoners and the liberation of slaves (Josephus, *War* 4.508). When recounting the burning of the Jerusalem archives, Josephus refers to them as the "sinews of the city." He might have said empire as well.

According to Josephus also, the Roman tax arrangements implemented when Judea became an imperial province in 6 CE were met with stiff resistance. Judas of Gamala (in Gaulanitis, the present-day Golan Heights to the east of the Galilean lake) and a certain Zaddok the Pharisee, insisting that there is no God but God and that paying taxes to Rome is a sign of servitude, advocated armed resistance. I quote briefly two passages from Josephus:

> But a certain Judas, a Gaulanite from a city named Gamala, who had enlisted the aid of Saddok, a Pharisee, threw himself into the cause of rebellion. They said that the [tax] assessment carried with it a status amounting to downright slavery, no less, and appealed to the nation to make a bid for independence . . .
>
> As for the fourth of the philosophies, Judas the Galilean set himself up as leader of it. This school agrees in all other respects with the opinions of the Pharisees, except that they have a passion for liberty that is almost unconquerable, since they are convinced that God alone is their leader and master.[15]

One cannot but be struck by the proximity of Judas and Jesus, and the similarity of their messages. At the time of the census, Jesus would have been about ten years old and living only thirty miles from Gamala. Moreover during the time of his own historical activity, Jesus spent most of his time in the environs of the Galilean lake. Capernaum is within eyesight of Gamala, and vice versa.

15. Josephus, *Ant.* 18.4, 23 (LCL).

Another significant datum about Jesus of Nazareth is his association with "tax collectors and sinners" (attested in Q and in Mark). "Why does he eat with tax collectors and sinners?" (Mark 2:16). Why indeed? John Kloppenborg, one of the preeminent North American scholars studying Q, offers a clue in terms of that document's origins:

> If one asks, who would be in a position to frame the Sayings Gospel as it has been framed, the answer would appear to be village and town notaries and scribes . . . There is ample evidence from Egypt to indicate the presence of a variety of scribes, of varying educational levels, in towns and villages, some serving in the apparatus of the provincial administration and others functioning as freelance professionals. The [village scribe] was concerned with tax and census matters.[16]

Jesus' association with "tax collectors and sinners" around the table, or as we will argue below "tax collectors and debtors," hence had to do with the sharing of real goods and perhaps with the mitigation or even elimination of burdensome debts and taxes.[17] The tax collectors possessed the social technology—writing—by which debt and tax collection was enforced. Ironically, the same technology enabled Jesus' oral Aramaic words eventually to be recorded for posterity. Jesus' message held special resonance with the fishingfolk, and Jesus' closest followers were fishermen like Simon and Andrew (sons of John), and James and John (sons of Zebedee). So a tax collector, Levi son of Alphaeus, turns up among Jesus' retinue. Interestingly, a fourth-century inscription found during the archaeological excavations at Capernaum reads: "Ḥalfu, the son of Zebidah, the son of Yoanan, made this column. May he be blessed."[18] It would seem from this inscription that the association of the Alphaeus, Zebedee, and John families persisted for many centuries. If so, then the tax collectors were the fishers' relatives, and Jesus' meal program gathered together to some extent both the indebted and their creditors. There was mutual benefit.

16. Kloppenborg [Verbin], *Excavating Q*, 200–201.

17. In a private communication, K. C. Hanson has suggested that "tax collectors and debtors" may have been employed as a merism. That is, Jesus associated with the full range of the marginal in the towns and villages (high and low)—from tax collectors (those with power and clients of the powerful, who were despised for their practices) to debtors (the marginal peasants who relied on subsistence loans).

18. Loffreda and Tzaferis, "Capernaum," 294.

The Radical Jesus

At the root of Christian origins, then, there stands a disaffected group and a social concern. Jesus proclaimed a socially transformative power, "the kingdom of God," which appealed to the indebted and the outcast. Lake-fishers were in debt to the tax-farmers; prostitutes were in debt to their pimps, who undoubtedly paid a regular tax; and village-farmers were obligated to the large estate holder. Rents and taxes meant debt and arrears, for sooner or later (and usually sooner) people fell behind on their payments and were permanently put on record. The Romans encouraged this situation by infusing coined money into provincial agrarian economies, which in turn led to money loans and further debt. The provincial banks, which in Greek are called "tables" (*trapezai*), were held by powerful-wealthy interests. These tables represented exploitation, while the table of Jesus promoted reconciliation and reciprocity.

Jesus was attempting to mitigate the situation of the indebted, and perhaps went even so far as to promote peasant resistance in the form of subversion of the imperial tax system in Galilee. This subversion would have operated both in terms of tax evasion and distortion of the tax records. Jesus also focused on debt-forgiveness in the name of God's ruling power in order to mitigate the situation of the indebted.

Additional corroborations for these assertions are found in a variety of excellent Jesus material. The remission of enormous tax debt in Matt 18:27 (special Matthew) is noteworthy, and the slaves are expected to follow suit. In a very different light, the political significance of Luke 16:1–7 lies open for scrutiny. A royal steward manipulates tax records in his own interests and against those of the *kyrios*, the master. These manipulations are viewed positively (in v. 8), and the steward anticipates "being welcomed into [villagers'] houses." More subtly, Mark 4:3–8 (The Sower) and Gos. Thom. 97 (The Empty Jar) intimate possible evasion tactics—when seed sown on impossible ground or lost meal becomes available for tax-free gleaning. The tax question is addressed ambiguously at Mark 12:17 and Matt 17:26 (M). Even at the redactional level of the evangelists, good evidence of such resistance might still be preserved, for instance in Luke's Zacchaeus (19:1–10) or in Luke 23:2 (both L), when Jesus is accused before Pilate of advocating tax evasion.

The evidence of the very earliest Q material, stemming as we have indicated from Tiberian scribes in the administration of Herod Antipas, is particularly important.[19] Early Q reflects on the ethos and largesse of God's alternate kingdom. With roots in Passover meditation (as I see the Q Beatitudes) and perhaps the example of Moses (who violently resisted Egyptian corveé, Exod 2:11–12), early Q has in view a liberation praxis.[20]

Indeed, early Q takes on a fascinating light when read against the concerns of "tax-collectors and debtors." "Love for enemies" (Q 6:27) and "Golden Rule" (Q 6:31) are not meant then as generalized ethical norms, but as supports for reversing the normal dynamics of imperial taxation. This value is stated positively in Luke 16:9, "*Make friends* with unjust Mammon." Behind both Q 6:32 and Q 11:4, Jesus' oral-Aramaic speech patterns are in view. As Matthew Black and others have noted, the Greek in both places reflects the ambiguity of the Aramaic *ḥov'*.[21] While the related Greek word *hamartōlos could* be understood within a Judean theological frame to refer to the morally disreputable, i.e. "sinners," *ḥovyn* could equally denote those in indebted circumstances. With this translation adjustment in view, Q 6:32 contrasts balanced reciprocity and the general reciprocity ethic of debt- and tax-forgiveness commensurate with God's ruling power. Jesus' prayer concretely brings into focus his praxis, especially through the petition "Release us (that is, tax-collectors) from debt, as we release those in debt to us (that is, those who owe taxes)" (Q 11:4).

Michael Rostovtzeff, the great ancient historian, remarks on the frequency during the Hellenistic period of those who turned in royal opponents (including tax-evaders): "[In Ecclesiastes, under Ptolemy II] The spies of Ptolemy, who are so ubiquitous that 'a bird of the air shall carry the voice' of him who cursed the king in secret, were presumably both fiscal and political *mēnytai* [Greek, 'informers']"[22] The same pattern continues into the Roman period. The Q-words of Luke 12:2–3 have in mind such damaging revelations of secrets, so the connection to bodily danger in 12:4 is not accidental. This consideration throws a striking light onto Judas Iscariot, the Betrayer of Jesus.

> Nothing is covered up that will not be uncovered, and nothing secret that will not become known. Therefore whatever you have said in the dark will be heard in the light, and what you have

---

19. See further Oakman, "The Lord's Prayer in Social Perspective," 202, 208.

20. Robinson, "The Jesus of Q," 259–74.

21. Black, *Aramaic Approach*, 140.

22. Rostovtzeff, *SEHHW*, 350.

whispered behind closed doors will be proclaimed from the housetops. (12:2–3)

I tell you, my friends, do not fear those who kill the body, and after that can do nothing more. (12:4)

Hatred of family members (understood ironically in Q 14:26) implies that one's actions for the sake of God's rule put family members at grave risk. Gospel of Thomas 55 and 100–101 juxtapose hatred of family with either the tax question or the cross. Besides Matt 18:25, there is the interesting story told by Philo about the actions of an Egyptian tax-collector:

Recently a man was appointed tax collector among us. When some of those who were supposed to owe taxes fled because of poverty and in fear of unbearable punishment, he carried off by force their wives, their children, the parents, and the rest of their families, striking them, and insulting them, and visiting all manner of outrages upon them in an effort to force them either to inform against the fugitive or else to make payment in his stead.[23]

Thus, Q 14:27 and Gos. Thom. 55 provide an important crux for this line of argument. For these sayings indicate very clearly Jesus' consciousness of the political consequences deriving from his praxis. The Q writers and Thomas hardly say a word otherwise about Jesus' death. If the cross saying is hyperbole, as some scholars think, why would it be associated with family and bodily danger? The saying's literal meaning must then be taken seriously. As the Roman jurist Julius Paulus wrote in the early second century CE, "People who plot sedition and riot or who stir up the masses are, according to the nature of their social rank, either crucified, or thrown to wild animals, or exiled to an island."[24]

Jesus' criticism of Mammon—the money and wealth stored at the bankers' tables, in creditors' storehouses, or in the imperial treasury—resonated with the concerns of other contemporary Palestinian documents focused especially upon the elites of Judea. The Damascus Document from the Dead Sea Scrolls records:

Unless [the priests] are careful to act in accordance with the exact interpretation of the law for the age of wickedness: to separate themselves from the sons of the pit; to abstain from wicked wealth

23. Philo, *Spec. Laws* 2.19.92–94, qtd. in Lewis and Reinhold, *Roman Civilization*, 400.

24. Julius Paulus, *Opinions* 5.22.1, qtd. in Shelton, *As the Romans Did*, 13.

which defiles, either by promise or by vow, and from the wealth of the temple and from stealing from the poor of the people, from making their widows their spoils and from murdering orphans . . .[25]

The Testament of Moses 7:3–8 likewise indicates a general feeling about Herodian Judea:

Then will rule destructive and godless men, who represent themselves as being righteous, but who will (in fact) arouse their inner wrath, for they will be deceitful men, pleasing only themselves, false in every way imaginable, (such as) loving feasts at any hour of the day—devouring, gluttonous.
. . . But really they consume the goods of the (poor), saying their acts are according to justice, (while in fact they are simply) exterminators, deceitfully seeking to conceal themselves so that they will not be known as completely godless because of their criminal deeds (committed) all the day long, saying, "We shall have feasts, even luxurious winings and dinings. Indeed, we shall behave ourselves as princes." They, with hand and mind, will touch impure things, yet their mouths will speak enormous things, and they will even say, "Do not touch me, lest you pollute me in the position I occupy . . ."[26]

Whether fictional or historical, the recollection in the gospels that Jesus attacked the tables in the temple points to an incompatibility of social perspective and interest. Forty years ago, Victor Eppstein supposed on the basis of Mishnah *Sheqalim* that Jesus would not have taken offense at money-changers because he "understood their necessity both in the provinces and, assuming that he had previously kept the Passover, in the Temple."[27] It is likely, on the contrary, that Jesus understood all too well the nefarious political consequences for provincials of the tables, money-changing, and debt. His attack enacts the basic idea of the Q saying "You cannot serve God and Mammon" (Q 16:13). The tables represented deposits of money in trust, bank deposits that could then be loaned out, *mamōnas*, and correspondingly something trusted to the detriment of other human concerns and values, such as familial sharing, which the Jesus movement championed. Moreover, the tables represented tax-collection points and

---

25. CD 6.14–17, García Martínez, *The Dead Sea Scrolls Translated*, 37.

26. Priest, "Testament of Moses," 930.

27. Eppstein, "Historicity," 45–46.

perpetual debt and arrears. Jesus' table, by contrast—consonant with his central concern of debt-forgiveness—was the gracious Passover table, the feast of the gracious and compassionate God of Israel to which all the hungry and indebted were invited.[28]

Jesus' historical activity, in this reading, was centrally about provincial politics, the social realities of Mammon or the wealth-concentrate in the hands of the powerful, and not centrally about theological debates. The activity of the historical Jesus signified debt-release and possibly tax evasion in the name of God's ruling power. While Jesus' historical resistance to imperial realities left its traces in early traditions, it is also true that later scribes shifted from Jesus' focus on political relations to theology. By Luke's day, Jesus could be seen as innocent of any Roman charges. In this sense, the New Testament made an early contribution to obscuring the meaning of Jesus' peasant resistance.

WWWD—What Would We Do?

How does any of this meet with our situation today? Certainly there are analogies. However, I do not think we can simply leap from the first directly into the twenty-first century without further considerations. So much has happened since then. Karl Polanyi gave important indications in his book *The Great Transformation*; Ernst Troeltsch traced other lines in his monumental *The Social Teaching of the Christian Churches*; H. Richard Niebuhr demonstrated complex historical possibilities in the relationship between *Christ and Culture*. But Robert Wuthnow's recent study, *God and Mammon in America*, indicates the ongoing resonance of these themes. Perhaps, therefore, the real question is not so much What Would Jesus Do, but What Would We Do now?

This kind of historical investigation places certain developments in the Christian tradition in a significant light. It suggests that we look for places in the Christian tradition that are socially and culturally resonant with Jesus' critique of Mammon. To name two examples ready to hand, Francis of Assisi and Luther come to mind. The wealthy Francis gave away his substance to stand in solidarity with the poor and all creation.[29] Luther

---

28. Oakman, "Economics of Palestine," 104; Oakman, "Models and Archaeology," 275–79.

29. Tawney, *The Rise of Capitalism*, 23; Troeltsch, *Social Teaching of the Christian Churches*, 355.

too came to a moment of theological clarity through the radical grace of God, and restated Jesus' radical aims thus (in the words of Luther's *Large Catechism*):

> the trust and faith of the heart alone make both God and an idol. If your faith and trust are right, then your God is the true God. On the other hand, if your trust is false and wrong, then you have not the true God. For these two belong together, faith and God. That to which your heart clings and entrusts itself is, I say, really your God.[30]

Luther further had none-too-kind things to say about money loans and usury, and he called bankers of his day "extortioners."[31] Arguably, the Lutheran Reformation itself had as a central concern the clarification of basic theological and human values that had been obscured by narrow economic interests. Exemplary figures in the Christian tradition, then, provide signs of the ongoing power and influence of Jesus' vision and commitment.

Relative to our time, Jesus' critique of Mammon suggests that a capitalism without equity and distributive justice has not measured up to his radical vision of human fulfillment. And his critique is not just for Christians. The engines of industrial and technological capitalism have produced the greatest boon in history, so as to provide the resources to address poverty and hunger on a global scale. But enormous imbalances in control and distribution of this cornucopia leave most on the planet in a state of abject poverty. Moreover, the great wealth of capitalism, in the name of security, is increasingly diverted into expensive weaponry, defensive social structures, and wars that perpetuate fear and misunderstanding. Necessary investments in the right kind of education—one that would promote genuine understanding and that perfect love which might finally cast out fear (1 John 4:18)—fall far behind. Meanwhile, the gross injustices of global capitalism and corresponding cultural dislocations give ready excuse for violent terrorism.

In this respect, the searching critique of individualism by Robert N. Bellah and his colleagues points to the tyranny of the isolated self that can only be the cultural consequence of capitalistic Mammon.[32] Critique of the social and environmental unsustainability of an economics promising endless growth in a world of limits has been powerfully advanced by Herman

30. Tappert, *The Book of Concord*, 365.

31. Tawney, *The Rise of Capitalism*, 74.

32. Bellah et al., *Habits of the Heart*.

Daly and John Cobb in their book *For the Common Good.* They urge a thorough reconsideration of arrangements that place wealth under control of a small elite, where the many hold tokens while the real dividends are paid only to the few.

Indeed, there is need to rethink in broadly representative democratic assemblies' arrangements of capital, trade, and taxation, and to pursue policies that promote a more just and humane social order. There is need for a new kind of leadership to move the debate in legislatures and congresses beyond draconian budget cuts and tax relief for the wealthy. And there is need to see fiduciary and trust arrangements not as mere opportunities for personal gain, or the stock market as a rich man's lotto, but to see wealth as a community-trust to benefit all.

Finally, in an age of increasing fear and insecurity, Jesus' critique of Mammon compels thought about how we might see, how we might live, and how things might *be* if the ultimate heart of the universe is loving mercy and grace. It was Jesus, after all, who was remembered as having said:

> If you love those who love you, what credit is that to you? For even debtors love those who love them. And if you do good to those who do good to you, what credit is that to you? For even debtors do the same. And if you lend to those from whom you hope to receive, what credit is that to you? Even debtors lend to debtors, to receive as much again. But love your enemies, and do good, and lend, expecting nothing in return; and your reward will be great, and you will be [children] of the Most High; for God is kind to the ungrateful and the selfish. (Q 6:32–35)

Hardly the sentiments of an Enron executive or a Pentagon general, but words that might still be taken seriously by Christians, a "Christian nation," or even a global civilization. Indeed, these are sentiments that do not sit comfortably at all in an age of corporate exploitation and the global politics of terror, but they might provide a radically different basis for rapprochement between very different cultures and peoples. If everything *has* been given in radical grace, what then will we do now?

CHAPTER 2

The Biblical World of Limited Good in Social, Cultural, and Technological Perspective

In Memory of Bruce J. Malina—Pioneer, Patron, and Friend

B RUCE J. MALINA WAS a pioneering scholar in the anthropological and cross-cultural study of the Bible.[1] While a critical analysis of the origins of this social-scientific approach remains to be written someday with the advantage of historical distance, it is fair to say that prior to Malina, few scholars had brought perspectives from Mediterranean and cultural anthropology to bear on the biblical texts.[2] It is also fair to say that Malina's work had influence far and wide in the field of biblical studies, whether acknowledged directly or not, especially by scholarship recognizing the core values of the biblical traditions. After Malina's work, it is difficult for credible biblical scholarship to ignore either the problematic ethnocentric lenses of postindustrial and post-Enlightenment societies or the need for more culturally appropriate reading scenarios.

1. The present chapter is a revised version of a paper delivered in 2009 at the International Context Group meeting in Tutzing, Germany; the original paper was translated and published in German as "Begrenzte Güter in der Biblischen Welt" (2014).

2. Partial contemporary accounts of the origins of social-scientific criticism can be found in Duling, *A Marginal Scribe*, 8–35; Elliott, *What Is Social-Scientific Criticism?* Elliott, "On Wooing Crocodiles"; Elliott, "From Social Description to Social-Scientific Criticism"; Esler, "The Context Group Project"; Esler, "Social-Scientific Models in Biblical Interpretation"; Esler, *Early Christian World*, 3–23; and Pilch, *Social Scientific Models*, 1–4.

Several salient factors played a role in Malina's oeuvre. First he was of Polish and Czech descent, but through his doctoral education in Italy and Spain (in Mediterranean cultural settings) and through experiences working in the Philippines as a Franciscan, he grew to appreciate deeply the problems of cross-cultural understanding. Malina's publications already in the 1970s show his advancing work on the cross-cultural study of the Bible. His 1981 classic *The New Testament World* brought sharply into focus the ways in which Euro-American biblical scholars missed important differences in the biblical cultures.[3] Importantly, false analogies can be redressed by cross-cultural models helping to overcome cultural ethnocentrism. For instance, honor and shame in collectivist or extended family contexts are core biblical values in contrast to individualist guilt or self-made persons; any claim to individual honor and worth has to be acknowledged by the larger group; dyadism means that group concerns and consciousness take precedence over individual choice and opinion; personalistic patronal relations govern both domestic and political societies in contrast to impersonal political offices; religion is not "freestanding" in churches or "separated by walls" from domestic or political settings; and economic production is largely agrarian and conducted within domestic units rather than impersonal factories. These contrasts could be multiplied many times, and have been in numerous books by members of the Context Group, including Malina and other scholars around the world. Malina proposed a method of using cross-cultural models and scenarios to navigate more effectively the cultural divide between modern readers and ancient biblical texts. This method is brilliantly demonstrated in *The New Testament World* (1981, 1993, 2001), *Christian Origins and Cultural Anthropology* (1988), and in the work jointly authored with Richard L. Rohrbaugh *Social-Science Commentary on the Synoptic Gospels* (1992, 2003). In short, it is difficult to read any biblical scholarship today without seeing the need to reckon with these issues and perspectives. Malina played a catalytic role in the emergence and development of the social-scientific approach, and he deserves to be remembered as a seminal scholar in the history of biblical scholarship.

Already in 1978 Malina had written about "limited good attitudes and beliefs."[4] The notion of limited good continues to provide an important and

---

3. Malina, *The New Testament World*, (2nd ed. 1993; 3rd ed. 2001); for a complete bibliographic listing of Malina publications up until 1999, see Pilch, *Social Scientific Models*, 381–97.

4. Malina, "Limited Good."

accurate heuristic for the biblical world, and for reasons that amplify the original model of George Foster (see below). In fact, *limited-good perspectives* are rooted in specific circumstances that regularly yield *actual limited goods* for most people, and such circumstances recurrently conditioned the cultural and social attitudes and values of the Bible. Moreover, biblical attitudes and values must continue to be appraised in relation to the economic/ecologic realities of the ancient circum-Mediterranean. Ancient social attitudes and cultural values of limited good were rooted in persistent social structures reinforced by ecological/environmental constraints.[5] This is why these attitudes and values recur over many centuries, in the writings of ancient moralists as well as in biblical material.

I invoke as something of a point of contrast and departure one of Ronald Reagan's famous statements about pies (from 1984):

> Our opponents . . . view our country not as people of varied backgrounds who share common values and aspirations; instead, they see us as warring factions and interest groups. They try to divide us, using envy, and playing people off against each other by telling us we're competing for a piece of a pie that is ever getting smaller. Well, that's not our way.
>
> . . . And about that pie—we also believe that we should work together to make a bigger pie, so everyone can have a bigger slice.[6]

Ronald Reagan obviously did not believe in limited good, nor did he apparently understand that a sharply stratified society of haves and have-nots would hardly allow all to benefit equally from greater productivity. But he did express a conservative commonplace of the postindustrial era: The economy must always grow. And this idea is rooted in technologically grounded beliefs that nature's limits have been permanently overcome in the industrial age, such that production can ever be increased.

Not only did most ancients *not* see ever-increasing pies, but they realistically understood that under the precarious conditions of agrarian production, increase of the essential goods of life was not to be had. Besides stringent natural limits, there were also social limits. The ancient world of the Bible was hardly industrialized, and in addition that world lacked key social values and arrangements that would encourage industrial organization on a wide scale or the productive attitudes that first gave rise to the

---

5. Schneider, "Of Vigilance and Virgins"; Gregg, *The Middle East*, 50, 92.
6. Reagan, "Remarks."

notion of "economic growth." This anti-industrial sentiment is illustrated in a nutshell by the following anecdote from Suetonius (*Vespasian* 18):

> To a mechanical engineer, who promised to transport some heavy columns to the Capitol at small expense, [Vespasian] gave no mean reward for his invention, but refused to make use of it, saying that he should not be forced to take from the poor commons the work that fed them.

This story points up what will be an important theme of this chapter. Ancient economies were built largely by human and animal labor, with limited inputs from mechanical or "labor-saving" technologies. Elites depended upon various means for controlling and organizing labor to their own advantage. Moreover, ancient societies offered a variant of Lenski's advanced agrarian societal type; that is, they were largely occupied with agrarian food-provision based upon iron plows drawn by oxen.[7] The productive capacity of agrarian societies limits the available surpluses for non-food-producing classes. Ancient technology and concomitant social organization must be an important aspect of ancient limited-good attitudes.[8]

Given the limited agrarian surpluses of Roman antiquity, social stratification and the urban locus of elites faced economic/ecologic constraints. Neither cities nor the numbers of elites whose lives were characterized by agrarian leisure could increase indefinitely. Indeed, the prosopography of elites in Roman antiquity is seen to have been quite limited: Although absolute quantification will always be uncertain, the *Prosopographia Imperii Romani* (1933–2015) lists 15,733 entries through seven volumes for the 253-year period 31 BCE to 284 CE.[9] For comparison in later Roman antiquity, Jones, Martindale, and Morris contains 3,740 pages with on average eight entries; this amounts to about 30,000 elite names over 381 years.[10] Consider also that the names listed for Josephus's entire *Antiquities* in the Loeb Classical Library edition number well under ten thousand. Life expectancy itself was a limited good, as "life expectancy at birth among the elite was of the order of twenty to thirty years."[11] Following Tim Parkin, on average nuclear family size (a family of five is typical), the imperial elites

7. Lenski, *Power and Privilege*, 189–210.

8. Finley, *The Ancient Economy*; Humphreys, "History, Economics, and Anthropology"; Scott, *Moral Economy*.

9. Rohden et al., eds., *Prosopographia Imperii Romani*.

10. Jones, Martindale, and Morris, eds., *Prosopography*.

11. Scheidel, "Emperors, Aristocrats, and the Grim Reaper," 280.

up until the third century amounted to no more than one hundred fifty thousand.[12] And this would suggest that the first-century "most rich and famous" in any one generation amounted to only several thousands out of approximately fifty million.[13] Lenski sees the entire agrarian governing class on average as about 1 percent, which would be around five hundred thousand for the first-century Roman Empire.[14]

Theoretical Resources

George Foster first formulated the model of limited good in 1965. He proposed in a response to critics that "the cognitive orientation of Limited Good goes farther than any other model yet advanced to explain peasant behavior."[15] He also referred to such social settings as "deprivation societies," where most are living under conditions of limited good, but gross inequalities between elite and non-elite are also broadly recognized.

While Foster receives primary credit for formulating the model, work of other students of classic peasant societies and comparative macrosociology provide support and perspective. I will draw here particularly upon Karl Wittfogel's *Oriental Despotism*. Wittfogel considered that whatever insights his seminal work had achieved were particularly dependent upon "the use of big structured concepts for the purpose of identifying big patterns of societal structure and change."[16]

Such large-scale approaches have fallen into disfavor in some scholarly sectors today, for various ideological reasons, but without such perspectives the forest is missed for the trees, or the exceptions are thought to be the rule. Explicit integration of large-scale social-scientific conceptions leads to useful generalizations, which raise counterintuitive questions and lend insights into regularities or even specific facts that would not otherwise be apparent to the inductive historian. Or as Foster stated it for the middle range:

> A good model is heuristic and explanatory, not descriptive, and it has predictive value. It encourages an analyst to search for

12. Parkin, *Demography*, 5, 112.

13. Scheidel, "Demography," 48.

14. Lenski, *Power and Privilege*, 245.

15. Foster, "Peasant Society and the Image of Limited Good"; Foster, "A Second Look at Limited Good," 62.

16. Wittfogel, *Oriental Despotism*, iii.

behavior patterns, and relationships between patterns, which . . .
may not yet have [been] recognized.[17]

Biblical Cultural and Social Values and Limited Good

Most of the discussions of limited good by biblical scholars have attended
to the cultural and social perceptions involved in the term. As mentioned
previously, Bruce Malina was the first biblical scholar to highlight limited-
good perspectives for the New Testament. His seminal treatments "Limited
Good and the Social World of Early Christianity" (1978) and *The New Testament World* (1981)—followed by John Elliott's 1988 *Forum* article "Fear of
the Leer" and 1991 review of evil-eye material related to the Hebrew Bible,
or Jerome Neyrey's "Bewitched in Galatia" (1988), Richard Rohrbaugh's "A
Peasant Reading of the Parable of the Talents/Pounds: A Text of Terror"
(1993), and Neyrey and Rohrbaugh's "'He must increase, I must decrease'"
(2001)—largely adhere to Malina's Interpretive/Verstehen approach in relation to the Mediterranean cultural system.[18] Although some aspects of
biblical limited good can be studied relative to accumulation of honor or
wealth, much else is hidden under various linguistic markers such as the
"evil eye."[19] The evil eye becomes an important index of limited-good beliefs. As these scholars point out, "limited good" implies a zero-sum view of
natural and social goods. Increase somewhere must imply decrease somewhere else. Hardly a Reaganesque view of life!

Rightly queried, the emic material of the Bible yields a variety of limited-good material. For instance, Ps 62:10 [MT 62:11], through *parallelismus
membrorum*, equates the increase of riches with extortion and robbery.
Psalm 73:12 suggests that only the wicked increase in wealth. The well-
known biblical passage in John 3:30 expresses the zero-sum attitude. The
idioms of Matt 20:15 and Galatians 3:1 attest to widespread evil-eye beliefs.
Alicia Batten perceptively discusses James's views of poverty and wealth
against the horizon of a limited-good economy.[20] Malina and Seeman as

---

17. Foster, "Peasant Society and the Image of Limited Good," 301.

18. Malina, *The New Testament World*, (1981) 75–76.

19. Neyrey, "Bewitched in Galatia," 72–75; Neyrey, "Limited Good," 103; Elliott, *Beware the Evil Eye*; Malina and Seeman, "Envy."

20. Batten, "Degraded Poor."

well as Elliott (2016) identify many more places in the Bible where limited good or the evil eye is mentioned.[21]

Ancient limited-good attitudes are not restricted to the Bible. There is for instance this anecdote in Augustine's *City of God* (4.4; originally from Cicero):

> Indeed, that was an apt and true reply which was given to Alexander the Great by a pirate who had been seized. For when that king had asked the man what he meant by keeping hostile possession of the sea, he answered with bold pride, "Exactly what you mean by seizing the whole earth; but because I do it with a petty ship, I am called a robber, while you who do it with a great fleet are styled emperor."

Neyrey and Rohrbaugh and Batten document these attitudes widely among the Greco-Roman moralists and other writers. Recently, Rivka Ulmer (1994) has examined the *ayin hara* in rabbinic literature. And we have recently received the fullest book-length treatment of the evil eye in world culture (including the biblical cultures) from John Elliott (2015–2017).

Besides the exegetical documentation of limited-good instances in the Bible, scholarship has explored the cultural mores determined by such attitudes and values. Malina, for instance, discusses the strategies of the ideal or wealthy man for preserving and protecting honor in a limited-good world.[22] It is important in this cultural scheme that everything be seen as "given." This conviction probably recurs within intransigent peasant thinking—whether of commoner or elite—which is fixated within a magical world. Max Weber stressed that peasant religion is bound up with magical thinking to influence nature; also, Heinz Werner showed that magical thinking deals in all-or-nothing propositions, and that one part of the whole cannot be disturbed without disturbing everything.[23] But since the elites value leisure, others must understandably work to provide "what has been given." Conversely, since increases in power or wealth achieved by less-honored families are always "new," these are generally difficult to rationalize within a limited-good world (consider aristocratic attitudes toward the nouveaux riches).

---

21. Malina and Seeman, "Envy," 53; Elliott, *Beware the Evil Eye*, vol. 2.

22. Malina, *The New Testament World*, (1981) 76–79; (2001) 90–93.

23. Werner, *Comparative Psychology*, 344; Weber, *Economy and Society*, 470, 482–83; see Horsley's critique of the notion of magic in *Jesus and Magic*.

Technological and Environmental Perspectives, and Limited Good

The importance of limited-good attitudes and values in the Bible seems adequately established by the scholarship of the last thirty years. Less attended to, however, and less successfully clarified have been the links between culture and the natural and social-structural bases of such attitudes.

Elliott provides some pointers in this direction when he refers to the "fragile and unpredictable ecological environment" that gives rise to evil-eye and limited-good beliefs. He documents exegetically that the evil eye in the Bible is often associated with the sharing of food, acquisition of wealth, or distribution of alms. Moreover, Deut 28:53–57 depicts "the most extreme illustration of Evil Eye behavior in all of scripture," based presumably upon the severe deprivations of the Neo-Babylonian siege. Elliott concludes that the evil eye "constituted a symbolical rendition of the ecological, economic, and social conditions in which the ancients felt themselves exposed and vulnerable," dependent upon a "precarious natural environment" where economic survival was uncertain and made more insecure by constant competition for resources.[24]

Yet even more needs to be done to explain the social recurrence of such perspectives over centuries. In order to accomplish this task, specific attention needs to be devoted to the actual working circumstances of our biblical writers, and macrosociological frameworks must effectively be brought to bear on the matter. The remainder of this chapter will offer a sketch as to what is meant by this (limited to the New Testament period and Greco-Roman world).

Applied to agrarian antiquity, limited-good attitudes and values expressed both acquiescence to extreme inequalities and a living protest against the exploitative conditions under which most lived. There was no source of unlimited goods in antiquity—at least for the vast majority. Wind, wheel, and lever technologies had limited application, and served the few; most useful work whether in agriculture or building was still the outcome of organized labor or animal power; elite taxation posed disincentives for increasing agricultural production. While Michael Rostovtzeff toyed with the idea of a "commercial Mediterranean" as a significant economic engine, imperial Mediterranean commerce really in the final analysis served only the Roman elites and their political agents (as sharply depicted by Rev 18

---

24. Elliott, "Evil Eye," 153, 159; Elliott, *Beware the Evil Eye*, 1:54–58.

or Gos. Thom. 64).[25] The agrarian masses toiled for limited goods under
the Italian boot. The preindustrial technoenvironmental conditions and the
organization of labor within an agrarian society must be the final court of
appeal in the explanation of limited-good attitudes and values.

Important for understanding the recurrence of limited-good notions
is incorporation of social-structural considerations and macrosociological
theory. Wittfogel provides a suggestive starting point. While his 1957 book
has been too simplistically characterized (or even dismissed) as a deter-
ministic study of irrigation societies, and its alleged defects noted by many
reviewers, it has also been very positively evaluated.[26] George Murdock
wrote, "This is a truly great book, one of the major contributions to the
science of man in our time. Its importance to anthropology in the area of
comparative political institutions parallels that of Tylor's *Primitive Culture*
in the field of comparative religion, and may conceivably even outrank that
of the entire corpus of theoretical literature in political science."[27] Wittfogel's work has broad application in understanding the social realities of
absolutist power, weak property, and coerced labor under low-productivity
conditions. It is an excellent comparative study of channeled power, not just
channeled water.

"Hydraulic society," as Wittfogel defines it, depends upon organization of labor, intensive cultivation, and large-scale cooperation. He includes
imperial Rome in the discussion as a loose and complex hydraulic society,
because the absolutist politics of Augustus drew upon examples of the "Hellenistic Orient," and "By laying the foundations for a salaried officialdom,
he initiated a bureaucratic development that rapidly gained momentum
in the 1st century A.D."[28] Wittfogel also calls this pattern "agromanagerial
despotism."

> Ecological determinism oversimplifies the relation between the
> natural environment and man's technical and economic activities
> by claiming that this relation is one-sided (with man passively re-
> sponding to the natural setting) and necessary. In fact, it involves
> a two-way process; and the ecological setting more often provides

25. Rostovtzeff, *SEHRE*, 3, 95, 772; Banaji, "Commercial Capitalism"; Brown, *Through the Eye of a Needle*, 14.

26. Venturi, "Oriental Despotism"; Toynbee, Review of Wittfogel," 196; Said, *Orientalism*, 89–107; Turner, *Marx*; Turner, "Outline"; Wittfogel, "Results and Problems."

27. Murdock, "Review of Wittfogel," 545; see also Eisenstadt's judicious review.

28. Wittfogel, *Oriental Despotism*, 210.

the possibility or probability, rather than the necessity for certain types of action.

But these differentiations do not eliminate the role of the natural factor. They only limit it. And the ecological approach remains central for the understanding of the 'Orient' in which only agro-managerial and state-directed action can solve the problems posed by the natural environment.[29]

As he makes clear, only absolute despotisms could compel the labor force necessary to feed numerous cities, erect monumental buildings or fortifications, or maintain extensive waterworks like aqueducts, baths, canals, or harbors. He also points to the weakness of property within agromanagerial empires (e.g., as revealed in partible inheritance arrangements or land grants by autocrats to their clients) as well as the introvert nature of architecture (one thinks of the windowless mansions at Pompeii).[30]

All of these features were characteristic of imperial Roman society, and the social contexts attendant to the writing of the New Testament literature. The Romans, like the Hellenistic rulers before them, promoted urban intensification in the East and intensification of agrarian production to supply those cities. Eastern cities as sites of delegated honor required adornments, and the archaeological record attests them aplenty! For instance, cities required secure water supplies, beautiful buildings, good roads, monumental tombs, and the like. Much of this was done in dressed stone, and required enormous investments of labor under preindustrial conditions. Cities required taxation and supply, so commercial development and agricultural intensification followed logically. Speaking directly about the agrarian situation, agricultural intensification required debt, alienation of traditional village lands, and growth of large estates controlled by the cities. As Foster has pointed out, and Marx and Sorokin before him, peasant villagers are always provincial and difficult to coordinate, and must be compelled into larger social endeavor. Debt and taxes, coupled with the threat of violent reprisals, are perhaps the best social leverage for labor and the surplus that villagers would otherwise devote to themselves and store up for the winter. Moreover, village labor needs to be harnessed directly for the benefit of the city-dweller. This is perhaps the most interesting aspect requiring further study. The city necessitated that village and craft labor be more intensively exploited. Interestingly, the Jesus and the Christ-follower

29. Wittfogel, *Oriental Despotism*, 361.
30. Wittfogel, *Oriental Despotism*, 78–86.

movements, bridging this social divide, addressed and incorporated people deeply affected by imperial labor exploitation.

Perhaps the matter can best be summarized under two aspects: (1) First-century Mediterranean social structures depended upon labor and agricultural surplus. These social entailments implied intensified agricultural production, and the organizational requirements to ensure surplus, as well as labor extraction. But under conditions of productivity within firm environmental limits, "surplus" would mean decrease of village edibles and "labor exploitation" marginal returns on agrarian production. (2) Ancient Mediterranean values centered upon honor. The city as the site of ascribed or achieved honor had political entailments. These entailments required increased monumental building to display that honor. We look at each of these selectively vis-à-vis the Jesus group and Christ-follower movement before concluding.

(1) The Attitude of the Jesus Group in Roman Palestine

The parable in Matt 20:1–16 often appears as exhibit A for limited-good perspectives and surely expresses attitudes of Jesus and his associates. Conventional commentaries (like Jeremias's) stress the graciousness of the estate owner, "the good employer."[31] Brandon Scott considers that the "lack in the parable of any absolute standard of justice undermines any human standard for the kingdom."[32] The synoptic commentary of Malina and Rohrbaugh handles the parable's meaning as a matter of a generous patron.[33] Of the existing treatments of which I am aware, only that of William Herzog comes close to the visceral Jesuanic situation: The "owner" arrogates to himself the prerogatives of God in his "ownership," and the true interests of the workers are confounded by the "divide and conquer" strategy in the payoff.[34]

In light of structural macrosociology, in other words, there appears a largely ignored dimension in this parable. First, village labor is vulnerable and readily available for the purposes of the elites on large estates. Second, the pay issue underscores that conventional village morals are irrelevant. The capriciousness of the pay underscores the vulnerability and exploitation

31. Jeremias, *Parables*, 136.

32. Scott, *Hear Then the Parable*, 297.

33. Malina and Rohrbaugh, *Synoptic Gospels*, (1992) 100, (2003) 377.

34. Herzog, *Parables*, 93–94.

of a coerced labor force. The picture brings into focus something like the degraded wage-labor conditions in the American South during the era of slavery. Third, the pay is in silver coin that will simply return to the tax collector in tribute. And fourth, the envy of the workers has less to do with the pay than with the distortion of village justice under conditions of coerced labor organization. This story encapsulates a statement about conscript labor, not the landlord's generosity. The evil eye has to do with the landlord's evil in destroying the integrity of the traditional village, as well as the entire situation of imperial exploitation.

In similar fashion, Rohrbaugh shows convincingly that the parable of the Talents/Pounds depends for its central evaluation on an appreciation of limited-good beliefs among Jesus' first-century Galilean audience, and a concomitant critique of money as associated with evil powers.[35]

The Jesus group conversely centered in a sense of Passover freedom and covenant justice, of familial sharing, and a table free from invidiousness. After all, Jesus assuredly said, "You cannot be a slave to God and Mammon" (Luke 16:13), and probably said something like, "It is more honorable to give rather than to receive" (Acts 20:35). Because these values challenged the Roman patronal order and allegiance to Rome, Jesus met the rebel's fate of Roman crucifixion.[36] Within a few decades, Simon bar Giora led an important segment in the rebellion against Rome's coercion and immediately declared freedom for slaves (Josephus, *War* 4.508). The Flavians made a special point of leading him in public triumph to his execution in Rome.

(2) Roman Honor, the Jesus Group, and the Christ-Follower Movement

Roman honor had a significant impact on the Jesus group and Christ-follower movement through its building and labor impacts. The Herods were continuous builders. Herod the Great rebuilt the Jerusalem temple and Caesarea Maritima; Herod Antipas founded Tiberias. When the Jerusalem temple was completed, Agrippa II was forced to establish a paving program to keep the labor occupied (Josephus, *Ant.* 20.222). Jesus of Nazareth's participation within this building system, and his historical activity needs much further appraisal along these lines. Both his critique of Mammon

---

35. Rohrbaugh, "Text of Terror," 111–16.
36. Oakman, *Political Aims of Jesus*, 94–111.

and his advocacy of an ethic of sharing express contrasting limited-good perspectives.[37] Since the royal power of God held eminent domain over all property, Jesus in effect subverted permanent inequality and the weak-property ideology supporting the ruling elites. This would explain why he showed no interest in land-redistribution schemes (Luke 12:13–15; whether Matt 5:5b and Mark 10:30 go back to Jesus is questionable).

Turning to the Christ-followers in cities, much more should be done to investigate the circumstances of their networks within the labor and urban structures of the East. Taking the case of Corinth, for instance, Rome's reshaping of the city embodied its claim to honor. That reshaping included significant temple-building and waterworks. Moreover, Rome attempted to build a canal to facilitate transhipment across the Isthmus of Corinth (Suetonius, *Nero* 19 on the ancient "railway" for hauling ships across called the *diolkos*).[38] This kind of project had enormous labor ramifications, and Paul's group drew upon those involved in the labor-system. Paul mentions Erastus the city treasurer in Rom 16:23; a Latin inscription, discovered in 1929, identified a city-aedile as Erastus, perhaps the same person.[39] If Corinthian baptismal practices had elements of "ritual inversion," as DeMaris suggests, namely, by subverting Rome's honor claims and replacing them with Christ's claims as the source of all good, then limited-good perspectives were clearly involved in shaping the social attitudes and values of these followers.[40]

The same kinds of study should be carried through for the movement in other cities, such as Syrian Antioch or Asian Ephesus where urban building and agrarian restructuring were equally significant. Moreover, attention needs to be given to Julio-Claudian and Flavian social policies that would affect the labor circumstances of the Jesus group and Christ-followers. At the time that Paul was dealing with the Corinthian problems, Claudius (in order to solve the problem of Rome's grain supply) refashioned the harbor at Ostia. Consonant with general Julio-Claudian policies, such a project implies greater centralization of the Roman administration and more rigorous taxation to maintain the annona (Rome's citizen-grain supply) and enlarged bureaucracy.

---

37. Oakman, "The Radical Jesus," chapter 1 in this volume; Oakman, *Political Aims of Jesus*, 91.

38. See Fraser, "The *Diolkos* of Alexandria," 134; *OCD*, 475.

39. Cadbury, "Erastus of Corinth," 42–58.

40. DeMaris, *The New Testament in Its Ritual World*, 32, 49.

The New Testament writers largely worked during the Flavian period. Much yet might be brought into focus about how Flavian policies regarding city and country affected the attitudes and values of the second-generation Christ-follower movement through its writings. Vespasian has already been mentioned. Though there was a revisioning in the New Testament of the social dynamics of the Jesus group (largely in the service of historical amnesia—since Jesus became honorable and increasingly clothed in the garb of developing christology), the texts still embody the everyday contexts and circumstances under Flavian labor coercion.

Conclusion

In sum, this limited review of limited-good attitudes and values in the Bible stresses past achievements, after the pioneering work of Bruce Malina and others, and the need for further inquiries into the ecological, natural, and macrosociological bases of such attitudes and values. Not only is such study needed for understanding the Bible, and its formulating social movements, but also for appraising the ongoing significance of the Bible. For while Reaganesque beliefs about unlimited goods and unlimited good continue to infect contemporary thinking, global warming and other environmental strictures impose increasingly formidable externalities on formal economistic theories hitherto untroubled by a naturally limited world. Regardless of the babble of political ideologues, the bubble of the myth of endless economic growth seems about to burst. Perhaps the clarity about social relations, ethical imperatives, and ultimate environmental conditions first formulated within ancient texts like the Bible become not less relevant, but even more relevant to our times when it comes to discernment of humane values. Indeed, it may be that biblical scholarship can play a genuinely significant cultural and social role in helping the twenty-first century to realize its constructive human potential within a world of real limits.

CHAPTER 3

Was the Galilean Economy
Oppressive or Prosperous?

*Socioarchaeology and Dimensions of Exploitation
in First-Century Palestine*

> What did you go out into the wilderness to look at? a reed shaken
> by the wind? But what did you go out to see? a man clothed in soft
> garments? Behold, those wearing soft clothing are in royal houses.
> —Q 7:24–25[1]

> The scholarship of antiquity is often removed from the real world,
> of the voiceless masses, the 95 percent who knew how "the other
> half" lived in antiquity. —THOMAS CARNEY[2]

RECENT SCHOLARSHIP ON GALILEE has focused intently on social matters. This chapter examines whether Herodian Galilee can be characterized as "socially oppressive," and whether Jesus of Nazareth and his early
followers were responding to perceived oppression.[3] While to date there is
no consensus, the answers here will be *yes* to both issues.

The alternative raised by the question in the chapter title presents
something of a false dilemma since both prosperity and oppression can be

1. Robinson, Hoffmann, and Kloppenborg, eds., *Critical Edition of Q*, 128–30 (my
translation; again Q is cited according to Luke). This chapter originally appeared as a
dialogical foil to Overman, "Picture of Relative Economic Health."

2. Carney, *The Shape of the Past*, xiv.

3. Jensen, "Herod Antipas," 7–32; for an earlier installment of this dialog, largely
concerned with Upper Galilee, see Horsley, "Villages of Upper Galilee," 1–16; also, Meyers, "Archaeological Response," 17–26.

true for first-century Galilee. The more appropriate question is *cui bono*? Who in fact benefitted from an obviously prosperous economic development in Herodian Galilee? Prosperity, if shared or controlled inequitably, could reasonably be perceived by some like Jesus of Nazareth as the other side of oppressive and exploitative social relations.

In this short essay, two main claims will be made: (1) Palestinian archaeology cannot ignore insights of comparative social science; in particular, Galilean archaeologists cannot simply work in pursuit of cultural artifacts; (2) early Roman Galilee was a hierarchically stratified society, and this social stratification is clearly visible in the archaeological record. In fact, specific archaeological features show the unequal distribution of power and wealth, and sensitive common people might feel oppressed and characterize their lot as exploitation. To support this second claim, appeals will also be made to the early Jesus material in the Q tradition.

The Importance of Comparative Sociotheoretical Frameworks

Archaeology like biblical studies is an interpretive discipline. No interpretation is "innocent," that is, absent of preunderstandings or conditioning from the modern environment. Further, the archaeological record like all historical records is more or less incomplete, which is why interpretation is always needed. Historians, biblical scholars, and archaeologists have to "posit" what is missing. Rogerson has put the matter well:

> while we do not invent the past, our narrative accounts of it are affected and shaped by factors such as our very limited knowledge of what happened in the past, and our situatednesses in nation, gender, class, political and religious commitment or lack of the same, and aims and interests in wanting to construct narratives about the past, in the first place.[4]

Comparative social sciences can help to correct anachronistic and ethnocentric interpretations, as well as to characterize typical social stratification patterns or other social relations.

A recent development in views on ancient social realia has been the declaration of a "post-Finley" thought world, bringing Roman antiquity much closer to the view that Roman rule was benign and Roman-period commerce and urbanization produced a kind of utilitarian greatest good

---

4. Rogerson, *Theology*, 18.

for the greatest number. This shift would seem to rule out a view of oppression or exploitation in provincial settings, or at least call for a measured testing of social conditions in various areas through artifact, inscription, and text. Still, the post-Finley view itself highlights, just as much as Moses Finley, Gerhard Lenski, or John Kautsky, that larger conceptual frames are always involved in identifying and interpreting data.

Partly because of scholarly disputes about the use of Finley, Lenski, or Kautsky in elucidating social relations in such an agrarian context, I invoked in my recent *The Political Aims of Jesus* the approach of David Christian and Big History to show that a bird's-eye view of all (advanced) agrarian civilizations show fairly static social themes with variations.[5] These agrarian societies have been the prevalent type since the end of the last ice ages, with predictable population structures—with so-called surpluses able to support only about 10 percent of the populace as non-agricultural producing elites (Carney's "other half"). Even if the 10 percent were to become larger, there are still numerous village and town dwellers with minimal resources, high infant mortality rates, low life expectancies, and dependence upon favors from the more powerful. A regular class of agrarian producers—invariably close to 90 percent—were compelled by adaptive necessities to produce or starve. Commerce complicates this picture, but raises questions about who benefits and what or how things "trickle down" to small towns and villages.

It is important to see that "exploitation" can be typical, built into ordinary structures of agrarian societies. Exploitative oppression is objectively normal, whether the 90 percent are subjectively aware of it or not, and has been so for most of historical humanity who have lived in agrarian villages and small towns. Oppression could occasionally grow.

To evaluate properly the lead question of this chapter, then, it is helpful to distinguish structural oppression, "inarticulate felt-oppression," and "articulate perception" about oppression. Preindustrial agrarian societies were based upon structural oppression in the form of exploitation of agrarian labor and so-called surpluses by relatively small leisured elites, with correspondingly constant food insecurity for the primary producers; peasants could feel this oppression without necessarily being aware of its systemic causes; under certain circumstances, individuals could become conscious of the injustices of exploitation and speak out or decide to resist, or at least criticize salient social aspects. Armed insurrections are rare among rural peoples; banditry is a more likely course of protest. Both of

5. Oakman, *The Political Aims of Jesus*; Christian, *Maps of Time*.

these are dangerous for primary producers since insurrections or banditry make an already precarious subsistence even more insecure.

The Importance and Consequences of Social Stratification

Some years ago, Eric Meyers and James Strange emphasized the cultural overlays in Greco-Roman Palestine.[6] Their analysis remains helpful, but I prefer to speak of political overlays. While there are many cultural variables in the picture of Roman Galilee, the primary social variable for social stratification is power, especially expressed through patronage to or from privileged families and concomitant social structures and stratifications. The Herods in Galilee are a clear example, but the elite Judean priestly groups also had strong interests in Galilee (as Josephus's mission demonstrates). In my mind, politics is primary; culture is embedded (i.e., a function of the ruling family's or families' preferences). Moreover, culture can support politics as in the case of religious legitimation of Roman power. Culture can become a powerful tool of empire!

David Christian speaks of "important characteristics" that, despite diverse cultures, provide underlying coherence to all agrarian societies. These are societies "based on villages," open to "epidemic disease," which evidence "new forms of power and hierarchy," and develop "enduring relations with nonagrarian peoples." Further,

> Although the crops, the technologies, and the rituals of villagers varied greatly from region to region, all such peasant communities were affected by the annual rhythms of harvesting and sowing, the demands of storage, the need for cooperation within and among households, and the need to manage relations with outside communities.[7]

Agrarian Prosperity and Endangered Subsistence

On the one hand, prosperity is indicated for Hellenistic-Roman Galilee in several respects. Josephus stresses that Galilee was intensively farmed and very productive (*War* 3.41–44). Wine development from the time of Ptolemy Philadelphus is attested in the Zenon Papyri (third century BCE); oil

6. Strange and Meyers, *Archaeology, the Rabbis, and Early Christianity*.

7. Christian, *This Fleeting World*, 32.

development in Galilee with Hasmoneans, and for export, but in Judea and Philistia from the Iron Age.[8] The appearance of larger and multitudinous presses for wine and oil during the Greco-Roman era indicate specialization. City and state garnered grain stores. Josephus mentions royal and imperial grain stores (*Life* 71, 73, 119). Acts 12:20 mentions Herod Agrippa's grain supply for Tyre and Sidon. Mendel Nun calls attention to the grain supply of Tiberias from lands of Susita.[9] The solid prosperity of Sepphoris and Tiberias is attested by both Josephus and archaeology. Houses on the acropolis of Sepphoris have storerooms aplenty.[10] For Tiberias, the fish of the lake were a ready resource.

On the other hand, the commoner population would have good reasons for perennial concern about subsistence. For peasant villagers, whose primary productive activity was agriculture, and who always needed to procure annual food, after rents, taxes, and other exchanges in kind, very little could be left of the annual harvest. Peter Brown recently has stressed that 60 percent of agrarian production by the 80 percent (according to Lenski, 70–86 percent of agrarian societies are peasants[11]) ended up in the storehouses of the "wealthy decile," and that typically one-third of the harvest was left for the annual peasant food stock. Brown claims that "granaries emerge as the economic villains of the ancient world."[12] Jesus is well aware of the storehouse (Q 12:42–46), and there is ample attestation of criticism (Q 16:13 "Mammon"; Q 9:58 "foxes have holes"; cf. Luke 12:16–20). One study suggests that the interannual storage in the ancient world may have been only 5 percent, meaning that most of the annual harvest was consumed in the year harvested.[13]

Some thought experiments can indicate important social variables in food security. Assume the arable land of Roman Palestine available for grain production to be 381,000 Ha.[14] If 5 Ha is an average subsistence plot in the Mediterranean world, then Roman Palestine would nominally support 76,200 subsistence farms. If land plots were less than 5 Ha, then farmers might have to draw in food resources from elsewhere. Eusebius (*Eccl. Hist.*

---

8. Aviam, *Jews, Pagans and Christians*, 54, 56–57.

9. Nun, *Ancient Anchorages*, 12.

10. Weiss, "Sepphoris," 1327.

11. Lenski, *Power and Privilege*, 243–85.

12. Brown, *Through the Eye of a Needle*, 12–13, 15.

13. Van Leeuwen, Földvari, and Pirngruber, "Markets in Pre-Industrial Societies."

14. Hamel, *Poverty and Charity*, 138.

3.20.1–2) says that Jesus' relatives held 39 *plethra* (*iugera* = 5 Ha) between two families. If some land were fallowed, then this would also mandate alternate food resources. If population grew beyond about 76,200 families (there are estimates of families between five and ten persons in size and Roman-era population in Palestine between two hundred fifty thousand and one million), then food insecurity might grow as well. If landlords put more area into commercial crops, leaving less production for subsistence, then this too would stress food security. Hence, land use and land tenure arrangements, and population pressure, could place significant straits on basic food resources for many.

Broshi approaches the issue from a different angle.[15] He says that 381,000 Ha produces 230,000 tons of grain = 230,000,000 kgs. With minimal average annual consumption (beggar) = 200 kgs, this estimate arrives at maximum population in Roman Palestine of 1,150,000. This estimate ignores animal feed.

Natural disasters would only compound the social-structural factors working against secure subsistence for the many. According to Josephus *Ant.* 15.299–316, in 25 BCE Herod imported 80,000 kors of grain from Egypt during a famine; 80,000 cors equal 24,218,000 kilograms, enough to feed 121,090 minimally for a year. Hamel cites Tannaitic tradition, "The real difference between rich and poor people was in terms of security. Richer people had a wide margin of safety . . . The Midrash on Lamentations puts it tersely: 'While the fat one becomes lean, the lean one is dead.'"[16] Thus, perennial food insecurity based upon the structural exploitation of an agrarian society could lead to felt oppression and from time to time also to overt perception of oppressive arrangements. Bones from commoner graves would certainly shed light on how often subsistence crises were encountered in the first century. As is known, in Palestinian archaeology there are difficulties related to bone studies.

Social stratification is clearly evident in the archaeological record. Fieldstone walls are typical in villages and towns, while ashlars are common in city public buildings. Jotapata/Yodfat shows social stratification within the site, as commoner houses with unplastered fieldstone walls were

---

15. Broshi's estimates as reported by Hamel, *Poverty and Charity*, 136 n. 242, 138–39. Calculations aided by the privately distributed Convert program of Stefan Kloppenborg © 2001.

16. Hamel, *Poverty and Charity*, 55.

found near a house with painted plaster.[17] The Herodian period witnessed numerous monumental building projects throughout Palestine (the Jerusalem temple, Caesarea Maritima, Herod's villas at Jericho, the Herodium, Sepphoris and Tiberias). These projects depended upon available labor and siphoned off labor from the villages and away from agricultural work. Considering also that these building projects were tied into the demonstration of loyalty and honor toward Rome, their implications for social pressure on the village is clear.

Downstream Patronage, Land Tenure, and Tenancy

Typically, peasant villagers engage in agricultural production with the aim of annual consumption. There is strong evidence that the late Hellenistic and early Roman periods produced changes in landholding and labor commitments detrimental to the village peasant but positive for the urban landlord and Herodian building programs.

Careful studies of landholding patterns in various periods of Greco-Roman Palestine may eventually settle the distribution between "large estates" and commoner/village smallholdings.[18] One problem with this dichotomy, which may frustrate archaeological inferences about land tenure, is that "large estates" are often comprised of patchworks of smaller holdings worked by various villages, and it seems that elites thought of villages as belonging to estates or cities. This was a ready way to organize agrarian productive labor, and given traditional hostility between villages, to divide and conquer (hinder mass organized rebellion).

John Kloppenborg's careful study, perhaps the best available now, indicates the growth of tenancy relationships in Hellenistic-Roman Palestine, and this would accord well with the (re)organization of large estate holdings, absentee landowners dwelling in urban areas, and heightened dependency of agrarian labor.[19] Douglas Edwards substantially denies this picture (see below on coins, markets).[20]

---

17. Aviam, "Yodfat," 2077.

18. See the study of Fiensy, "Large Estates"; Hirschfeld, "Fortified Manor Houses," 197–226.

19. Kloppenborg, "Agricultural Tenancy," 33–66; see Strickert, *Philip's City*, 165, concerning the impact of the city of Tiberias upon land tenure.

20. Edwards, "Roman Galilean Villages," 362–63.

Upstream Patronage, Money, and Markets

Work of Keith Hopkins has urged us to see that Roman provincial policy allowed a fair amount of the tax/rent-take to "buy" the loyalty of provincial elites. In the first century, this system worked for a good while for the Herods and elite Judean priestly families. Peter Brown concurs but sees urban town councilors as the heavy lifters in the later empire. All provincial elites expressed their loyalty by building monuments favorable to Rome, so Herod: Caesarea Maritima; Antipas: Tiberias; Philip: Bethsaida. Moreover, the Herods shipped significant resources out of their territories in Palestine.[21]

The key issue in this picture is the elite control of productive decisions and resources, particularly control of agriculture, fishing, and small industry (*ergasteria*). Control of land by city elites and estate-tenancy is indicated in the pages of Josephus and the New Testament gospels. Further, that Antipas built Tiberias on the lake suggests his interest in tighter control of the fishing industry.[22] Elites controlled production of ceramics and textiles, as evidenced in Galilee by common pottery made at Kefar Hananiah, Kefar Shichin, and Yodfat. Loom weights may tie Sepphoris and Jotapata together. Jerusalem interests controlled production and distribution of Herodian lamps, while chalk vessels seem to have been a concern of priestly groups.[23] Ceramics have been central to discussions of markets and trade in Galilee, but they also hold information about social status and stratification. Commoner houses do not as a rule yield fine wares or stone vessels. It is interesting to consider that stone vessels are often found along with hard-fired ceramic vessels (subject to impurity). Magan gives information that the craftsmen at Ḥizma near Jerusalem prepared their lunches in common vessels![24] Stone vessels thus are also status and not just purity-concern indicators and equally supply evidence for social differentiation.

With regard to money and markets, coin counts at Jotapata, Kefar Qana, and Gamla show that bronze coinage flowed to political centers, thus indicating its predominant function of keeping the countryside in debt.[25] Indeed the bimetal money system of the early empire worked in accordance

---

21. Oakman, *The Political Aims of Jesus*, 66.

22. Strickert, *Philip's City*, 91, 165.

23. See Aviam, "Distribution Maps," 120 (map includes 25 sites).

24. Magen, *Stone Vessel Industry*, 52–61, 138–41.

25. Oakman, "Execrable Peasants!" 139–64 (chapter 4 in this volume).

with Gresham's law, i.e., driving the good silver to political centers and leaving the countryside holding less valuable copper money. Jesus was critical of money's power, and again warned of enslavement to Mammon (money on deposit or loan). So Jesus also said (Q 12:58), "As you are underway with your creditor, make a deal (take pains to be free of him), lest he remand you to the judge, and the judge hand you over to the bailiff, and you be thrown into (debt) prison." So Hamel is of the opinion, "Debt was a permanent feature of the economic structure . . . From the point of view of the landowner, the existence of debt was a sign that the correct degree of extraction was being applied to his tenants."[26]

Markets too showed political overlay. While MacMullen's 75 percent of ancient exchanges were local is perhaps correct—since peasants sometimes need to exchange for other necessities—commercial markets were under the control of royal or urban elites.[27] In Peter Brown's judgment, "Farmers could bring their produce into the nearest town. But the rich had privileged access to wider and more lucrative markets. They alone could defeat distance."[28] City markets and local fairs were controlled by elites (see *agoranomoi*).[29] Again, Jesus lamented a situation in which everything now had a price: "Are not five sparrows sold for two *assaria*? And not one of them is forgotten before God. Indeed, even the hairs of your head are all numbered. Fear not; you are worth more than many sparrows" (Q 12:6–7).

There are good reasons finally for seeing both prosperity and oppressive exploitation as interrelated social realities conditioning the Galilean material record and the concerns and activities of the historical Jesus (and others). To a degree, the debate continues unresolved because of differing ways of viewing both textual and artifactual data. Neville Morley has written (just as John Rogerson has[30]):

> The problem with this long-running debate [about the 'primitivism' of Finley, Paulina et al.]—the reason why it has yet to be resolved, and why historians are becoming increasingly frustrated with it . . .—is that the available evidence is inconclusive, because

26. Hamel, *Poverty and Charity*, 156–57.

27. MacMullen, "Market-Days," 333–41.

28. Brown, *Through the Eye of a Needle*, 14; this general picture is corroborated by Snell, "Trade and Commerce (ANE)," 625–29 and Sidebotham, "Trade and Commerce (Roman)," 629–33.

29. Chancey, *Greco-Roman Culture*, 135.

30. Rogerson, *Theology of the Old Testament*, 18.

the interpretation of any individual example depends on prior assumptions about the nature of the ancient economy.[31]

The interpretation of Herodian Galilee through text and spade can show material prosperity, exploitative relations benefitting the power elites, and reasons to believe the commoner felt oppression and sometimes perceived its social mechanisms with utter clarity. For the future, the fuller inclusion of comparative social sciences is necessary to test assumptions and pose more precise social questions. Both historians and archaeologists can benefit from "big picture deductions" as well as "induction from detail"—at the very least, having both types of approaches in situ will allow sharper questions. The kinds of social questions asked of excavation can sharpen the interpretive results, but *caveat lector*—interpretation must reckon always with an incomplete record!

31. Morley, *Trade*, 5.

CHAPTER 4

Execrating? or Execrable Peasants!

Well, ours is not a maritime country; neither commerce nor the intercourse which it promotes with the outside world has any attraction for us. Our cities are built inland, remote from the sea; and we devote ourselves to the cultivation of the productive country with which we are blessed.[1]

Herod was a shrewd businessman, who took advantage of many commercial enterprises, both domestically and internationally.[2]

MY RESPONSE TO MORDECHAI Aviam's excellent survey article will be to offer selective ruminations about peasants and political economy in first-century Galilee, including definitions and models drawn from peasant or agrarian theorists, along with some observations or questions about the archaeological data, especially money, in the light of these models.[3]

What Is a "Peasant"?

The word "peasant" has been securely attested in the English language since the fifteenth century.[4] Karl Marx, Werner Sombart, and Max Weber

---

1. Josephus, *Ag. Ap.*, 1.60 (LCL).

2. Dar, "Agrarian Economy," 305–6.

3. This chapter appeared originally in the Southeast ASOR meeting 2010 conference volume *The Galilean Economy* as a response to Aviam, "First-century Galilee." Christian, *Maps of Time* provides the largest framework and plausibility for the ideas of my response, especially the chapters on agrarian civilizations.

4. Borrowed from the French language, *OED* 594.

wrote early scientific works on the social life and values of the German peasantry.[5] Others were producing more anecdotal and impressionistic studies of peasants.[6] For instance, Elihu Grant wrote on *The Peasantry of Palestine* in 1907.[7] Gustaf Dalman's *Arbeit und Sitte in Palästina* appeared from 1928 to 1942.[8] Dalman cataloged the details of everyday Arab peasant life. In the 1930 collection of Sorokin, Zimmerman, and Galpin, the three-volume *A Systematic Source Book in Rural Sociology*, the terms "peasant" and "farmer" still are used rather interchangeably.[9] Mintz points to Robert Redfield's *Tepoztlán* (1930) as an early study by an anthropologist.[10] The study of the history and anthropology of peasantry took firm shape and flourished after World War II, reaching perhaps an apogee with the work of Eric Wolf and James C. Scott in the 1980s and 1990s. Impetus for study came not only from historical and ethnographic interests, but also from postcolonial and development policy issues.[11] Traditional peasantries have been disappearing for some time now under the impact of global markets and urbanization.[12] Recently, postmodern trends and the turn to the emic subject in social sciences have brought the term "peasant" into doubt as a general category (see the section "Accursed Peasants" below).

The ancients certainly had words for agricultural types that we could better understand through the literature on peasants—the Latin *rusticus* or *agricola*, the Greek *geōrgos* or *agroikos*, the Semitic *'ikkar*, and so on. Rural types are often praised by Roman writers as those most to be honored. These agrarian viewpoints, for the most part, represented the ideals

5. Marx, "Eighteenth Brumaire," 229–37; Sombart, *Der moderne Kapitalismus*, excerpts in Sorokin, Zimmerman, and Galpin, *Systematic Source Book*, 1:170–84; Weber, *Economy and Society*, e.g., 90 or 468.

6. Foster, "What Is a Peasant?" 2–14.

7. Grant, *Peasantry of Palestine*; subsequently revised as *The People of Palestine*.

8. Dalman, *Arbeit und Sitte*.

9. Sorokin, Zimmerman, and Galpin, *A Systematic Source Book in Rural Sociology*.

10. Mintz, "Definition of Peasantries," 92.

11. The readings in Shanin, *Peasants and Peasant Societies*, provide a sense of the rise of peasant studies; Redfield, *Peasant Society and Culture*, 15–39, gives a brief history of anthropological recognition of peasants.

12. Plattner, *Economic Anthropology*; Bernstein and Byres, "Agrarian Change," 1–56; Christian writes, "In the late agrarian era, most households lived in the countryside and engaged in small-scale farming. Today, small farming has vanished in many regions and is declining where it still survives" (*Maps of Time*, 348). So, I note in my *Jesus and the Peasants*, 1–2 that urbanization since 1900 has left most biblical scholars with little feel for or experience of the lives and realities of peasants.

and prejudices of elite "gentlemen farmers." For instance, Cato writes, "And when [our ancestors] would praise a worthy their praise took this form: 'good husbandman,' 'good farmer.'"[13] Varro likewise comments

> And not only is the tilling of the fields more ancient—it is more noble. It was therefore not without reason that our ancestors tried to entice their citizens back from the city to the country; for in time of peace they were fed by the country Romans, and in time of war aided by them.[14]

There was also the snobbish view of the peasant as a rube. Theophrastus says of the *agroikos*:

> He will sit down with his cloak above his knee, and thus expose too much of himself. Most things this man sees in the streets strike him not at all, but let him espy an ox or an ass or a billy-goat, and he will stand and contemplate him. He is apt also to take from the larder as he eats, and to drink his wine over-strong; to make secret love to the bake-wench, and then help her grind the day's corn for the whole household and himself with it . . . When he receives money he tests it and finds it wanting; it looks, says he, too much like lead; and changes it for other. And if he has lent his plough, or a basket, or a sickle, or a sack, he will remember it as he lies awake one night and rise and go out to seek it.[15]

Perhaps a more realistic view of the peasant comes from Jesus ben Sira in the early second century BCE (38:24–26 RSV):

> The wisdom of the scribe depends on the opportunity of leisure; and he who has little business may become wise. How can he become wise who handles the plow, and who glories in the shaft of a goad, who drives oxen and is occupied with their work, and whose talk is about bulls? He sets his heart on plowing furrows, and he is careful about fodder for the heifers.

Sirach also gives a sense of limited labor specialization in Hellenistic period Judea, naming craftsmen (especially the makers of signets), the smith, and the potter. Again, this is a depiction of villagers, village life, proletarian and rural labor from the vantage point of elites.[16]

13. Cato, *De Agri Cultura* 2 (LCL).

14. Varro, *Rerum Rusticarum* 3.1.4 (LCL).

15. Theophrastus, *Characters*, 4.4–11 (LCL).

16. Jeremias gives some idea of urban division of labor at the time of Jesus (*Jerusalem*, 4–27). By the Middle Roman period, the list could include at least "forty kinds of

Josephus, as is well known, gives us every expectation of having to deal with conditions and arrangements of agrarian production:

> For the land [of the two Galilees] is everywhere so rich in soil and pasturage and produces such variety of trees, that even the most indolent are tempted by these facilities to devote themselves to agriculture. In fact, every inch of the soil has been cultivated by the inhabitants; there is not a parcel of waste land.[17]

Of course, use of "farmer" versus "peasant" could be seen as merely a semantic issue. But this is not the best approach from the standpoint of the comparative social sciences. There have been good reasons to identify under the term "peasant" a general agricultural phenomenon through much of world history.[18] One of these reasons has been the synthetic and comparative work of macrosociology—for instance, exemplified in the early twentieth-century work of Weber, then in the 1950s and 1960s in work of Gideon Sjøberg, Karl Wittfogel, and Gerhard Lenski, and then in the 1980s by work of John Kautsky.[19] Further, the historically and ethnographically informed works of Barrington Moore, Robert Redfield, George Foster, Teodore Shanin, Eric Hobsbawm, Eric Wolf, and James Scott have provided us with a very persuasive set of studies on the variations on a theme we call "peasantry."[20] In addition, post-war work of Karl Polanyi was especially

---

craftsmen," Klausner identifies "Tailors, shoemakers, builders, masons, carpenters, millers, bakers, tanners, spice-merchants, apothecaries, cattlemen, butchers, slaughterers, dairymen, cheesemakers, physicians and bloodletters, barbers, hairdressers, laundrymen, jewellers, smiths, weavers, dryers, embroiderers, workers in gold brocade, carpet makers, matting makers, well-diggers, fishermen, bee-keepers, potters and platemakers (who were also pottery dealers), pitcher makers, coopers, pitch-refiners and glaze-makers, makers of glass and glassware, armourers, copyists, painters and engravers" (*Jesus of Nazareth*, 177).

17. Josephus, *War* 3.42–43 (LCL).

18. Kearney, "Peasantry," 195–96; von Dietze, "Peasantry," 48–53; see Van der Spek, "The Hellenistic Near East," 414. Van der Spek makes it clear that subordinate rural labor was typical in the eastern Mediterranean world.

19. Lenski, *Power and Privilege*; Kautsky, *The Politics of Aristocratic Empires*; Sjøberg, *The Preindustrial City*; Weber, *Economy and Society*; Wittfogel, *Oriental Despotism*.

20. Foster, "Peasant Society and the Image of Limited Good," 300–23; Hobsbawm, *Primitive Rebels*; Hobsbawm, "Peasants and Politics," 3–23; Moore, *Social Origins*; Redfield, *Peasant Society and Culture*; Scott, *Moral Economy*; Shanin, *Peasant Societies*; Wolf, *Peasants*. James C. Scott writes to me (private communication) that he still considers Wolf's *Peasants* one of the best synthetic treatments.

important for characterizing premodern economics as "substantive" and embedded within noneconomic social and political concerns.[21]

Marx proposed the cultural and social isolation of peasants: "The small-holding peasants [of France] form a vast mass, the members of which live in similar conditions but without entering into manifold relations with one another. Their mode of production isolates them from one another instead of bringing them into mutual intercourse."[22] Chayanov emphasized in his theory that the family was the economic producing and consuming unit, while Wolf stressed that the peasant had to balance subsistence concerns with outside demands. Raymond Firth (1950) argued that the word "peasant" includes "other small-scale producers, such as fishermen and rural craftsmen, pointing out that 'they are of the same social class as the agriculturalists, and often members of the same families.'"[23] Here are some other representative definitions from significant peasant theorists: Barrington Moore (1966):

> A previous history of subordination to a landed upper class recognized and enforced in the laws, which, however, need not always prohibit movement out of this class, sharp cultural distinctions, and a considerable degree of *de facto* possession of the land, constitute the main distinguishing features of a peasantry.[24]

George Foster (1967):

> prepeasants [in ANE] were turned into peasants with the appearance of the first towns or incipient cities . . . in which political and usually religious control began to be exercised over the hinterland.[25]

---

21. Polanyi, Arensberg, and Pearson, *Trade and Market*; Polanyi, *Livelihood of Man*. The critique of Polanyi by North represents the formalist position (*Structure and Change*, 106). However, the formalist critique fails to appreciate that rational choice theory or maximization of self interest does not encompass all human economic motivations.

22. Qtd. in Shanin, *Peasant Societies*, 230.

23. Qtd. in Foster, "What Is a Peasant?" 4. Wolf took issue with this broad definition, "It [definition of peasant] does not, however, include fishermen or landless laborers" (*Peasant Wars*, xiv). He also differentiated peasants from farmers, who fully enter into the market (while as we argue, peasants do not).

24. Moore, *Social Origins*, 111.

25. Foster, "What Is a Peasant?" 7.

James Scott (1976):

> The distinctive economic behavior of the subsistence-oriented peasant family results from the fact that, unlike a capitalist enterprise, it is a unit of consumption as well as a unit of production.[26]

Finally, John Kautsky (1982):

> I have sought to confine use of the term "peasants" to agriculturalists exploited by aristocrats, . . . There can be no aristocrat without peasants and no peasants without aristocrat.

Regarding "The Aristocracy in the Economy" he says,

> Exploitation is, indeed, the principal and only necessary link between the peasants' societies in their villages and the society of the aristocracy, regardless of who "owns" the land.[27]

"Peasant" as a Model for Agrarian Rural Labor

Table 4.1 provides contrasting ideal types to define some of the salient differences between premodern peasants and modern farmers.[28]

Peasant	Farmer, "agricultural entrepreneur"
Technology: iron plows and tools, human and animal energies, village cooperation	**Technology**: steel plows and tools, machinery, petrochemicals, farm cooperatives
Strong familism: Rigid family codes and hierarchy, mistrust of outsiders, strict gender roles	**Weaker familism**: Family codes upheld in the face of cultural change, works with outsiders for business purposes under terms of limited trust, gender roles more open

26. Scott, *Moral Economy*, 13.

27. Kautsky, *The Politics of Aristocratic Empires*, 271; on aristocrats and the economy, Kautsky, *The Politics of Aristocratic Empires*, 103.

28. The notion of "Great" and "Little" Traditions of religion derives from Redfield, *Peasant Society and Culture*, 41–42.

Politics: The state is always an enemy to the subsistence margin; little-to-no participation in politics, localism, payment (or evasion) of taxes and dues	**Politics**: Some participation for the sake of promoting rural interests (cf. Jefferson—farming as basis for democracy), broader horizons, government liens upon profits
Family production: Self-sufficiency, subsistence, production for consumption	**Family production**: Market orientation, production for sale, buying of food
Economic exchange: Household economy; generalized reciprocity within the family, balanced reciprocity with villagers or other villages, negative reciprocity with strangers or agents of the elites	**Economic exchange**: Market-orientation; generalized reciprocity within the family, universalizing of balanced reciprocity; local cooperatives, appeals to the courts
Culture: Traditional, no education, very limited literacy (if any)	**Culture**: Traditional, some education and literacy, openness to technological innovation—modern scientific farming requires a high degree of technical knowledge
Traditional religion: Local (little) traditions; great tradition cared for by distant priests (cf. M. Weber, *Economy and Society*—religion of peasants is magic)	**Traditional religion**: More integrated into great traditions (cf. H. R. Niebuhr, *Social Sources of Denominationalism*)

Table 4.1: Ideal Type Definitions of Premodern "Peasant" and Modern "Farmer"

Further, Table 4.2 contrasts typical peasant values and attitudes with those of modern farmers.

Peasant Household Embedded in Imperial Politics	Farming Embedded in Modern Capitalist Economy
Production for consumption, self-sufficiency the ideal, but some labor specialization in the village, limited exchange between villages and towns	Production for market profit, production and consumption separated, modern farmer depends on a range of labor specializations

Peasant subsistence "mortgaged" by requisitions by outsiders	Taxation on profits
Local markets are in kind or simple products that peasant household cannot make for itself; markets require permission to enter; distinguish local markets from translocal or long-distance commerce	Land, labor, capital markets open to those with capital
Money—limited economic utility for most; money barter with copper tokens, silver needed for tax payments, distribution dependent on political forces and patronage	Money—generalized economic utility, "everything" is for sale for money
Debt—peasants are inevitably in debt, which usually expresses relations of long-term political indenture, extensive tenancy likely in early Roman Palestine	Debt—the farm can be foreclosed on, but some debt can periodically be assumed in order to invest in the operation or increase productivity (heavy machinery)
Politics structured through patronage; patrons control real wealth; elites control markets, banks, commerce	Politics structured through democratic systems

**Table 4.2: Peasant Values and Economic Orientation
in Contrast to Modern Farmer**

These tabular models are my own, representing the opposite ends of a spectrum of agrarian possibilities. They are constructed to highlight a significant issue in the discussion of the conference papers collected in *The Galilean Economy in the Time of Jesus*—the characteristics and situation of the typical first-century Galilean peasant family (household economy) embedded within Roman political-economy (involving imperial patronage politics and commercial interests). Max Weber would never allow us to say that peasant villagers in Roman Galilee were in every respect like the ideal types in the left-hand columns. The models are not reality. But they help us to think about the social dynamics in Roman Galilee in significant ways.

Peasants in Early Roman Galilee

Why should we think that rural cultivators in first-century Galilee were peasants? Here are several reasons. Rural families were the basic producing units. Considerations of technology and comparative social typology suggest that agriculture in early first-century Palestine was low-yield, based as it was upon the animal-drawn iron plow and iron hand implements (hoe, scythe, and so forth). Helmuth Schneider concurs: "In ancient agriculture, certainly, much of the work hardly changed over long periods of time: for example, ploughing with a pair of oxen, hoeing of the ground to eliminate weeds, harvesting the grain with a simple sickle, winnowing, or harvesting olives with long sticks." Schneider goes on: "Under the conditions of ancient technology, human muscle power remained one of the most important energy sources. Agricultural work in particular was highly physical work, done with simple tools such as hoe, sickle, or scythe."[29]

Archaeological surveys of Galilee also show varying agricultural plot sizes, but with the majority of the populace farming very small plots. Some time ago, David Fiensy and I respectively tried to estimate the size of a first-century subsistence plot. My result came to 0.6 hectare (1.5 acre) per adult.[30] Joel M. Halpern has shown for mid-twentieth-century Serbian peasants, 5 hectares (12.4 acres) was the threshold between "pure agriculturalist" families and "mixed agriculturalist" families.[31] Smaller plots on average would imply many families on the subsistence margin.

Lenski would classify large portions of the Roman East as fitting the macrosocietal type of the "advanced agrarian society," in which peasants and (iron) hand tools were the foundation of agricultural production. Proximity to the Mediterranean led to interconnections between agrarian society and maritime society, and commercial opportunities for elites.[32]

---

29. Schneider, "Technology," 149, 150; Greene, "Agriculture," 75 (based upon work of M. Jones) gives a sense of the slow rate of technological innovation in agricultural tools. Further information on the simple agricultural technology of antiquity can be found in White, *Technology*, 58–72.

30. Oakman, *Jesus and the Economic Questions of His Day*, 62; Fiensy, *The Social History of Palestine*, 93–94.

31. Halpern, *Serbian Village*, 73, 75.

32. "Agrarian society" and "maritime society," Lenski, *Power and Privilege*, 191; "advanced agrarian society" denotes the move from bronze to iron implements, Lenski and Lenski, *Human Societies*, 219.

We could think of Herodian Palestine as a whole as a "peasant society." Daniel Thorner once proposed that such societies had these major structural features:

(1)   "One half or more of the total production must be agricultural";

(2)   "More than half the working population must be engaged in agriculture";

(3)   Within a territorial state, having an administration with "at least five thousand officers, minor officials, flunkeys, and underlings";

(4)   With towns and a break between town and country that is "simultaneously political, economic, social, and cultural"; urban population is at least five hundred thousand or "at least 5 per cent of the entire population . . . reside in towns";

(5)   Agrarian production is accomplished by family household units.[33]

By Thorner's yardsticks, Roman Galilee would have most if not all of the salient features. Conditions 1, 2, and 5 are met (Josephus, *Ag. Ap.* 1.60). For condition 4, population estimates for early Roman Palestine are available, with five hundred thousand being a credible figure. Five percent of this [(3) and (4)] gives twenty-five thousand elites and their retainers, not difficult to imagine. Consider that this is at the right order of magnitude if populations of Jerusalem (twenty-five thousand), Sepphoris and Tiberias (five thousand to ten thousand each), and all other urban and town areas are added together.[34] Finally, (4) there is certainly a political, economic, and cultural break between the Herodian regime and the village Galilean/Judean cultivators.

It should not be forgotten that peasants always exist within political, city, or commercial systems that put varying degrees of stress on traditional peasant subsistence concerns. A period of increased commercialization and urbanization, such as we see in early Roman Palestine, would involve such stress. The model "A Dynamic Model of the Causes of Agrarian Conflict"

---

33. Thorner, "Peasantry," 508.

34. Hamel sees a possible population range for Roman Palestine between 250,000 and 1,000,000 (*Poverty and Charity*, 139). Reed estimates the populations of Sepphoris and Tiberias as between 8,000 and 12,000 (*Archaeology and the Galilean Jesus*, 89). Fiensy gives a population figure of 175,000 for Galilee, but only 3,500 elites in both Sepphoris and Tiberias (*Jesus the Galilean*, 40). Still, with retainers and town populations included, this estimate of Galilean urban population would likely cross the 5 percent threshold. See further below in this chapter on settlement populations and orders of magnitude.

shows how the economic development efforts of Judean and Galilean elites, with interest in translocal or Mediterranean commerce, would negatively impact peasant attitudes and values.[35]

FIGURE 4.1

A DYNAMIC MODEL OF THE CAUSES OF AGRARIAN CONFLICT

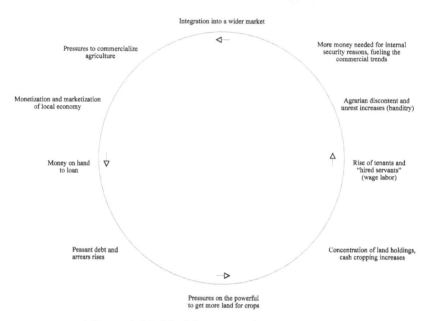

A Dynamic Model of the Causes of Agrarian Conflict

Tables 4.1 and 4.2 and figure 4.1 indicate that at least four important interpretive dimensions should be considered for non-elite Roman Galilee: (1) The relative extent of "pure agriculturalists" (subsistence agriculture), "mixed agriculturalists" (agriculture plus wage labor), and landless workers or rural proletariat; (2) taxation and the political impact of patronage politics; (3) the degree to which and the ways in which agrarian sectors of Galilee were drawn into Mediterranean commerce; and (4) the influence of peasant culture and values in the lives of the non-elite landless or rural proletariate (like Jesus or the fishers of the lake).

35. Model 4.1 is derived from comments of Henry Landsberger, taken from Oakman, *Jesus and the Peasants*, 168.

The entire situation of Galilean agriculturalists and non-elites, shaped in the first place by subsistence concerns and political realities, is best elucidated by theory informed by comparative study of peasants and agrarian societies. Interpretations without models informed by comparative social science will miss crucial social dynamics.[36] Interpretations without models will have a basis in uncertain social categories, or simply be anachronistic. The regularity of premodern patterns of elite organization of political economy based upon the labor of subsistence-oriented ruralites would urge against reading Galilee too much in terms of postcapitalist or postindustrial modernization. Ancient commerce and economic development served the interests of elites and their storehouses. Participation at the village level was more in terms of labor exploitation, mortgages on subsistence, and distortion of traditional/local/peasant values. David Christian borrows the term of William H. McNeill for this relationship: parasitism. The broad lines of "agrarian civilizations," Christian claims, are founded upon a multitude of primary producers and relatively small number of elite tribute-takers. Perspectives of "Big History" would argue in favor of the main definitions and historical findings of peasant studies.[37] Closer to the first-century Galilean soil, we have clear evidence in the early Jesus traditions, such as the parables (Talents/Minas, Unjust Steward) and some of the red-letter Q material (Lord's Prayer, pericope addressing anxiety about food and clothing, saying about God and Mammon), that subsistence and debt concerns were wrapped up with the Jesus movement. Social tensions also account for the appearance of Judah of Gamla. And there are very good indications that agrarian problems played a prominent role in the genesis of the Judean–Roman War; if Galilee is socially articulated to Judea as the archaeologists say, then such agrarian problems were likely also entailed in Galilee.[38]

36. On the importance of explicit models, see Carney, *The Shape of the Past*, 1–43; more recently, Morley, *Theories, Models and Concepts*, 1–31.

37. Christian, *Maps of Time*, 283–89; further, Christian writes, "Though the Chinese countryside was highly commericalized in the eighteenth century, structures of ownership and control of the land limited the extent to which the majority of the population could be involved in commercial networks" (*Maps of Time*, 389).

38. Goodman, "The First Jewish Revolt," 417–27; Applebaum, "Economic Causes," 237–64.

Accursed Peasants: The Current Critique

It is clear (from the 2010 conference discussion) that the category of "peasantry" has come into disrepute among some Galilean historians and archaeologists. Mordechai Aviam completely rejects the use of "peasant" as an interpretive category. He would use biblical terms like *'ish 'obed 'adama* (Zech 13:5). Sharon Mattila spoke from the audience during the brief panel discussion to urge that the term "peasant" simply be dropped. She has just published a very thorough account of why she believes the term is no longer helpful.[39] Her main conclusions are that peasants are often significantly differentiated by socioeconomic inequalities (not simply Marx's "potatoes in a sack"); also, rural cultivators have often utilized a "multiplicity of economic strategies" (not just subsistence agriculture).[40] Fiensy warns against reifying models, or supplying missing data from models.[41] Part of the concern in these critiques is that a social-science category replaces inferences solely from historical or archaeological data; part of the concern is that a social-science category like "peasant" is too simplistic in accounting for first-century Galilean social dynamics.

Among social scientists, of course, the terminological critique or questionable status of generalizations about rural peoples is not entirely news.[42] Already in 1934, von Dietze could write, "The term peasantry has undergone many changes in meaning in the past and is still subject to various interpretations. Common to all the shifting meanings, however, is a view of the peasant as a tiller of the soil to whom the land which he and his family work offers both a home and a living."[43]

Historical studies and ethnography show that "peasant" is not a simple category; nonetheless, social scientists continue to use the term. Part of the reason for this is that the social sciences concern themselves by definition with the typical; part of the reason for this is that social dynamics are otherwise unintelligible. Marc Becker, for instance, makes the following helpful observations:

---

39. Mattila, "Middle Peasants?" 291–313. Mattila's article gives an excellent history of some aspects of peasant studies and a focused critique of Richard A. Horsley.

40. Mattila, "Middle Peasants?" 301, 313.

41. Fiensy, *The Galilean Economy*, 177–81.

42. Mintz writes of "a persisting lack of consensus among scholars about the definition of the peasantry" ("Definition of Peasantries," 91).

43. Von Dietze, "Peasantry," 48.

It is difficult to establish a precise definition of the word "peasant" and, as Sidney Mintz noted in a 1973 essay in the *Journal of Peasant Studies*, this issue has invoked a lengthy debate. Issues of self identity, created identity, and situational identity all complicate a definition. On one hand, some scholars favor tightly restrictive definitions that limit peasants to a nineteenth-century rural French population, while others have broadened the term to include virtually anyone involved in agriculture, from hunters and gatherers to small landholders, whatever the economic mode of production involved. Increasingly, many historians who study peasants in Latin America have largely eschewed issues of terminology in order to focus on deeper and more significant questions of power and the role that the peasantry played in nation building. Collapsing diverse economic modes of production into a simplistic catch-all category of "peasant," however, tends to hide certain forms of rural consciousness. Not only has the term become so commonly used that it can hardly be avoided, but also a more critical inquiry into what it means to be a "peasant" helps to understand rural protest movements.[44]

Despite critical doubts, the *Journal of Peasant Studies* is still being published after nearly forty years. Yet, the people known historically under the label "peasants" are becoming extinct. David Christian quotes Eric Hobsbawm, "the most dramatic and far-reaching social change of the second half of [the twentieth century], and the one which cuts us off for ever from the world of the past, is the death of the peasantry."[45] Kearney remarks: "Until the mid-twentieth century, most of the world's population could be characterized as peasant, but since that time peasant communities have tended to become more complex, due largely to ever increasing rates of permanent and circular migration from agricultural communities to urban areas." Bernstein and Byres note the difficulties of a "peasant essentialism" and provide a lengthy discussion of the reasons for a shift "From Peasant Studies to Agrarian Change."[46] More recent studies of peasants thus move away from the traditional or historical to study rural peoples under

44. Becker, "Peasant Identity," 118; also available on line. In a private communication, Professor Becker has written to me, "[I see] all of the terminology I use as socially constructed and contradictory, but continue to use them with all of their vagueness anyway because of how they function as convenient shorthands for much more complicated concepts."

45. Hobsbawm, qtd. in Christian, *Maps of Time*, 453.

46. Kearney, "Peasantry," 196; Bernstein and Byres, "Agrarian Change," 4–5, 7–8.

the impact of modernization and globalism. This shift in the social situation of contemporary rural groups and in the focus of agrarian social sciences does not invalidate the use of comparative agrarian macrosociology or models inspired by peasant studies applied to the study of ancient rural social realities.

The concerns of Aviam, Mattila, and Fiensy can also be answered by several other considerations: First, "peasant" denotes a multidimensional concept, backed by a significant social-scientific literature, as both the models of this chapter and Marc Becker's comments show. The term "peasant" and related models, in other words, provide an important index into both comparative social-science literature and the agrarian realities on the first-century ground.[47] Particularly important, given that family is the basic institutional domain of Mediterranean societies, is the interpretive articulation *Family (peasant households)—Politics (elite households and others)—Economics/Religion.* What is noticeably missing from Aviam's interpretive account is the extension of family networks and patronage and the political structuring of socioeconomic relations as the basis for Hellenistic-Roman political economy. Economy and Religion are embedded in family and politics, not the other way around.[48] While the term "peasant" is a shorthand conceptual model for a great variety of rural cultivator situations, it points to a complex of many typical features. Second, all of our interpretations of the past are "etic," and without the use of explicit, clearly (con)tested interpretive models—better fitting for understanding the politics, economics, and culture of agrarian societies—some other interpretive framework will be imposed. Third, all of us have to supply missing elements in the data, since historical and archaeological data are always incomplete. Further discoveries of texts and artifacts can correct previous interpretations, of course, but the main lines of social interpretation are best informed by comparative social-scientific models and theory.

In sum, it is not a matter of discarding a term or a whole body of social-scientific work, but utilizing it with care to elucidate the agrarian conditions of early Roman Galilee, especially the familial-political-economic and religiocultural dynamics of that time and place.

---

47. The "indexical" value of a model has to do with its incisive isomorphic qualities, in terms of Carney's distinction between "homomorphic" (abstract) models and "isomorphic" (representational) models.

48. Hanson and Oakman, *Palestine in the Time of Jesus, passim.*

Peasants and Money, Markets, Commerce in Early Roman Galilee

The Hasmonean kingdom of Alexander Jannaeus, as the archeological accounts of Aviam and Berlin indicate, was an insular kingdom. Berlin shows that the Judean crown retained its simple cultural assemblages, eschewing the fancy imports from the Mediterranean.[49] Aviam shows that Jannaeus developed Migdal as a fishing harbor on the Kinnereth Lake; Jannaeus must have viewed the lake as a royal monopoly.[50] Surely, the economic aims of Herod the Great, Herod Antipas, and Philip would have claimed no less. It is clear that Herod the Great abandoned Hasmonean isolationism and embraced commerce. This is dramatically signified by the building of Caesarea Maritima. But Dar also shows that Herod had economic interests in balsam plantations, copper mining, and tax farming in Nabataea, Syria, and Asia.[51]

Even if there is a rapidly developing commercial-type economy in first-century Galilee, it must be asked, *Cui bono*? Lenski clearly sees the Mediterranean littoral as a mixed-type, a combination of advanced agrarian society (with peasants) and commercial society (with seaborne commerce and cities). The key articulation between the two is politics and patronage. Commerce does not automatically mean that all participate or benefit; it is important to clarify who controlled the commerce, and how product distribution in Galilee (ceramics, clothing) relates to imperial patronage and Galilean social stratification.

Ancient peasants preferred barter in kind. They knew money as a political reality with extremely limited economic utility; copper money or product had to be exchanged "up" to pay taxes or debts. This was always at a disadvantage to the villagers and even townspeople. Galilean peasants evaded taxes by hiding produce (in underground tunnels) and if possible by deceiving the tax collectors.[52] Likewise, literacy worked against peasants

49. Berlin, "Hellenistic Period," 25–26.

50. Aviam, "First-century Galilee," 13. Rostovtzeff lists fishing among the numerous tightly controlled concessions of Ptolemaic Egypt: "[accounts show] how small a share went to the actual fishermen" (*SEHHW*, 296–97). Usual royal monopolies in the ancient world were hunting preserves, special forests, salt, mines, and the like; i.e., monopolies were political, not "economic" realities. See Millett, "Monopolies," *OCD*, 994; see also Hanson, "Galilean Fishing Economy," 99–111.

51. Dar, "Agrarian Economy," 306.

52. Aviam claims that we cannot be certain about the purpose and use of these underground chambers. Ronen, Gal, and Aviam, "Galilee," 454; Aviam, *Jews, Pagans and Christians*, 123–32.

in terms of debt contracts and records of tax arrears. Peasants and their villages were incorporated into the Roman patronage systems and territories of elite estates or cities. The towns played a crucial role in this articulation process. The elites owned or controlled all the major factors of production. If there were such entities as "'free' smallholding peasants" in the early Roman period, they were rapidly becoming a rarity.[53]

I have argued that the Roman monetary policy, at least by effect if not by intention, maintained by imperial client elites around the Mediterranean, was to "leverage" real goods through reserving silver for tax and debt payments and wide distribution of copper tokens. Gresham's law ("bad money drives out the good") helps us to understand that bad copper money drives out the good silver money, and I add drives out the goods (to the imperial towns and cities). The Romans and their agents obviously exploited money through location of mints. The coin profiles of all archaeological sites show that copper coins were aplenty, but silver was preciously rare in situ.[54]

The Romans must have learned something about bimetallic money systems, and their convenience for handling agrarian debt and taxes, from the Hellenistic kingdoms. Rostovtzeff years ago wrote the following about Ptolemaic money policy:

> The copper coinage of [Ptolemy] Philadelphus was consequently another symbol and expression of the dualism which was established in Egypt by the Ptolemaic system of organization: old Egypt, the Egypt of the natives, with its heavy and clumsy old-fashioned copper, coexisted with the new Egypt, that of Alexandria and the Greeks, with its elegant and handy silver and magnificent gold. But to satisfy the requirements of the natives was not the only aim of Philadelphus in introducing the new bronze coinage. He foresaw that the new coins would drive silver and gold out of circulation, and that the coins made of these two metals would gradually come to be hoarded in the royal treasury and used by the king for his own purposes. And that, without doubt, was what happened, especially after his time.[55]

53. Kloppenborg, "Agricultural Tenancy, 33–66.
54. Oakman, "Batteries of Power, 171–85.
55. Rostovtzeff, *SEHHW*, 400.

The detailed numismatic study of Danny Syon provides some additional corroborations and support for these assertions.[56] Syon does note the operation of Gresham's law in regard to the circulation of the less pure Eagle Tetradrachms in 60–66 CE. However, he does not extend this principle in relation to the ubiquity of coppers and the rarity of silvers in the excavations. Coin hoards are another illustration of the operation of Gresham's law.

The systematic coin-counts done by Syon can tell us something about the distribution—I do not say circulation—of money in Galilee during our periods. We can take Gamla, Yodefat, and Qana to heart here. We know that Yodefat and Gamla were never rebuilt after 67 CE. Based on the tabulations of Syon, the coin counts for these uninhabited places for the 70–138 CE period are: Gamla 0?; Yodefat 13; Qana for comparison 2. An uninhabited period, on average, will yield about ten coin-finds or less. Compare with this the Hasmonean period, 125–63 BCE: Gamla 4912; Yodefat 397; Qana 9; and for the early Roman period, 63 BCE—70 CE: Gamla 692; Yodefat 84; Qana 2. Qana's profile is consistent and unremarkable, almost no different from the uninhabited average. However, Yodefat and Gamla have noticeable volumes before destruction.[57]

What this shows, I believe, is the *political (not the economic) importance* of money. The profiles show accumulations at strong-points, towns which we might identify as the administrative-juridical-security nodes. Not surprisingly, the Romans had to take Yodefat and Gamla with force. By contrast, Qana was untouched by the war, unwalled, and apparently the domicile only for agrarian labor and some local gentry.[58]

---

56. Syon, *Small Change.*

57. Syon, *Small Change,* 169, 198, 210.

58. There are unadorned, rock-cut tombs at Qana, indicating a wealthier class there. Mattila calls Yodefat and Gamla villages ("Middle Peasants?" 309–10). Interestingly, the typology of Galilean settlements could also use more critical discussion. In my view, Yodefat and Gamla are towns with administrative roles in the political structures of Galilee. Therefore, one would expect to find painted-plaster houses and signs of wealth at each site. See my classification of settlements by rank-size distribution of population in *Jesus and the Peasants,* 46–52. Nazareth, with population of the order of magnitude 10^2, would represent a typical Galilean village. Yodefat, Capernaum, and Gamla by contrast were towns with important political-economic roles and populations of the order of magnitude 10^3. Cities (Jerusalem, Sepphoris, Tiberias) would be closer to the order of magnitude 10^4.

There were periodic fairs and markets that peasants could enter; however, they entered only with permission and always at a disadvantage.[59] Conversely, peasant "cunning" typically looked for ways to deceive and cheat to an advantage. Trade in these occasional markets or the town *agorai* is not to be confused with translocal or long-distance commerce carried on by elites and their agents. "Banks" or tables were controlled by the elites of Roman Palestine. The tables were for loans at interest, based upon money on deposit or *mamōnas*, or money exchange (with disadvantageous fees). Archives in Jerusalem and Tiberias, what Josephus called the "sinews" of the city (*Life* 38), maintained records about family lines and debts.[60]

This picture is certainly not entirely that of the isolated peasant family of other times and places. But neither is it the modern farmer or democratic, free-market system read back into the first century. The Early Roman economy in Galilee is a political-economy, and in many senses, only a semi-economy. Economic development functions for the sake of the urban and imperial elites, but only in basic and limited senses at the village level or on the lake. Distributed money does not circulate so much as effect the political will of the elites in keeping the masses in debt and the goods flowing toward the cities and the seacoast.

I hope this response serves to explain why I believe Galilee holds plenty of evidence for execrable first-century peasants and their landless or rural proletariat offspring within an economy that existed essentially for the benefit of Rome and her regional agents. My guess is that Jesus of Nazareth, Judas of Gamla, and Simon bar Giora—all might have sympathized with the remark of Calgacus in Tacitus's *Agricola*, "To plunder, butcher, steal, these things [the Romans] misname empire; they make a desolation and they call it peace."[61]

---

59. Morley, "Distribution," 586.

60. Consider the controlling presence of the *agoranomos*. Rathbone says "Monetized exchange functioned, and grew across time, through credit arrangements" ("Roman Egypt," 715). "Credit arrangements" for peasants are the obverse of perennial debts. Rathbone mentions that private Egyptian banks played an important role in arrangements of on-going "credit."

61. Tacitus, *Agricola* 30 (LCL): *Auferre trucidare rapere falsis nominibus imperium, atque ubi solitudinem faciunt, pacem appellant.* Thanks to Motti Aviam and the 2010 conference panelists for the excellent stimulus and provocation to consider these matters. I am indebted to Professor David Gowler for his independent critique of this essay response. His questions and suggestions helped in refining the text for publication. The essay's faults and limitations of course are mine alone.

CHAPTER 5

The Galilean World of Jesus

In Memoriam Seán Freyne

Interpretation in [history and archaeology] . . . necessitates a degree of guided conjecture, but, to quote Max Weber, "an ingenious
error is more fruitful for science than stupid accuracy." —SHIMON
APPLEBAUM[1]

For such a small region of the globe, Galilee has surely had scholarly and world impact all out of proportion to its size. Over the last
few decades, the understanding of the social world and imperial realities
of Roman Galilee have become ever more important for narratives about
the emergence of early Christianity and Judaism. Since the magisterial
synthesis of Professor Freyne in the first edition of this work [*The Early
Christian World*, 2 volumes, published between 2000 and 2002], both social
theory (or its lack) and archaeological information, as well as studies of the
Roman social world, have played ever more prominent roles in historical
interpretation. Freyne expressed concern that then-current historical Jesus
research was too theologically motivated. Certainly, recent scholarship has
raised and struggled with a variety of new questions related to the Galilean
world of Jesus. These questions arise, not only from theology, but also from
various ideological commitments, social preconceptions, and interpretive
assumptions.

1. Applebaum, "Economic Causes," 237. Professor Freyne lamentably died in 2013.
He provided judicious assessments of Galilee studies in "Galilean Studies," and his final
comprehensive views on the Galilean world of Jesus have been published posthumously
in *The Jesus Movement*.

This chapter situates Jesus of Nazareth especially within the pre-70 CE realities of Roman Galilee. Of course, this setting also holds importance for the emergence of rabbinic Judaism in the late first century. Yet both Christianity and rabbinic Judaism took on more distinctive shapes in the post-70 CE period after the Jerusalem temple's destruction, and especially in the second century CE with rabbi and synagogue on the one hand and bishop and church on the other. Jesus lived under the overlays of Roman imperial, Herodian, and Judean political cultures, and his historical activity held profound political ramifications.

The Ecological Setting of Hellenistic-Roman Galilee

Both Josephus and the Mishnah subdivide Galilee into Lower Galilee, Upper Galilee, and the valley of Tiberias.[2] Presumably, these sources also include the Galilean lake. Good general accounts of the physical character-istics of Galilee are available.[3] Most of Galilee is made up of sedimentary limestone (hard and soft), though volcanic basalt dominates the eastern areas near the Galilean lake and Huleh Valley. Buildings in Lower and Up-per Galilee are primarily made of limestone; on the north end of the lake, buildings, stone presses, and grinding stones are made of basalt. Lower Galilee is crosscut by fertile east–west valleys and low mountains (Mount Kamon peaks at 598 meters above sea level); Upper Galilee reaches about 1200 meters at Mt. Meiron.[4] The lake is on average about 210 meters below sea level, covering an area of about 21 by 13 kilometers. The geology of the lake region is subject to the plate tectonics that have also created the Jordan River Valley.[5]

The total area of Galilee is estimated at about 2,073 square kilome-ters, of which 65–70 percent was cultivated at the turn of the eras.[6] The natural vegetation is Mediterranean woodland (including especially ever-green thickets and oaks). Lower Galilee receives on average 600 millimeters of rain, while Upper Galilee receives 800 millimeters, quite adequate for all kinds of agriculture, viticulture, and arboriculture. Soils and rainfall

2. Josephus, *War* 3.35–40; *m. Sheb.* 9:2; Strange, "Galilean Road System," 263–65.

3. Goodman, *State and Society*, 17–40; Aviam, "First-century Galilee."

4. Ronen, Gal, and Aviam, "Galilee," 449.

5. See Shroder and Inbar, "Geologic and Geographic Background," 65–98.

6. Applebaum, "Economic Life in Palestine," 646; Strange, "Galilean Road System," 265.

encouraged grain in the valleys and vines and olive trees on the rugged hill- and mountainsides. Deuteronomy 8:8 already names the fundamental products of the land: "a land of wheat and barley, of vines and fig trees and pomegranates, a land of olive trees and honey." Many types of other crops were possible, including pulses and fruit trees. The lake offered rich fare in edible fish. Indeed, the two prominent staples in the Galilee of Jesus were bread and fish (Mark 6:38). In the poorly drained eastern Beit Netofa and Huleh Valleys, flax could be cultivated. But equally, malaria was a problem in those areas.[7]

Settlements generally are sited on the hills to provide maximum agricultural land and to rise above the mosquitoes carrying malaria. If natural springs were not nearby, watertight plastered cisterns were necessary. Josephus remarks that the Galilee of his day was fully under cultivation (*War* 3.42–43) and populous with 204 settlements (*Life* 235). For Galilee, considering the agricultural carrying capacity, the population was at maximum around 175,000. Further considerations of agricultural production and population will be pursued below.

Galilean Social Systems and Conflicting Interests

The understanding of the context of Jesus of Nazareth has been enormously enriched in the past forty years by interdisciplinary engagement with comparative social sciences. This engagement has made ever more clear that historical interpretation is hazardous; but interpretation in historical narrative is unavoidable. If interpretation can be characterized as "reading between the lines," or "connecting the dots," then the fact that much of the past is lost to us will indicate the absolute centrality of interpretation in historical work. Moreover, preconceptions of the interpreter must be critically examined in order to avoid the twin dangers of anachronism and ethnocentrism. Rogerson puts the matter this way:

> while we do not invent the past, our narrative accounts of it are affected and shaped by factors such as our very limited knowledge of what happened in the past, and our situatednesses in nation, gender, class, political and religious commitment or lack of the same, and aims and interests in wanting to construct narratives about the past, in the first place.[8]

7. Reed, "Mortality, Morbidity, and Economics."

8. Rogerson, *Theology*, 18.

The current state of Galilee research stands in much flux precisely because of competing interpretations, problematic anachronisms, and ethnocentrisms. Over the almost twenty years since the original article of Seán Freyne for *The Early Christian World* (1st ed.), work on the social world of Galilee and the involvement of archaeological data have required the rethinking of almost all the old verities. Gone is the sunny, innocent Galilee of Ernest Renan. Galilee the hotbed of revolutionaries has now become a hotbed of reinterpretation. Galilee is no longer "the circle of the nations," but in the minds of some a monochrome "Jewish" region. Culture is given uncritical precedence over politics, and anachronistic economic ideas befuddle the question.

The New Testament gospels and Josephus all postdate 70 CE. Of course, the rabbinic sources do as well. While all have memories and recollections of the pre-70 situation, the danger of anachronism looms very large. For instance, the dictum of Julius Wellhausen over a century ago is well known: "Jesus was not a Christian, he was a Jew" (1905).[9] Today, the notion of Judaism as a first-century "free-standing religion" is under intensive scrutiny. The nomenclature "Jew" or "Judean" has spawned numerous scholarly arguments and explicit appeals to social identity theory.[10]

Furthermore, archaeology has played an increasingly important role in interpreting the Galilean world of Jesus as well as Jesus in context.[11] Important archaeologists working in Galilee have eschewed the use of comparative social sciences, such as appeals to Gerhard Lenski's *Power and Privilege*.[12] A prominent development over the last decade, however, is the claim that Galilee at the turn of the eras enjoyed prosperity for all, under moderate Herodian rule, with insignificant social stratification, and such that social problems and dislocations can hardly be invoked to explain the appearances of John the Baptizer in Peraea or Jesus of Nazareth in Galilee.[13]

---

9. Wellhausen, *Einleitung in die drei ersten Evangelien.*

10. Berlin, "Household Judaism," 211; Cromhout, *Jesus and Identity*; Cromhout, "Galileans"; Esler, "Intergroup Conflict and Matthew 23"; Mason, "Jews, Judaeans, Judaizing, Judaism." On this whole debate, see chapter 7 in this volume, which presents additional perspectives.

11. Reed, *Archaeology and the Galilean Jesus*; Crossan and Reed, *Excavating Jesus*; Fiensy, *Jesus the Galilean*; Oakman, *The Political Aims Of Jesus.*

12. For an exception, see Magness, *Stone and Dung*, 13–15.

13. Aviam, "First-Century Galilee"; Jensen, *Herod Antipas in Galilee*; Mattila, "Middle Peasants"; Mattila, "Revisiting Jesus' Capernaum."

How to locate Jesus in Galilee, then, has been a matter of strenuous debate. Was Jesus a "Peasant Jewish Cynic," a "Jewish Galilean," or simply a Galilean?[14] Was he Torah observant or not? What were his views of Judean eschatology or the Jerusalem temple? Did he think of himself as a Messiah? Was he literate or illiterate? Was he wealthy or poor? Was he a "middler" or a vagabond? These are the kinds of questions being given a complex variety of answers. In the midst of this flux, then, it is impossible to avoid the hazard of interpretation. The quest of the historical Jesus, as Freyne held, has indeed become also the quest of the historical Galilee, but prospects for a consensus seem more remote than at the time of the first edition of this chapter.

Power and Culture

All of these scholarly conversations involve assumptions about how power and culture were related in the early Roman Empire and in Roman Galilee. Perhaps one of the most persistent disagreements in the study of the social world of the Roman Empire, including Roman Galilee, has been over the use of comparative social science and macrosocial models. Historians and archaeologists tend to like detailed narratives based upon inductive inferences, and there has been the frequent accusation that comparative social models supply missing data inappropriately.[15] However, even archaeologists and social historians have to supply missing data since the data of antiquity is always incomplete.[16]

In recent archaeological approaches to Galilee, for example, cultural interpretations have prevailed. However, these approaches have to a high degree ignored the question of the relationship between power and culture. It is important, therefore, to make an a priori decision about whether power precedes culture, that is, culture is embedded within power, or vice versa, that is, power is embedded within culture. Of course, religion has been a central feature of human cultures, so the question of priority also pertains to the relationship between religion and politics.

---

14. Crossan, *The Historical Jesus*, a peasant Jewish Cynic; Freyne, *Jesus, A Jewish Galilean*; Fiensy, *Jesus the Galilean*.

15. Fiensy, *Christian Origins*, 81–84; Fiensy and Hawkins, *The Galilean Economy*; Freyne, *The Jesus Movement*, 6, 91–93; Oakman, "Galilean Economy" (chapter 3 in this volume); Oakman, "Execrable Peasants!" (chapter 4 in this volume).

16. Fiensy and Hawkins, *The Galilean Economy*, 173–77.

In the Mediterranean world of Rome, Galilee, and Jesus, extended families (natural and fictive) provided the central institutional structures. Caesar could view the empire as an extended household (Phil 4:22). This implies that "power" in the world of Jesus had to do with how elite families controlled and treated everyone else. This understanding can be modeled as in Figure 5.1.

FIGURE 5.1

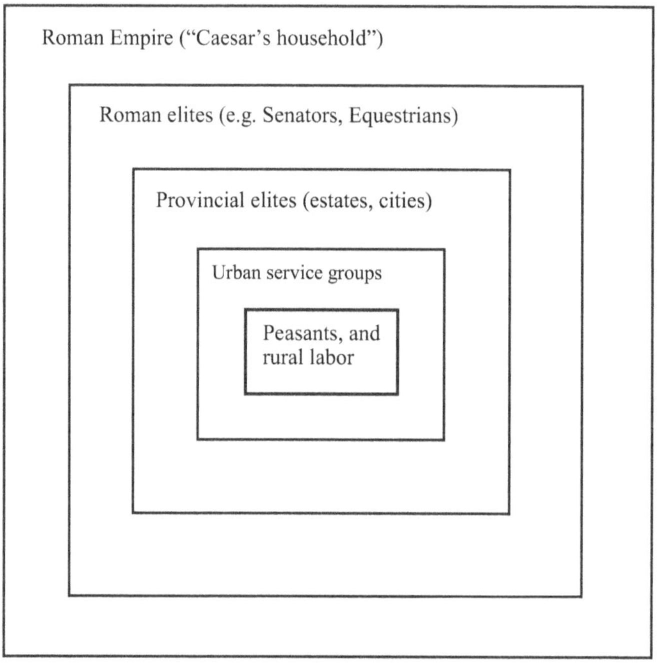

Roman Empire ("Caesar's household")

Roman elites (e.g. Senators, Equestrians)

Provincial elites (estates, cities)

Urban service groups

Peasants, and rural labor

Power in the Early Roman Empire

This diagram suggests that the culture of the leading family becomes the dominant culture. Power determines Culture. This does not preclude subcultures of other families from functioning within or contesting the culture of the ruling elite. No social power is absolute, and non-elites had various forms of power for negotiating life from below. From a different point of view, if religion provides meaning to the cultural world, then political religion is the religion of the ruling elite, which legitimates the way things are.

Further, religious politics of the non-elites may contest the way things are in the name of a higher power. In this respect, Culture determines Power. While the ways of the elites tend to be imprinted in the grand traditions of the dominant culture, the little traditions of families and regions tend to bolster countercultures and contest the dominant power. These considerations will become important in the case of Jesus of Nazareth when it is perceived that for his in-group God is Father (the absolute householder and patron), but for Jesus' worldly action in early Roman Galilee his guiding idea was that God is King.

Power (and consequent privilege) must be the more-or-less "independent variable" in the interpretive proposals of this chapter. Non-elite families, local cultures, economic realities, and religion all are embedded in the fields of force exerted by the ruling families. In the Galilean world of Jesus, power relations were by and large vertical in structure. Not surprisingly, then, the literature of patronage has become more prevalent in recent work on the gospels.[17] The politics in the Galilee of Jesus was patronal, and the dependency relations thus spawned affected all aspects of society. This is especially important when considering the politics and political economy of Roman Galilee.

Provincial Elites: Judeans and Herods in Galilee

The political history of Galilee has been unfolded in numerous scholarly places. The literary sources are clear that Palestine was a political bone of contention between the Ptolemies and the Seleucids, which terminated in favor of the latter by the definitive conquests of Antiochus III (Panion 200 BCE; Jerusalem 198 BCE).[18] Subsequently in 167 BCE, the policies of Antiochus Epiphanes provoked the uprising of Mattathias and his sons. The wars of the Maccabeans included the campaigns of Simon and Jonathan to the north and the annexation of Galilee (1 Macc 5:15–23; 10:30; 11:63). Ideologically, Hasmonean aspirations may have aimed at establishing the borders of Ezekiel's ideal Israel.[19] Recent archaeology correlates the disappearance of Hellenistic period Galilean Coarse Ware (GCW) storage jars

17. Elliott, "Patronage and Clientage"; Malina, *The Social Gospel of Jesus*, 31–35; Malina, *The New Testament World* (2001), 94–96.

18. Tcherikover, *Palestine under the Ptolemies*.

19. Cromhout, "Galileans," 12–87.

with this expansion.[20] Yodefat likely originated as a Persian or Ptolemaic fort and was taken by the Hasmoneans along with other such forts; it later became an administrative town for Lower Galilee and was destroyed in 67 CE at the beginning of the Judean–Roman War of 66–70 CE.

It has been debated as to how populous Galilee was before the Hasmonean take-over, and whether Israelites of the northern kingdom survived down to the times of the Hasmoneans. Richard Horsley has argued vigorously that descendants of Israelite peasants remained in Galilee throughout the Persian and Hellenistic periods and preserved northern Israelite traditions in Galilee, but Reed and Cromhout speak against this.[21] Archaeological surveys suggest that Galilee was sparsely populated during the Persian and early Hellenistic periods.[22] Yet this makes it difficult to understand how Judeans got there to be liberated by the Maccabees. It also would imply that agricultural land, which was considered highly valuable by the Hellenistic monarchs preceding the Hasmoneans, would have been mostly abandoned. Archaeologists like Aviam can document the power of Akko/Ptolemais before the Hasmonean conquests. Fortresses guard the agricultural territory.[23] If royal estates of the Seleucids, inherited from the Ptolemies, endured up until Hasmonean times, then there had to be peasants working the best land. After 100 BCE, Hasmonean policy in Galilee encouraged settlement by Judeans.[24]

First Maccabees 12:1–3 also recounts that the Hasmoneans made a treaty with the Romans. Their appearance in the east would have enormous consequences for Palestine in the first century BCE with the conquests of Pompey, the demise of Hasmonean rule, the reorganization of taxation districts by Gabinius (Josephus, *War* 1.170), the favors of Julius Caesar and Mark Antony during the Republican civil wars, and eventually the rise of the house of Herod. Herod consolidated his power by killing prominent Hasmoneans and expropriating their estates. He also expropriated estate

20. Aviam, *Jews, Christians and Pagans*, 44–50; Aviam, "First-century Galilee," 6.

21. Horsley, *Galilee: History, Politics, People*, 25–33; Horsley, *Archaeology, History, and Society in Galilee*, 23; Cromhout, "Galileans"; Reed, *Archaeology and the Galilean Jesus*, 25.

22. Reed, *Archaeology and the Galilean Jesus*, 23–61, based on Gal's survey.

23. Aviam, *Jews, Pagans and Christians*, 29.

24. Without a doubt, however, both Q and Mark (see below and chapter 6) reflect scribal readings of Jesus that do in fact invoke northern Israelite keynotes (Moses, Elijah) and scribal interests not entirely sympathetic with Judean interests in Galilee.

lands of the Sadducean (wealthy) faction of Jerusalem priests. Applebaum gives a comprehensive survey of estate lands under the control of the Herods: Sadducean estates in Samaria; domains of Berenice on the Esdraelon Plain, in southwestern Samaria, and in the Golan; Antipas in the eastern Hepher Plain and in northwestern Samaria; Yavneh, belonging to Salome; Herod the Great's estate lands in eastern Perea, estates on the Jericho Plain; Herodian interests in Bashan and Hauran. Temple and priestly lands were probably under the purview of Sepphoris.[25] After 70 CE, many of these estates came under the control of the imperial authorities.

Herod the Great at the beginning of his rule as king of the Judeans subdued banditry in Galilee, suggestive of very unsettled agrarian conditions up to that time. At Herod's death, Hezekiah led an armed insurrection that had to be put down by a Roman legion under Varus. Strongman rule continued in Galilee under Herod's son Antipas. He ably controlled things through his patronage networks (Mark 6:21). Powerful-wealthy Judeans also had significant interests in Galilee during Jesus' lifetime. Sepphoris was a Judean-oriented city, which may suggest why Herod Antipas wanted to found Tiberias as a more Hellenized capital.[26] The Gospel of Mark indicates that Jesus' most important Galilean opponents were the clients of these powerful interests, namely, the Herodians (Herod partisans and clients) and the Pharisees (Mark 3:6).

Galilee's Agrarian Political Economy

Political history alone is inadequate to understand the context of Jesus. Political histories based on ancient literary sources, or archaeology focused solely on cultural artifacts, have tended merely to follow the perspectives and interests of the elite factions at the top of the social ladder. Further theoretical nuance can be gained by taking seriously the general character of "agrarian civilizations." The models of Lenski, Kautsky, and Sjoberg have been deployed in previous work to understand the context of Jesus. To them now can be added the perspectives of world systems and Big History. In the words of Christian, drawing upon ecological metaphors,

25. Applebaum, "Economic Causes," 245; Fiensy, *Christian Origins*, 98–117.

26. The Hebrew University excavations have dated the outer wall of the theater at Sepphoris to post-70 CE, but this does not preclude the founding of an earlier inner portion in the days of Herod Antipas; see Fiensy and Strange, *Galilee*, 2:67 and n. 22.

> agrarian civilizations [are] large societies based on agriculture,
> with states and all that that implies (literacy, warfare, etc.) . . .
> Human society became the "niche" in which elites foraged for the
> resources they needed. Society became multilayered, with a base
> level of those who exploited nature (the primary producers) and
> upper layers of those who exploited those who exploited nature.[27]

Homomorphic macromodels become necessary to highlight important general features of the agrarian social world. These abstract models have to be selective in order to be informative. Though they do not satisfy the social historian's desire for detailed isomorphic micromodels, they can help to correct anachronistic assumptions about social processes and cultural details.[28]

For the greatest clarity about the agrarian social situation of Galilee, it is necessary to model Jesus' world from the bottom up. Figure 5.2 gives a sense of how this all works at least for agriculture (leaving out of consideration for now the fishing industry of the Galilean lake).

27. Christian, *Maps of Time*, 248–49.

28. Carney, *The Shape of the Past*; Elliott, *What Is Social-Scientific Criticism?*; Finley, *Ancient History*; Morley, *Theories, Models and Concepts*; Rohrbaugh, "Models and Muddles."

FIGURE 5.2

FIGURE 5.2: A Model for Early Roman Galilee

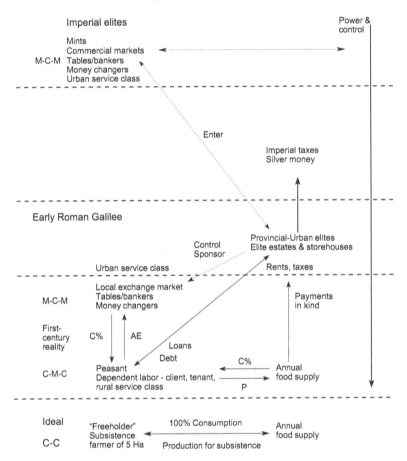

An Economic Model for Early Roman Galilee

In this model, **M-C-M** means the purchased commodity (**C**) is used to produce more money (**M**); **C-M-C**, commodity is sold and money is used then to reacquire commodity; **C-C**, commodity used only as item for barter.

Elite power and politics frustrate the small-farmer ideal of self-sufficiency and subsistence agriculture along with the possibility of consuming 100 percent of the harvest. This is the clear meaning of the term "peasant"—someone not living according to the self-sufficiency ideal, but rather subject to vertical power relations that frustrate that ideal. After all, elite rents and taxes extract so-called surpluses. *So the emphasis must be on "so-called."* Dependency relations and patronage politics were the Galilean rule and norm. The idea of a "free peasant" or "freeholder" seems hard to sustain if this is the case.[29] All preindustrial agriculture after the appearance of cities and states was accomplished by some form of dependent labor.

And under the early Empire, the elites themselves seek resources to repay their own provincial and imperial patrons, and the elites themselves hold to the ideal of their own self-sufficiency—which entails the control over the productive resources of land and other people's labor. This entails Mammon, that is, money in the treasure house—on loan, or on deposit— and the building of storehouses (Luke 12:18)! Elites have the power to modify productive decisions away from subsistence farming and toward cash crops and commerce. These decisions impact the subsistence margins of the dependent labor that works the land. Bad years and poor productive decisions can yield a crop of landless peasants and a harvest of banditry.

Debates continue on the level of rents and taxes in early Roman Galilee.[30] Hopkins has argued that the Roman authorities allowed a sizable "take" to the provincial elites, precisely to buy their allegiance, but also with the expectation of costly demonstrations of loyalty.[31] The Herods obliged with extravagance. Josephus notes the hatred for Herod the Great for de- spoiling the country, but also hatred for both Agrippas I and II for largesse to Berytos (*Ant.* 17.306; 19.335–336; 20.211–212). Ehud Netzer, of course, discovered Herod's tomb a few years ago, with his sarcophagus broken into hundreds of small pieces by the insurgents who held the Herodion during the 66–70 revolt.

Broshi notes the importance of the Babatha Archive for assessing the question of the typical extraction level. Babatha paid half the dates per tree in her contracts, and 1 Macc 10:30 suggests that this level may have been a standard for rents and taxes on tree crops throughout the Hellenistic- Roman period.[32] First Maccabees also mentions one-third of the grain per annum. The rents implied in the Luke 16 story of the Dishonest Steward are sizable. They were also burdensome, for why else would falsifying the

---

29. On tenancy, see Kloppenborg, "Agricultural Tenancy."

30. Udoh, "Taxation"; also see, Oakman, *Jesus and the Economic Questions of His Day*, 57–72.

31. Hopkins, "Rome, Taxes, Rent and Trade."

32. Broshi, "Agriculture and Economy," 236. See also Esler, *Babatha's Orchard*.

books be acclaimed in the villages? And patronage politics, the return obligation and loyalties incurred by the villagers, are clearly in view.

As for any taxes imposed in money, what would the villager have left
from so-called surpluses on the threshing floor to sell for cash? Hamel calls
attention to the following interesting passage in the *Tosephta*:

> The renter of a field harvests, makes sheaves, [threshes], and win-
> nows. [Then] the measurers, diggers, bailiff, and steward come
> and take from the middle (before the product is shared by the
> landowner and sharecropper). The well-master, bather, barber,
> boatsman, when they come [to collect] by the owner's authority,
> they take from his share; if they come [to collect] by the sharecrop-
> per's authority, they take from his share. The customs of the region
> are not to be changed . . .[33]

It is absolutely essential to realize that rents and various kinds of local taxes
always had to be paid to a significant extent in produce. The reason for
this is that these so-called surpluses line the larders of the landlords and
urban elites. Correspondingly, the "stores" of the village and the peasant
household shrink, and beyond harvest time, subsistence anxiety must have
been a persistent reality. Peter Brown has called storehouses "the economic
villains of the ancient world."[34]

Literary sources and archaeological finds do offer some information
about elite storehouses in Roman Palestine.[35] An early midrash reports that
Nakdimon ben Gorion, Ben Kalba Sabbua, and Ben Zizit Hakeset "could
provision Jerusalem for ten years" (*Midrash Lamentations Rabba* 1); *b. Git.*
56a confirms that these three were remembered as fabulously wealthy.[36]
The *horreum* at the Northern Palace of Herod the Great is a prominent sign
of the costs of the royal house to the agricultural producers. Josephus refers
to an imperial granary in upper Galilee (*Life* 71) and to wheat of Queen
Berenike stored at Besara (*Life* 119). Acts 12:20 reports that Agrippa I supplied Tyre and Sidon with food. It has been reported that there were large
granaries at Sepphoris, and most likely at Tiberias as well. Mendel Nun calls

---

33. Quoted in Hamel, *Poverty and Charity*, 154; he notes that *t. B. Meṣ.* 9.14 and *y. B. Meṣ.* 9.1.12a add the salaries of town watchmen.

34. Brown, *Through the Eye of a Needle*, 14.

35. See Borowski, *Agriculture*, 82.

36. Applebaum, "Economic Life in Palestine," 659.

attention to the talmudic phrase "from Susita to Tiberias" as indicating the regular conveyance of grain by boat to the Galilean city.[37]

Moreover, the Herods and the chief priests under the Romans developed commerce far beyond the level achieved in the Hasmonean kingdom. Herod built the emporium Caesarea Maritima and had commercial interests also with the Nabateans.[38] The megalithic building programs of Herod the Great, Antipas, and Philip, especially seen in building and expansion of cities, would place much strain upon the country dwellers. The temple required enormous resources from Palestine, and Galilean wheat and oil supplied the ongoing temple rituals.[39] The wealthy high priests were involved in various kinds of business ventures—both private and temple-related. Eleazar ben Zadok and Abba Saul ben Batnith controlled wheat flour, wine, and oil interests. Eleazar was also involved in the sale of Ennion glassware to pilgrims.[40] Tyrian silver money held sway in Jerusalem and Galilee; Antipas was only allowed to mint copper coins. Mediterranean seaborne commerce made possible accumulation of luxury goods, but also for cities on the coast trade in bulk goods (esp. wine and oil, but also grain). Overland transport was difficult and expensive, but clearly possible for powerful wealthy families.

What about the food supplies and food security of the villager? Based upon studies of Serbian peasant economics in the 1950s, Joel Halpern determined that the north Mediterranean peasant (with some degree of modern technologies) could reach self-sufficiency on 5 Ha of land.[41] Anything less than this area would require supplemental wage income—but this would imply that additional food surpluses were available to be purchased. And if landlords and urban elites were to extract exorbitant taxes and rents from the produce, then what would be left to the smallholder to be sold for money in the market? Low-paid labor done for others would have to compensate. Estimates of plot sizes in ancient Palestine are in accord with this comparative instance. Ben-David "supposes an area of 7 hectares for a family of six to nine people."[42] Eusebius relates in *The Ecclesiastical History*

37. Nun, *Ancient Anchorages and Harbours*, 12.

38. Dar, "Agrarian Economy," 306.

39. Hanson and Oakman, *Palestine in the Time of Jesus*, 127–45.

40. Engle, "Amphorisk"; Oakman, *The Political Aims of Jesus*, 105.

41. Halpern, *Serbian Village*, 74–75.

42. Qtd. in Hamel, *Poverty and Charity*, 134.

(3.20.1–2) that relatives of Jesus shared a 2.5 Ha plot between two families. 2.5 Ha also seem to be a standard plot size from Dar's survey of Samaria.[43]

There are further systemic issues to be reckoned with. As inheritance customs require plot-divisions into smaller and smaller parcels, the 5 Ha self-sufficient minimum is no longer possible. Animal fodder, seed requirements, the necessity for fallow periods—all press against subsistence. With no refrigeration, food preservation and storage is a significant issue. Low to zero interannual storage rates for most peasants are the rule. Belt-tightening is the ordinary![44]

Population pressure and land scarcity add additional danger. The available arable land in ancient Galilee has been variously estimated. The best recent estimate is 2,073 square kilometers.[45] Abstractly, say 145,110 cultivable hectares (70 percent of 207,300 Ha) are available in the Galilee of Herod Antipas.[46] This amounts to 29,022 subsistence plots of 5 Ha each. If family sizes on average were five to six people, then the Galilean population correspondingly would maximally amount to around 175,000 people at any one time. Viewed from a different angle: The 145,110 Ha, assuming 30 percent fallowing and fields entirely sown to grain at 150 kg per Ha, and a yield of 1:5, would produce 76,183 metric tons. One-fifth of this would need to be set aside for the next seeding. 200 kg per annum is a starvation ration. Assuming 250 kg for a working peasant, an absolute subsistence population would be around 244,000.[47] And when all agrarian production decisions are made by the elites who own (control) the land, subsistence crops compete with cash cropping!

The feedback model here can illustrate the factors endangering villagers and perhaps strategies embraced by villagers to protect peasant subsistence.

---

43. Dar, *Landscape and Pattern*; see also *m. B. Bathra* 1:6; DJD II, 145 cited in Applebaum, "Economic Life in Palestine," 657.

44. But, see Wilson, *For I Was Hungry*, 81–132.

45. Strange, "Galilean Road System," 265.

46. See Applebaum, "Economic Life in Palestine," 646, based upon Reifenberg.

47. Broshi, "Population of Western Palestine," 7; Hamel, *Poverty and Charity*, 138.

Enemies of Peasant Subsistence (Factors having negative impact on village subsistence, i.e., negative feedback)	Ideal of Production for 100 Percent Consumption (Factors having positive impact on village subsistence, i.e., positive feedback)
Social threats • Taxes & rents—visible diminishment of annual consumption • Elite storehouses • Absentee or "single-strand" landlords • Corvée labor—labor siphoned away from the fields • Monumental building programs—labor conscription or "wage slavery" • Money (leading to loans, debt)—what is produced has to be repurchased • Chronic debt • Markets—what is produced can be sold to the highest bidder • Translocal markets • Cash cropping, commercial interests • Partible inheritance • Banditry *Natural threats* • Land pressure, marginal plots • Population pressure • Contamination • Pestilence or blight • Drought • Soil depletion (inadequate fallow periods) • Soil salinization	*Tactical measures* • Hiding produce • Contaminating in-kind tax produce, keeping the good produce • Surreptitious cultivation *Social measures* • Patron, "multistrand landlord" (clientship, loyalty, and obligation) • Tax and debt relief • Sharecropping vs. fixed rents • Agrarian revolt? *Natural opportunities* • New or more land available • Foraging during periods of famine

Table 5.1: Factors in Ancient Food Security and Insecurity

Given very small cultivable plots and perennial elite exactions, local exchange markets or fairs become a necessity, but these are controlled and staged by people with resources.[48] Once a "middle man" (whether personal, money, or market) is interposed between peasant and consumable produce, the primary producer is at a distinct disadvantage. Long-distance commerce is no help since it is solely an elite game. Brown has expressed it this way: "Farmers could bring their produce into the nearest town. But the rich had privileged access to wider and more lucrative markets. They alone could defeat distance . . . The rich alone could also defeat time. They could store the abundance of the harvest and wait to sell when the prices were at their highest."[49] And in accordance with Gresham's law, "bad" copper (i.e., token) money in the provincial Roman bimetallic monetary system drives out the "good" silver money. This fact is amply attested by coin hoards and the prevalence of copper coinage at archaeological sites. The Romans may have sensed the power of money to work in this way—engendering ever-more debt and dependency at the agrarian bottom.[50] Bad money will drive out the good, and only the good can support commercial ventures. Bad money, in effect, drives the goods to the urban and provincial storehouses. The villager's room for maneuvering for viable annual subsistence becomes very small in this social world.

These systemic considerations underscore the important point that the ancient provincial elites held all the power and productive levers in early Roman Palestine. They controlled land through estates and labor through debt, client loyalty, and obligation. The significant Galilean elites at that time, of course, derived from the Herods and their clients (the Herodians) and the Jerusalem priestly elites and their clients (temple scribes and Pharisees).

Jesus In His Galilean World

It is crucial to remember that almost all of our written sources view Jesus and his Galilee from a later temporal distance, after the catastrophe of 70 CE. While Josephus mentions Jesus of Nazareth in the famous Flavian Testimony (*Ant.* 18.3), the report has been embellished through the hands of later Christian copyists. And, of course, Tacitus mentions the execution of "Christus" at the hands of the provincial governor Pilate (*Annals* 15.44).

---

48. MacMullen, "Market Days"; Safrai, *Economy of Roman Palestine*, 239–69.

49. Brown, *Through the Eye of a Needle*, 14.

50. Goodman, "The First Jewish Revolt"; Hamel, *Poverty and Charity*, 156–58.

Various early rabbinic traditions provide information largely about second-century Galilee.[51]

The earliest written records to provide substantial information about Jesus stand in the reconstructed document Q and the Gospel of Mark. Parallel sayings of Jesus in the Gospel of Thomas may be as old as those in Q, or at least in more original forms. Not all scholars are persuaded about a written document Q; and even more debate focuses on a Q stratified into at least two editions.[52] But the reasons for seeing a sayings source used by both Matthew and Luke are very strong, and the alternate hypotheses for explaining the relationship of the Synoptic Gospels have many problems.[53] Moreover, earliest or wisdom Q is distinctive in its use of simple chreiai (aphorisms) and concern for economic issues; the later or deuteronomic Q edition incorporates more elaborated chreiai as well as strong elements of Judean eschatology (for instance, the Danielic figure of the Son of Man, also notable in the Gospel of Mark). Earliest Q seemingly was the product of scribes in the administration of Herod Antipas;[54] the deuteronomic recension, with its decidedly Judean color, probably took shape after the transfer of the royal archives from Tiberias to Sepphoris during the reign of Nero (54–68 CE).[55]

It is most probable that Jesus was born in Galilee. Moreover, the Synoptic Gospels indicate problems surrounding his paternity, so it also seems highly probable that Jesus was illegitimate.[56] As such, his honor rating would have been low in the eyes of contemporaries, especially in the conservative ethos of the village, and this may have been one reason for his departure from Nazareth (Mark 6:1–6; Matt 4:13). Contemporaries of Jesus familiar with Deut 23:2 may have considered him a non-Israelite. Early traditions associate him with "tax collectors [telōnai] and sinners" (Q 7:34; Mark 2:16). The genealogies of Matthew and Luke, or the making explicit of Joseph's paternity in Matthew, Luke, and John, show the tendency to

51. Goodman, *State and Society*; Safrai, *Economy of Roman Palestine*.

52. The reconstructed Q by scholarly convention is cited by position in the Gospel of Luke. See Robinson et al., *Critical Edition of Q*. For details on the stratigraphic hypothesis, see Kloppenborg, *Excavating Q*, 143–65; for critique of the stratified Q hypothesis, see Tuckett, *Q and the History of Early Christianity*, 69–74.

53. Kloppenborg, *Excavating Q*.

54. Arnal, *Jesus and the Village Scribes*.

55. Josephus, *Life* 38–39; scribes are treated more fully in chapter 6.

56. Schaberg, *The Illegitimacy of Jesus*; van Aarde, *Fatherless in Galilee*; Oakman, *The Political Aims of Jesus*, 67–68.

rescue Jesus' honor (despite the information in Q and Mark that Jesus was alienated from his family).

Jesus and the Galilean Fishers

Given land scarcity, a landless peasant from Nazareth would be forced into wage labor. Jesus is called a *tektōn* in the Gospel of Mark (6:3). The meaning of this trade has been debated; it probably refers to a worker in wood or stone and a building generalist (although Justin, *Dialogue with Trypho* 88 reported that Jesus made yokes and plows).[57] It is possible that passages in Q 6:41–42 or 48; Luke 13:4; 14:28–30; or Gos. Thom. 77 reflect Jesus' experiences in his trade. It is probable that Jesus' travels and experiences, reflected in the parables especially, had more to do with finding work than conducting a religious mission.[58] Moreover, the parables and sayings also show knowledge of estates and markets in the cities.

In the Synoptic Gospels, Jesus leaves Nazareth and takes up residence in Capernaum. When not wandering elsewhere, Jesus spent considerable time in the environs of the Galilean lake and in the company of fishers. As a peasant artisan, he could perhaps find work in the local building trade and in boat repair.[59] The Galilee boat recovered in 1985 showed numerous patches and repairs, demonstrating the necessity of woodworkers. Moreover, the boat attested the use of both oars and sails, with a capacity of up to fifteen persons.[60]

Archaeology has shown that development of harbors on the lake began in the Hellenistic period; a harbor was established by the Hasmoneans at Magdala.[61] This suggests that in the late Hellenistic period the lake was considered a royal monopoly. Herod Antipas and Philip probably held the same (competing) view on the lake's resources. Both built cities on the lake (Tiberias and Bethsaida/Julias respectively), which probably attests a desire for greater control over the fishing. Both cities also signify through their names the loyalty and obligation shown toward Rome by the Herods.[62] Nun

57. Fiensy, *Jesus the Galilean*, 69.
58. Fiensy, *Jesus the Galilean*, 74; Oakman, *The Political Aims of Jesus*, 83.
59. McCown, "*Ho Tektōn.*"
60. Wachsmann, *Galilee Boat*, 315.
61. Aviam, "First-century Galilee," 13–14.
62. Hirschfeld et al. "Tiberias"; Arav and Freund, *Bethsaida*; Strickert, *Philip's City*, 165–68.

has identified at least fourteen harbors around the lake and commented that they would have required substantial building labor.[63] These might have been constructed with conscript or corvée labor.

The fishing syndicates were not exceptionally wealthy and paid their fixed "rent" in fish to *telōnai*, that is, agents who contracted rent and tax collection from the Galilean elites. Figure 5.3 shows how control over the lake resources can be represented.[64]

FIGURE 5.3

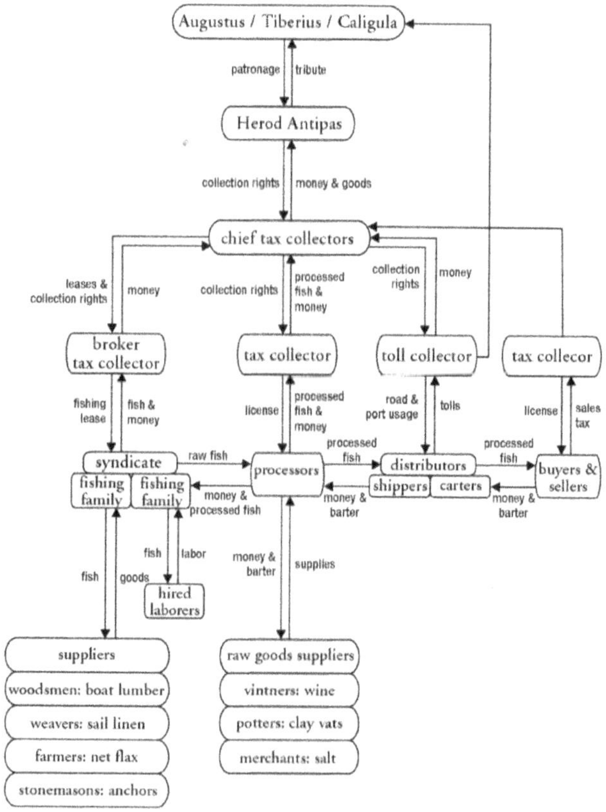

The Galilean Fishing Industry (after K. C. Hanson 1997)

63. Nun, "Ancient Anchorages," 27.

64. Hanson, "The Galilean Fishing Economy"; Hanson and Oakman, *Palestine in the Time of Jesus*, 101.

The vertical structures and flow of goods *replicate* the patronal structures and relations of the landed estates under elite control. Fish were salted in Magdala; some Galilean fish were processed for Mediterranean commerce.[65] As with bulk commodities or luxuries, only the powerful-wealthy could (through agents) conduct circum-Mediterranean commerce. It is clear, however, that the fishers themselves were not in a position to carry on long-distance trade. Like their agricultural relatives, the fishers lived precariously and had to buy back from their own catch!

Jesus and Judeans in Galilee

The incorporation into recent discussion of ethnic identity theory, and careful philological analysis of *Ioudaios*, has urged that the translation "Judean" is to be preferred for the first century over "Jew"; and that the more accurate translation of *Ioudaismos* is "one embracing ethnic markers and customs of Judea."[66] The usage of the terms "Jew" and "Judaism" as exclusively religious or cultural terms in the early first century further ignores the overdetermining realities of power and "political identity."[67]

Based on an important synthetic study of archaeological materials, Andrea Berlin has argued for a "household Judaism" in Galilee during the early Roman period.[68] Central to her proposal are *miqva'oth* (ritual purity baths), a common simple cooking assemblage, unadorned Jerusalem oil lamps (also called "Herodian lamps"), and burial customs. The cooking assemblage contains a cooking pot form found at Judean sites as well as in Galilee stemming from Kefar Hananya.[69] Bag jars made at Kefar Shikhin are also a part of this profile. She also includes simple stone cups and plates, and at sites like Gamla Eastern Terra Sigillata plates made in the coastal cities. Her argument is that this material culture evidences a heightened "Jewish piety" up until the time of the Judean–Roman War. However, this

65. Nun, "Sea of Galilee," 51; Hanson, "The Galilean Fishing Economy"; Freyne, *The Jesus Movement*, 95.

66. Additionally on this, see chapter 7 in this volume.

67. Berlin, "Household Judaism," 211; Cromhout, *Jesus and Identity*; Cromhout, "Galileans"; Elliott, "Jesus the Israelite"; Esler, "Social Identity Theory"; Esler, "Intergroup Conflict and Matthew 23"; Feldman, "Flavius Josephus"; Mason, "Jews, Judaeans, Judaizing, Judaism"; Moxnes, "Construction of Galilee."

68. Berlin, "Jewish Life"; Berlin, "Household Judaism," 208–15.

69. Berlin, "Household Judaism," 210.

interpretation can be contested in several respects. First, the pottery uniformity and limited production locations suggest the interests of controlling
families. In particular, the lamps point to Jerusalem interests. Furthermore,
Berlin acknowledges that while Galileans are eating with very simple cooking technology, wealthy Jerusalem houses contain imported wares from
the Mediterranean and Nabataea. Would it not be more natural to think
that Galileans are very poor and positioned within distribution networks
of powerful Judean and Galilean families? As for *miqva'oth*, it is claimed
that over three hundred are known.[70] However, the rush to see these as
ritual purity baths seems anachronistically to read in rabbinic values and
institutions from the second century CE. Ritual baths in the upper city
of Sepphoris are credible as Sepphoris was a priestly city. Large *miqva'oth*
such as at Gamla may have functioned like showers in modern electronics
manufactories—that is, to cleanse workers for the production of pure wine
for the temple.[71] This could also make sense of other *miqva'oth*, as evidence
of production for the temple.

Still, Berlin's synthesis does not mention where grain would be stored,
and at least some of these *miqva'oth* could be reservoirs with other functional purposes. (In the Hebrew Bible, the word *miqveh* can refer to collections of other things besides water, and even figuratively of associations of
people.) That peasants stored grain in underground areas is known from
excavations at Nazareth. Underground areas at other Galilean sites may
likewise have functioned as food storage areas.[72] Arabs in the late Ottoman
period stored dry figs in a hiding place called *mikhba*.[73] Likewise, stone
vessels in Galilee have not displaced hard-fired ceramics in commoner
contexts. If these vessels are evidence for priestly purity concerns, then it
seems most probable that they are restricted to domestic contexts of those
families or to priestly clients and domains in Galilee. Many Galileans were
either disinterested in purity laws or were incapable of observing them.
Yohanan ben Zakkai's question about why Galilee hated the Torah needs
to be kept in mind (*y. Shabbat* 16:7, 15d). And certainly, even in the second century the rabbis berated the *'amme ha-'aretz* ("people of the land,"

70. Berlin, "Jewish Life," 253; count of 700 according to Magness, *Stone and Dung*, 16.

71. Magness, *Stone and Dung*, 16–17.

72. Aviam, *Jews, Pagans and Christians*, 123–32.

73. Grant, *The People of Palestine*, 139.

i.e., either landowners or villagers) for their disregard of Torah strictures. Through most of the second century CE, the rabbis were not very influential in Galilee.[74]

It is notable, then, that neither Q nor Mark identifies Jesus as a "Judean," nor employs the explicit term *Ioudaios* in any significant measure. In the Q story of the centurion's slave (7:1–10), the centurion (understood here as commanding a unit in Herod's mercenary army) is shown as a patron of *Ioudaioi* who built the synagogue in Capernaum. Such patronage of local building projects is well known in the inscriptions of Syria and Arabia.[75] Then, the centurion addresses Jesus directly to broker God's healing patronage for the benefit of the slave (and centurion). Regarding the faith of the centurion, Jesus remarks that he has not found such faith *in Israel*. Israel is the more comprehensive term, with scope far beyond the ethnos of Judea.[76] Q and Mark otherwise associate Judeans only with John the Baptizer, and Mark uses the term in relation to Jesus only in the title "King of the Judeans." This information is obviously important in showing that "Judeans" were more an elite presence in Galilee and expressive of the projected power of Jerusalem elites. Conversely, it says something about the interests of the scribes of the earliest Jesus traditions, and how their interests may have coincided with those of Jesus.

Pharisees from Jerusalem are mostly in conflict with Jesus in deuteronomic Q and Mark. These Pharisees, as temple retainers, were there to look after priestly and temple interests in Galilee.[77] Their scribes promoted especially strict sabbath observance, tithing (extra temple liens), and ritual purity at meals. Sepphoris was a home for priestly elites, and their lands presumably were spread across Lower Galilee. Further, they controlled the pottery industry at Shikhin, and for their loyalty in the Judean–Roman War their villages (such as Khirbet Qana) were spared destruction. There is no mention of Pharisees in earliest wisdom Q. Deuteronomic Q includes the "Woes" against the Pharisees in relation to tithing and purity (11:41–42).[78] For Mark, conflicts more frequently center on sabbath observance (Mark 3:2), though there is also concern over purity (Mark 7:1–8). The same

74. Goodman, *State and Society*, 102–11; Hezser, *Rabbinic Movement*, 386–99; Freyne, *The Jesus Movement*, 133, 156.

75. Grainger, "Village Government."

76. Freyne, *The Jesus Movement*, 143, 168.

77. See Saldarini, *Pharisees, Scribes, and Sadducees*, 296. See further below, p. 109.

78. Magness, *Stone and Dung*, 21–24.

tensions are felt in Josephus's *Life*, as he leads an armed force and comes into conflict with Galilean elite factions. Josephus is in Galilee precisely to defend the interests of powerful Jerusalem priestly groups, and it seems more that he is on the side of those who will surrender to Rome to preserve their own privilege. (This certainly is how things played out for Josephus himself; he was rewarded for surrender.)

The scribes of the latest stage of Q can be characterized by their interest in John and Jesus as eschatological prophets in the line of deuteronomic prophets. If earliest wisdom Q was produced by scribes in the Herodian administration of the lake, then deuteronomic Q most likely emerged from scribal groups in Sepphoris after the transfer of the archives from Tiberias under Nero and Agrippa II. Deuteronomy emphasizes the sole worth of the God of Israel and "all Israel." The Gospel of Mark likewise "reads" John and Jesus as eschatological prophets in the mold of Elijah (Mark 1:2; Mal 4:5). Zvi Zahavy has identified non-Jerusalem scribes in early rabbinism who emphasized the *Shema*ʿ and the Exodus over against Jerusalem scribes who sponsored the Amidah.[79] The Q scribes of Sepphoris likely affiliated in Galilee with the former groups. Their conflict with scribes of the Jerusalem Pharisee groups is thus understandable. Their interest in Jesus ostensibly derived from his central concern with God's Kingdom and with the Exodus at Passover. Consider Mark 12:28 for an example of a scribe who probably would be sympathetic as well to the Q tradents. Hence, the scribes and Pharisees in Galilee representing the interests of Jerusalem, the temple, and priests came into conflict with Jesus in ways that involved both ideology and material concerns.

Jesus and the Kingdom of God in Galilee

All contemporary Jesus scholars concede that Jesus' central concern was expressed through the metaphor "kingdom of God." How to construe this has long been discussed. The two major options are first the eschatological rule of God as found in Second Temple literature like Daniel 7 or in the Dead Sea Scrolls. This is indeed how Jesus is presented in both Q and Mark. However, the second option is that Jesus sees this rule as "real and present" in the fields, natural world, and human relations of his Galilee. In the one view, Jesus' parables and sayings will warn of imminent catastrophe and reveal the opportunity to respond before the final Judgment; in the other

79. Zahavy, *Studies in Jewish Prayer*.

view, the parables and sayings invite hearers to decide how they must act in the presence of this Power.

The tension between the eschatological outlook of the Synoptic Gospels (and deuteronomic Q's and Mark's construal of John and Jesus as eschatological prophets) and the natural theology elements of the earliest Jesus traditions in wisdom Q has led to extended arguments about the relationship between Jesus and John the Baptist. For Meier, Allison, and Freyne, for instance, Jesus' apocalyptic eschatology is largely in accord with the Baptist's.[80] Paul Hollenbach and John Dominic Crossan, by contrast, argue that Jesus broke with the Baptist.[81] This alternative seems more likely, and the peasant artisan Jesus is hardly an eschatological prophet.[82] This, rather, is the portrayal of him given in the earliest sources, Q and Mark. Peasant theology (ideology) is immediate and concrete.[83] The Prayer of Jesus is about immediate human need, in particular the deadly mortgage of debt upon adequate subsistence and free life. Jesus the peasant artisan seems best understood as a village sage whose wide travels garnered a unique social experience and wisdom. Under the dominant metaphor of the kingdom of God, Jesus spoke of the real presence of God in the midst of perceived Galilean social problems.

For Jesus, God's kingdom is closely associated with Israel's story of liberation in the Exodus. Jesus identifies himself with the Passover bread and wine in the traditions of the Passion Narrative. And these political interests eventually call Jesus to the attention of the authorities as well as the scribes behind Q.

Though the meanings of the parables of Jesus will continue to be debated, it is generally conceded that they had to do with Jesus' central interests, concerns, and praxis. The parables and sayings of Jesus again and again point to the everyday situations of Galilee. The eschatological readings of the parables are demonstrably secondary. So, sociological imagination is called for to place their meanings firmly in the context of a colonized Galilee. Fundamental here is that God's ruling presence pertains substantively to subsistence anxiety brought on by the conflicting social goals of Galilean elites (Q 12:22–32; cf. Mark 2:19). Patronage politics

---

80. Meier, *A Marginal Jew*, 2:19–181; Allison, *Constructing Jesus*, 31–220; Freyne, *The Jesus Movement*, 134–39.

81. Hollenbach, "Conversion of Jesus"; Crossan, *The Historical Jesus*, 237–38.

82. Oakman, *The Political Aims of Jesus*, 81.

83. Oakman, *The Political Aims of Jesus*, 75.

imply debt and obligation, as well as required expressions of loyalty. The exploitive practices of the elites are clear (Q 19:12–27; Mark 12:38–44; Luke 16:19–31). Jesus appears to advocate a "reverse patronage" (Q 11:4; Luke 16:4). The two revolutionary cries of antiquity were abolition of debts and redistribution of land.[84] Jesus says little about the latter issue; only Mark 10:30 or Luke 12:13–14 seem to address land issues. However, there is a clear concern for debt in the Prayer of Jesus (the Lord's Prayer), and radical sayings about making loans without expectation of repayment appear in Q 6:30 and Gos. Thom. 95.

The parable of the Sower takes on an interesting light when one considers that it reflects sowing on marginal ground, not on fertile bottomland. In relation to the ruling power of God, what can the Sower signify? The harvest "despite" all the bad odds has often led to claims that it is about growth and signifies Kingdom success in face of great odds. This approach ties into concerns about temporal eschatology. More likely, the story indicates the foolhardiness of the Sower and the preposterousness of the food situation facing the average Galilean. The bottomlands invariably belong to elite estates. The peasant is forced to eke out a living even on marginal lands and rocky soils. In sum, the Sower signifies "the Ruling God has compassion over subsistence anxiety." Q 9:58 again suggests that the *ho huios tou anthrōpou* (Aramaic *bar 'enasha*), "the Galilean commoner," is homeless! Interestingly, the term *ho huios tou anthrōpou* also appears in a wisdom Q context at 6:22 and need not signify there the eschatological figure of deuteronomic Q. Both 6:22 and 9:58 show that Jesus as vexed about the shameful plight of commoners. There is a sense of this meaning as well in the suffering Markan *huios tou anthrōpou*.[85] Of course, wisdom Q contains the discourse on anxiety 12:22–32.

In addition to the parables, Jesus' sayings and maxims especially found in the early Q material point to social and political meanings. Q 9:58 saying "foxes have holes, the birds of the air have nests" can be a veiled comment about the ease and plenty of both Herod Antipas and the people of Sepphoris. Their stores are full, and they perch (like birds, *zipporin*) securely. That foxes and birds are also a natural threat to the fields will not go unnoticed by the villagers and villages owned by Sepphoris! The elites are parasites

---

84. Lev 25:10; Oakman, *The Political Aims of Jesus*, 102.

85. In past scholarship, *[ho] huios tou anthrōpou* (Aramaic *bar 'enash[a]*) has either been considered as an apocalyptic figure "The Son of Man" or a circumlocution for Jesus "I." This matter of interpretation is considered in more detail in chapter 6 of this volume.

upon the countryside! Interestingly, Brown points to a parallel to Q 9:58 in Plutarch's biography of Tiberius Gracchus: "The wild beasts that roam over Italy have a hole, to each is its lair or nest; but the men who fight and die for Italy have no share in anything but air and sunshine."[86] Were the early Q tradents then familiar with agrarian problems in other parts of the Roman world? Their concern for wisdom would suggest a broader horizon of knowledge.[87]

Q 16:13, "You cannot serve God and Mammon," stands in close connection with the Dishonest Steward parable where rents in kind would naturally imply need for storage. Far from being advice on investment strategies, Mammon here signifies more generally than money the security arrangements—the treasury and storehouse—that the provincial elites trust (which seems to be at the Semitic root of the word) to hedge about their estates. Luke's Rich Fool (Luke 12) will build more barns (*apothēkai*), and in the end trusts the wrong things and has the wrong investment calculus. These suggest that Jesus was more interested in immediate access to adequate food resources or in acquiring it for others.

The critiques of Mammon and Debt are leveled at the patronage politics of Galilee that keep most everyone in dependent and servile status. The Prayer of Jesus encapsulates the concern with debt as it endangers secure subsistence. In particular, the second table links the interlocking concerns of inadequate bread, debt, and courts that serve creditors.[88] This concern is also visible in wisdom Q 12:58–59 where the creditor's court and debtor's prison are mentioned in the same breath.

The feeding stories associate secure food with God's ruling power. The feeding of the five thousand men centers on adequacy of bread and fish, which were the staples of Galilee. (Five loaves and two fish are probably a "subsistence unit," perhaps for a day for a peasant family or a week for a single person.) In general, the stories of healing and exorcism express Jesus' ability to broker help in the name of the kingdom of God. So Crossan has said on the basis of Q 10:8–9 and parallel in Gos. Thom. 14 that eating and healing were at the center of Jesus' concerns.[89] God's presence indeed can be compared to a wedding feast (Mark 2:19).

---

86. Brown, "Prometheus, the Servant of Yahweh, Jesus" after Toynbee.

87. Kloppenborg, *Excavating Q*, 200.

88. Oakman, "The Lord's Prayer in Social Perspective"; Oakman, *Jesus, Debt, and the Lord's Prayer*, 42–91.

89. Crossan, *The Historical Jesus*, 332–33.

For Jesus' in-group, God's patronage was expressed in the address to God as 'Abba', Aramaic for Father. This implies that Jesus' group and network were a fictive family, though not exclusive about membership. Jesus' conflict with the purity standards of the Pharisees in part had to do with his willingness to accept the outcasts, the "tax collectors and sinners," and to cross lines that Judean purity standards would not allow. The sharing ethic of the Jesus network counteracted the threats to adequate subsistence by so to speak building capacity to supply acute need. The healing and feeding narratives express this capacity. Jesus as broker of God's ruling power developed a network of powerful friends among the "haves" and the reputation for brokering real goods for the "have-nots." Upon this fictive kin network and reputation of effective connection with God's present power would later be built the earliest christological claims and Christ-believing communities. Central to the life of their assemblies (*ekklēsiai*) was Jesus' Passover table and his continuing mediation (as a broker) with God even after his death (Heb 8:6; 9:15).

Developments after Jesus

Jesus' lasting influence in Galilee seems to have been minimal. His failure to address land redistribution or land tenure issues, despite his concerns about debt and insecure subsistence, made his vision unattractive to conservative peasant villagers. For the elites, calls for debt release were enough to indict and convict. There is no evidence of a Galilean Jesus movement after Jesus' death. Close associates like Peter leave Galilee after the crucifixion; James the son of Zebedee and James the brother of the Lord are killed in Judea. The "Jesus movement," it seems, takes form and shape in the post-Easter period in Jerusalem. From there, of course, it moves to Syria and Egypt, and via Paul and others to Asia and Europe. Christians are first identified as a distinct group in 1 Peter 4 in Roman Asia and in Syrian Antioch (Acts 11:26). How Christianity reached Rome is uncertain, but it was certainly there when Paul wrote his letter to Rome ca. 56 CE. The most remarkable thing to remember, and perhaps one of the greatest events in the history of religions, was the transformation of the message and influence of a provincial and rural peasant artisan into a predominately urban movement and universal salvation religion that eventually triumphed over Roman imperial power!

CHAPTER 6

In the Beginning of the Gospels
Was the Scribe

Scribal Interests in the Earlier Jesus Traditions—
an Exploration

> The wisdom of the scribe depends on the opportunity of leisure; only the one who has little business can become wise. —Sir 38:24[1]

> [Pinemʼe] caused the people to penetrate the secret of writing and the use of ink and paper; on account of this matter, there are many who have erred from eternity to eternity, until this very day. —1 Enoch 69:9

> He said to them, "For this reason, every scribe educated for the Kingdom of Heaven is like a householder who draws out of his treasury new things and old things." —Matt 13:52

JESUS OF NAZARETH ENTERED the pages of history due to the work of sympathetic scribes. This article investigates, through tradition-historical and social-scientific criticisms, the confluence of interests between Jesus of Nazareth and the early Jesus- or Christ-believing scribes who inscribed him. While initially the illiterate Jesus may have been "written up" within

---

1. Biblical and pseudepigraphic quotations in this chapter will be drawn usually from the NRSV and Charlesworth, *OTP*. In places some translations are my own. Consultation of the Charles classic, *Pseudepigrapha*, has also been made. Citations of Q as already mentioned refer to the location of passages in Luke.

the administration of Herod Antipas as a threat to the crown, at some point scribes sympathized with him, concurred with his interests, and recounted his words and deeds.

It is that interface of sympathetic interests within specific social locations and situations that this essay intends to explore in the earlier Jesus traditions. Tradition-historical criticism pursues the analytic investigation of blocks of tradition in literary form that exhibit identifiable themes and motifs. These express identifiable concerns and ideological interests of literate scribes, which in turn may provide *indices* to the originary social connections to Jesus. The social-science criticism approach attempts to develop models or provide comparative social perspectives on the scribes; elucidates geographic and social locations of groups; and identifies prevailing social interests, as well as locates the study of writing and the biblical writings within agrarian societies in general. Texts emerge out of definite contexts, but their interrelationships can be complex. This dual-pronged method assumes the procedure that Bruce Malina has called "abduction," i.e., hermeneutical work that is both inductive as historians desire, but also deductive as social theory and constructed models can entail.[2]

The entire picture of "early Jesus scribalism" needs to be put into social perspective because of the nature of literacy in preindustrial agrarian settings. Literacy rates were very low in the ancient world, and consequently literate scribes, perhaps 3 percent, constituted a very small percentage of the population.[3] Reading literacy was probably higher than writing literacy. Moreover, scribes served elite interests—in the case of biblical-period Palestine: kings and priests. However, scribes were also attached to cities and

2. Malina, "Interpretation: Reading, Abduction, Metaphor," 259, 357 n25: Abduction was first discussed by the philosopher Charles Peirce as a circular process involving both induction and deduction. Historians frequently complain that the social-scientific approach with theoretical models is either a cookie-cutter approach, a "procrustean bed," or full of illicit assumptions about missing data. However, no historian is a tabula rasa in terms of "pre-understanding" the historical data, nor is the historical data self-evidently meaningful without relation to the larger social-systemic gestalt or context. Actually, models help the historian to see the relevant data for interpretation. See Morley, *Theories, Models and Concepts*, 5–31. The hermeneutical circles live on! On "dialogue with history," see Bultmann, *Jesus and the Word*, 3–15.

3. The best discussion of this issue for early Roman Palestine is Hezser, *Jewish Literacy*. She argues that the literacy rate in Palestine at the turn of the eras was less than the general Roman society average of 10–15 percent claimed by William Harris; most likely, the average was closer to Bar-Ilan's estimate of 3 percent. See *Jewish Literacy*, 23, 496. Of course, scribal literacy also included a range of writing abilities as the chapter epigraphs suggest.

towns; in Galilee, the important Herodian-era cities were Sepphoris and Tiberias. And at the village level, scribes served a variety of social functions, as will be discussed. As Lenski has well said about "retainers" of elites, among whom would be the scribal groups: "Collectively the retainer class was . . . important because it performed the crucial task of mediating relations between the governing class and the common people. It was the retainers who actually performed most of the work involved in effecting the transfer of the economic surplus from the producers to the political elite."[4] Studies of writing in agrarian contexts, where illiteracy and orality are prevalent among peasantry, have also indicated that villagers typically tend to distrust or even hate writing. After all, scribes provide elites with the power of written memory, and contracts or debt and tax records were mortgages upon the peasant's labor power and freedom.[5] Conversely, scribes can also serve the interests of the village or small groups of non-elites. This seems to be the point to begin with the earliest Jesus traditions.

Tradition-Historical Criticism and the Interests of Early Jesus-Scribes

Form and redaction criticism of the Jesus traditions and gospels held central scholarly attention through the twentieth century until about 1960. These criticisms were concerned mostly with biblical theologies or ecclesiastical settings. In a 1964 article, James M. Robinson introduced a new consideration by tracing the trajectories of genres (*Gattungen*).[6] At that time, the entire conversation had been enormously enriched by the discoveries of the Dead Sea Scrolls (1946) and the Nag Hammadi Codices (1945). Scholarship moved away from a strictly "theological" or "canonical" approach in order to consider the wealth of written materials at the root of Jewish and Christian origins. Investigations also moved in a more comprehensive historical direction beyond the boundaries of the traditional canons of the Hebrew Bible, the New Testament, and the issues of orthodoxy and heresy.

---

4. Lenski, *Power and Privilege*, 246. Scribes of any sort were to be counted among the "retainers" of all historical agrarian societies.

5. James Scott commented on this mistrust in my hearing during an oral presentation to the nation SBL Q Section about twenty years ago. Consider the tensions and conflict implied in *m. Sheqal.* 1:3 "pledges" and Matt 17:21; and Josephus, *War* 2.427–428; 7:61, burning of debt archives in Jerusalem and Antioch.

6. Robinson, "*Logoi Sophon*: On the Gattung of Q," 71–113.

In more recent days, the social-scientific study of the Bible as noted in the Introduction has raised additional questions about the contextual origins and social meaning of biblical texts and interest groups.[7]

Q1, the Formative Stratum of the Sayings Source Q

In respect to Jesus of Nazareth, this stratum of the earliest written record documents Jesus' importance and meaning to a scribe or group of scribes and their community. It is here that scholarship must reckon with an initial match of interests that could explain why any scribe or scribes would be concerned with the words and activities of an illiterate peasant. In the attempt to identify those social interests, peculiar *indices* are sought that can give meaningful definition to them.[8]

The formative stratum of Q (hereafter Q1) is comprised of five sayings clusters with form-critical marks of aphoristic wisdom in simple chreiai (aphorisms introduced by "Jesus said").[9] Again, it can be asked why these sayings were first inscribed. Why were the originary scribe(s) interested in Jesus, or how did their interests converge? Ancillary questions arise as to why the scribe(s) of the Sayings Source Q collected sayings of Jesus, and why they attributed them to Jesus and not someone else.

Q's redactional stratum, Q2, excoriates Capernaum, Chorizin, and Magdala (10:13–15), which allows Arnal to argue for an origin of all Q editions by the Galilean lake.[10] If this is so, then Q1 most likely would have

---

7. Elliott, *What Is Social-Scientific Criticism?* See further on the work of the Context Group chapter 2, note 2.

8. Just as smoke is an index of the presence of fire, by analogy, chronological schemes can be seen as an index of eschatological interests or Kingdom-of-God speech as an index of political interests. On the distinctions between index, sign, and symbol, see Heisig, "Symbolism," 198–208; see also chapter 11 in this volume for Tillich's analysis.

9. Not all scholars accept the view that a stratified Q can be reconstructed from Matthew and Luke. The present volume throughout assumes the perspectives of Kloppenborg, *The Formation of Q*, 317–28, and Kloppenborg [Verbin], *Excavating Q*, 146, 151. Ronald Piper, *Wisdom in the Q-Tradition*, 15, independently discusses five aphoristic clusters, all of which fall within Kloppenborg's Q1. This core wisdom material thus meshes with the wisdom forms characteristic of Jesus.

10. Arnal, *Jesus and the Village Scribes*, 164, claims that both formative and redactional stages of Q originated at Capernaum; while in general agreement, Kloppenborg [Verbin] raises critical questions, *Excavating Q*, 173–75. The argument to follow in this essay argues for a slightly different scenario for the location of Q1 and Q2. The dating of these two strata also will be addressed further. Suffice it for now to say that both are

been penned by lower-level scribes in the administrative structure of Herod Antipas (4 BCE—39 CE). Herod certainly receives oblique mention in Q2 (7:19–28). The date of the formative layer, Q1, is uncertain, but most likely inscription began as early as the lifetime of Jesus. In terms of themes and interests, Q1 does not claim the status of revelation, but aims at persuasion. Jesus is perceived as a purveyor of wisdom, an oral sage of town or village, one whose words require serious consideration in regard to worldly action. His words are often simply introduced as "Jesus said," the unadorned chreia. As with biblical wisdom traditions in general, "revelation" here is by observation and reasoning. Reference points are found in the natural and social worlds of that time. This type of wisdom is deliberative, i.e., to encourage the contemplation of right action in the world. Important indices of Q1 scribal interests, both natural and social, can be selectively exemplified in the Q Beatitudes and Sermon (especially Q 6:20–21 and Q 6:27–28, 35); the two "Son of Man" references (Q 6:22; 9:58); the parable of the Rich Fool (Luke 12:16–20, likely in Q);[11] the saying on God and Mammon (Q 16:13); the Lord's Prayer (Q 11:2–4); and the sayings cluster on anxiety (Q 12:22–31).[12]

The Q Beatitudes (Q 6:20–23) mark the opening lines of the formative stratum of Q, and the opening lines of the Sermon. Assuming synonymous parallelism, the Beatitudes promise the destitute (*ptōchoi*) the possession of the Kingdom, and when coupled with the second beatitude about hunger highlight the concern of people without secure material sustenance. Weeping in the third beatitude will be transformed into laughter. That these same sentiments can be seen in other ways in the Sermon (Q 6:20–49) and the Lord's Prayer (Q 11:2–4) indicates a situation where scribes are in contact with landless people or village peasants living without a secure subsistence. This point shines an unusual light on Q 6:27–28, 35 (and, as will be seen, Q 6:22) for a change in address may be suspected—to those who have the means to oppress but are enjoined to love of "their enemies" the oppressed. In the critical reconstruction of Q1, Q 6:35 adds a motive clause enjoining generous behavior patterned on the natural benefaction of God "the Father" (cf. Q 11:2, the Address in the Lord's Prayer). This other audience

---

pre-70 CE (as Q gives no indication of the Roman destruction of Jerusalem).

11. Kloppenborg [Verbin], *Q Parallels*, 128.

12. Piper takes a slightly different view about the meaning of these topics, arguing that they are all to be interpreted "internally" to depict Q's attitudes toward the world, "Wealth, Poverty, and Subsistence in Q," 219–64.

(not the *ptōchoi*) would have means as implied by Q 6:34 (see Gos. Thom. 95). The rhetorical question of Q 6:32 seems to raise a problem for the interpretation that Q also addresses the concerns of the scribes, revolving around whether Q read *telōnai* (Matthew) or *hamartōloi* (Luke); *The Critical Edition of Q* chooses the former but notes the uncertainty.[13] For reasons discussed later, reference to tax- or rent-debtors as *hamartōloi* would be more appropriate.

The two instances of the term "[The] Son of Man" (*[ho] huios tou anthrōpou*) in the formative stratum of Q (Q 6:22 and Q 9:58) likewise assume something radically different from the more familiar scholarly meanings.[14] Considering Q 9:58 first, the term is part of a political allegory. The "fox" and the "birds of the air" refer obliquely to Herod Antipas and to Sepphoris, the political center in Lower Galilee. On this recognition, then, the Son of Man is not Jesus himself, but the common person of Galilee (especially the landless). Likewise in Q 6:22, the fourth Beatitude—"You are honorable when men hate you . . . for the sake of (*heneka*) the common man"—is not about Jesus, but is addressed to those who suffer on account of their concern for the commoners. This reading will take on more flesh in consideration of other Q1 material.

The parable of the Rich Fool (Luke 12:16–20, likely from Q) identifies the dishonorable behavior of the selfish landlord, who is only concerned with self-sufficiency. This is the reverse of God's generosity, and taken together with Jesus' Q-word, "You cannot serve God and Mammon" (Q1? Q 16:13), contrasts the generous benefactions of God's "family" or "kingdom" with the landlord ethos of first-century Galilee that leaves the *ptōchoi* in mourning.

In the Lord's Prayer, the Father is addressed directly (Q 11:2), implying that the children request God's direct solicitude (there is no mediation). Elsewhere,[15] I have argued that the Second Table of the Prayer (Q 11:3–4) is closer to the Prayer of Jesus, but here it might also be suggested that the Address and the Second Table comprised the version in Q1 and that the petitions for hallowing God's name and the arrival of the Kingdom likely

13. Robinson, Hoffmann, and Kloppenborg, eds., *Critical Edition of Q*, 68–69.

14. All Son of Man references in the gospels are on the lips of Jesus. Three scholarly meanings are usually assumed: 1) Jesus' self-reference, i.e., a circumlocution for "I"; 2) the suffering Son of Man in Mark; 3) the future Son of Man who will judge the world. See Nickelsburg, "Son of Man," 137–50.

15. Oakman, "The Lord's Prayer in Social Perspective"; Oakman, *Jesus, Debt, and the Lord's Prayer*.

come from the hands of Q2 scribes. Again, the petitions for bread, debt remission, and avoidance of the creditor's court (see Q 12:58–59) apply to the *ptōchoi* quite well, but petition five "forgive our debts as we also forgive others" (Q 11:4, Matt 6:12 is probably closer to original Q wording) suggests that the interests of a creditor are also in view.[16] This point will lead below to a consideration of the term "tax collectors and sinners" that comes into prominence in Q2 and Mark.

The material on anxiety Q 12:22–31 further continues the emphasis upon material security. It is notable that the first two metaphors (ravens, "lilies") refer to scavenger birds and weeds (if the lilies are actually anemones in wheat fields). God's natural provision seems the relevant point, over against a social order that is not providing adequately or justly. But what does "seeking the Kingdom" (Q 12:31) mean when it has already been promised in the opening Beatitudes?

Excursus: Q and the Gospel of Thomas

> The work of Arnal and Patterson indicates that Q and Thomas both contain two redactional layers, and, as is well known, a good number of sayings in common (about forty percent, often with slightly diverging forms). Both originated with scribes interested in deliberative wisdom, but the respective redactional levels diverge—in Q2 toward apocalyptic and in Thomas toward Gnosticism. Arnal sees a Galilean location for Q; Patterson argues for an eastern Syrian origin for Thomas. Both Q and Thomas lack a Passion Narrative or resurrection account of Jesus. However, Q manifests a good deal of conflict with Judean groups like the Pharisees, while Thomas contains little such polemic. In what follows, more will be said about Q's context(s) in relation to Jesus.[17]

Q2 and Mark

New scribal elements come into view when considering the redactional level of Q (hereafter Q2) and its nearly contemporary text, the Gospel of Mark. Q2 takes on very specific ideological and rhetorical features that

---

16. Robinson, Hoffmann, and Kloppenborg, editors, *Critical Edition of Q*, 210.

17. Arnal, "The Rhetoric of Marginality," 471–94; Patterson, "The View from Across the Euphrates," 411–31. Arnal, "The Rhetoric of Marginality," 471, on common material.

differentiate it from Q1. Here are several notable accents: Developed chreiai with more narrative tissue are present; John the Baptist is introduced at the beginning of this later layer; Q2 insists that both John and Jesus are children of wisdom; but even more so, there is an increase of prophetic pronouncements, a critique of "this generation," a deuteronomic concern for the fate of the prophets, and notable features of apocalyptic such as the reference to the coming Son of Man as Judge. Thus, both Jesus and John in Q2 announce the impending judgment against "this generation," serving the one main idea that their pronouncements are eschatological wisdom in preparation for the final judgment.[18]

Arnal posited that all editions of Q originated around the north shore of the Galilean lake. However, this notable shift in emphasis in Q2 suggests a change of social and perhaps geographical setting. The redactional layer of Q incorporates material more akin to that of Judean scribes concerned with the true prophets of Israel (a deuteronomic emphasis) and to apocalyptic judgment like that found in the Enochic literature. In 54 Nero (54–68) came to power in Rome and granted certain benefactions to Agrippa II, including the incorporation of Tiberias into his kingdom (61 CE?).[19] Josephus reports that at this time the royal archives were relocated to Sepphoris. This could logically imply that scribes with more Judean interests, i.e., those of Q2 within the administrative catchment of Sepphoris, inherited the first Jesus inscriptions. Their redactions of Q1 show an interest in condemning what they saw as a corrupt Israel ("this generation"). Arnal notes that Q2 mentions Jonah, a northern Israelite prophet, and that (as pointed out by Jonathan Reed) a shrine to Jonah existed on the road from Sepphoris to Tiberias.[20]

---

18. Kloppenborg [Verbin], *Excavating Q*, 187, 212–13, adds a Q3 at the latest stage of Q before its incorporation into Matthew and Luke. Q3 is most clearly evident in the Temptation narrative, where both Jesus and the Devil quote Deuteronomy. After incorporation, Matthew continues much of Q's apocalyptic interests and Q3's Torah interests while Luke attenuates them.

19. Schürer, *History*, 1:473, notes that "When exactly Nero's gift was made, cannot be determined with certainty," but that Josephus, *Life* 37–38 and coin evidence point to 61 CE. Kloppenborg [Verbin], *Excavating Q*, 237, citing A. H. M. Jones, assumes 54 CE. A date in the 60s CE, however, and the disturbed social conditions leading up to the Judean–Roman War, would accord well with the prophetic-apocalyptic rhetorical shift in Q2. On Sepphoris as a Judean city, see Schürer, *History*, 2:174; Chancey and Meyers, "How Jewish Was Sepphoris?," 18–33, 61.

20. Arnal, *Jesus and the Village Scribes*, 161.

In addition to contrasting Q1 and Q2, it is equally important to read the Gospel of Mark in relation to Q2. Both texts articulate the figures of John and Jesus in similar ways. In both cases, Mark and Q2 understand John and Jesus as prophets (Q 7:26; 11:49; 13:34; Mark 6:15; 8:28). Both embed John and Jesus within apocalyptic scenarios. Both are nearly contemporaneous in the contexts of the run up to (Q2 in the 60s) or the likely aftermath of the Judean–Roman War (Mark in final form). Both Mark and Q contain the term "Son of Man," but Mark's idea is more complicated.

The composition of Mark, like Q, is multilayered. Where Q2 moves from the "worldly wisdom" of Q1 to revealed prophetic-apocalyptic or eschatological concerns, Mark has classically been called a passion narrative with an extended introduction (Martin Kähler).[21] Moreover, the Markan narrative after Jesus' baptism by John moves into Galilee up until chapter 10, then moves to Jerusalem. This spatial movement has been classically discussed by Lohmeyer and Lightfoot.[22] Whether geography and text can have a meaningful homology is debated, but traditional and contextual considerations trace substantive Markan material and interests to Galilee, and other Markan interests to Jerusalem in the Synoptic Apocalypse and the Passion Narrative. Eric Stewart documents a strong scholarly tendency today to consider geography and space in Mark as serving only narrative interests. Stewart himself focuses on narrative perceptions and the social nature of space in Mark.[23] However, the present tradition-contextual study argues that the "extended introduction" contains tradition-blocks that originated in a Galilean context, and that the Passion Narrative is more likely a Jerusalem scribal product. These facts would seem to argue that Mark was produced by a scribal group or groups with feet on the ground both in Galilee and in Jerusalem. Central to this argument will be the traditions of and interest in the "Son of Man" shared by Q and Mark.

As stated in the previous section, the provenance of Q is without much doubt the Galilee of Jesus. This makes historical sense if Jesus as previously described domiciled around the Lake in the company of fishers, telōnai (tax collectors like Levi), and others. Q1 makes little reference to Judean traditions or Torah; further, it is uncertain as to whether the Q tradents knew

21. Kähler, *The So-Called Historical Jesus.*

22. See Stewart, "Mark and Space in Recent Discussion," in *Gathered Around Jesus,* 1–29.

23. Stewart, *Gathered Around Jesus,* 17–29. For a detailed analysis of the Markan Passion Narrative, see Mack, *A Myth of Innocence,* 249–312.

of a baptism of Jesus by John the Baptist, who preached an eschatological message of repentance (in Q2 and Mark).

EXCURSUS: JOHN'S BAPTISM, Q, AND JESUS

> Critical work on Q has not reached consensus on whether Jesus is reported in Q2 to be baptized by John; for Mark, there is no doubt. Many scholars consider Jesus' baptism an assured historical fact about him (criterion of embarrassment). What is clear literarily is that the Baptist material in Q2 forms an "inclusio" around the first formative layer cluster (the Q1 sermon introduced by the Beatitudes). Further, the inconcinnity of John's question in Q2, are you the one to come? (Q 7:19), and the focus upon John's preaching (only in Q2, not in Q1), give strong evidence that there is no report of a baptism. The location of Q 16:16 has been debated, since it logically belongs with the material of Q 7. The Gospel of Thomas mentions the Baptist in saying 46 (as in Q 7:28), but has no reference to Jesus' baptism.[24]

There is no similar "inclusio" in Mark. Jesus' baptism by John implies that Jesus is a sinner who needs it, Mark 1:4. John's disciples ask about fasting (Mark 2:18–19). John makes a reappearance in the context of Herod's banquet (Mark 6:15–17). Jesus asks about John's origin in a question about his authority (Mark 11:30–38). Matthew follows Mark on the baptism, but with the dialog with Jesus as to its necessity (3:14). Significantly, Luke does not mention Jesus' baptism by John explicitly (3:19–20 and 21), and in the Gospel of John there is no baptism at all (but John 3:25–26 raises interesting questions about Jesus that will not to be pursued here). There are good reasons then to suspect that the ambiguous linkage of Jesus to John's baptism is the literary result of scribal interests. Have Q and Mark, then, associated the two both in the interests of giving the peasant Jesus greater honor, and thereby setting up the Elijah motif (Q 7:27; Mark 1:2, 6)? Mark is the text that carries this motif most thoroughly throughout his narrative.

Before considering the Elijah motif, it is helpful also to consider baptism or John's baptism as referenced in Paul and Acts. Acts 18:24—19:5 connects Apollos the Christ-preacher only with John's baptism; but when

---

24. Kloppenborg, *Q Parallels*, 16 (on baptism), 56 (on text location of Q 16:16); Robinson, Hoffmann, and Kloppenborg, eds., *Critical Edition of Q*, 18 (on baptism), 464 (on Q 16:16).

he is informed that the Spirit is bestowed uniquely with baptism in Jesus' name, he undergoes a second baptism by Paul (19:5). Here are echoes of the earlier fractious issues in Corinth, where apparently baptisms were undergone in various names including Apollos. Further, washings were effected on behalf of the dead (1 Cor 15:29). Paul disclaims any necessity of baptism in 1:14–17 (ironically, in a reversal of the portraits of Apollos and Paul in Acts). These aporias in the early traditions about Jesus' baptism and Christ-baptism give rise to historical doubts. Paul's experience of the risen Lord was unmediated. Further, the significant issue in Antioch and Corinth was table fellowship, precisely the focus of Jesus' praxis (see below). Since 1 Thessalonians and Galatians make no mention of the rite of baptism, it seems highly unlikely that Paul required baptism as a *communal entry rite*, substitute for circumcision, or eschatological washing (Gal 2:1; 5:6; cf. 1 Cor 1:14–17; 7:18–19). Paul does acknowledge baptism as a *participatory rite*, like those of the mysteries, in Rom 6:3–4. It therefore seems plausible either that Paul was ignorant of Jesus' baptism, or that Jesus was not baptized by John the Baptist, and that baptism only became an essential rite of *Christ-follower entry* after the respective lifetimes of John and Jesus. It is reasonable to think, therefore, that scribes with Baptist sympathies associated Jesus with John's baptism in the first place.

Elijah in Q and Mark[25]

A strong connection inheres in the relationship between Elijah in Israelite tradition and God's Spirit (apart from the baptism question, although John's baptism may have been conjoined with a reenactment of the parting of the Jordan in the Elijah-Elisha traditions). Famously, Elijah was assumed into heaven and a double measure of his (i.e., derived from God's) spirit was bestowed upon Elisha (2 Kgs 2:9–12). Where in Q the John–Elijah association is related to preaching (and most likely not to a baptism rite), in Mark the John–Elijah announcement is about the anointing by God's Spirit (Mark 1:8). Mark 1:8 and 9:9–13 become key texts that unlock Mark's Elijah interest, especially in the traditions with Galilean setting (though Jesus is thought to call for Elijah in the Passion Narrative, Mark 15:34–35).

For Malachi, adduced by Mark 1:2, Elijah will come to prepare the way for the great and terrible day of the LORD (Mal 4:5; cf. Q 7:27). Just as in the Elijah traditions of Kings, where Elijah is a bestower of God's Spirit

25. This idea is developed also in chapter 11 in this volume.

(1 Kgs 19:15–16; 2 Kgs 2:9–15), John announces that the One Coming will anoint with the Spirit of God (Mark 1:8). John wears coarse clothing, like Elijah. Jesus, like Elijah, is driven into the wilderness by the Spirit and ministered to by angels (Mark 1:6, clothing; 1:12–13, wilderness; cf. 1 Kgs 17–19). Thus, the word *christos* in Mark is to be understood as prophetic-eschatological anointing, and the gospel explicitly rejects a royal-Davidic understanding of messiah (Mark 12:35–37; but see 2:23–28 where Jesus and his entourage practice royal freedom in the name of David). Q2 identifies John the Baptist with the Coming One in Q 7:26–27, but connects his activity with prophecy ("more than a prophet"). Likewise, Q does not mention the word *christos* at any point. Mark's "christology," however, functions like the wise ethos and action communicable in Jesus' Q-words by promoting the communal preparing of the Way. The "anointing" of Jesus at the baptism empowers him to anoint others (grant *exousia*, Mark 6:7) to prepare the Way—which includes preaching repentance, power to exorcise, and the effecting of healing through anointing with oil (Mark 6:13).

The central theme and interest, then, in the Galilean traditions of Mark at least, is that the role of Elijah redivivus is being played out not only by John, but also definitively by Jesus and his delegates. Note that the delegation story marks an inclusio around the Herod story (Mark 6:7–13, 30), where Herod remarks that Jesus is John raised from the dead, and that "others" see Elijah or one of the other prophets of old (Mark 6:14–16). Again, Jesus' question near Caesarea Philippi is answered in a similar way, John the Baptist, Elijah, or one of the prophets (Mark 8:28). As is often noted by scholars, Peter's response "you are the Christ" is not affirmed as in Matt 16, nor is Peter praised for his rebuke of Jesus (Mark 8:30, 32–33). And here in Mark appear the three so-called passion predictions (8:31; 9:31; 10:33–34). Their meaning may become clearer by laying out parallel traditions in Mark chapters 4–8 and especially in Mark 9:9–13.

Two cycles of Jesus' mighty deeds or actions, Mark 4:46—6:44 and 6:45—8:10, immediately follow Mark's parables account and recall Elijah- or Elisha-like scenarios. Moreover, the chief authority figures and structures in Palestine represented by Herodians (partisans of the Royal House) and Pharisees (retainers of the Jerusalem temple) stand in disapproval. Just as Elijah was scorned by Ahab (1 Kgs 18:17; 21:20), so Jesus meets with rejection by the Pharisees and Herodians.

Mark 3:6 Pharisees and Herodians plot Parables that convey the secret of the kingdom of God (Mark 4:11)	
Mark 4:36–41 Stilling of the storm 5 Man among the tombs, Jairus' daughter, Woman with flow of blood	Mark 6:45–52 Jesus walks on the sea 7 Controversy with Pharisees over sabbath observance, the Syrophoenician woman, Ephatha—opening man's ears and speech
6 Jesus' hometown, Sending of the Twelve, Herod Antipas thinks John raised from dead, return of the Twelve	
Mark 6:34–44 Feeding of the 5,000	8:1–10 Feeding of the 4,000 8:15 The leaven of the Pharisees and Herod
Cf. for comparison 1 Kgs 17:8–16; 19:19–21	

Table 6.1: Two Cycles Evoking Memories of Elijah and Elisha

The parallel members of Mark 9:9–13 are especially important for this argument. They can be represented in a second table:

Mark 9:12a Elijah does come	12b the Son of Man, that he should suffer many things and be treated with contempt
Mark 9:13a Elijah has come	13b They did to him whatever they pleased

Table 6.2 Elijah and the Son of Man

These synonymous parallels indicate that, for Mark, Elijah is the "Son of Man." Hence, this information suggests that "Son of Man" designates *the role* to be played by Jesus (functional praxis), and that the Elijah-anointing (Mark 1:8) is communicable to Jesus' delegates (Mark 6:7). Moreover, Mark 9:39 and 9:41, if construed *hos poiesei dynamin epi to onomati mou* "who will perform an [act of] power in my [Elijah's] name" . . . *en onomati hoti christou este* "because you are by name of the Anointed [Elijah]," indicate that others are summoned to the work of preparing the Way, not only Jesus' immediate delegates. Elijah-anointing conveys the Elijah role. The communal preparation of the Way is the mission, not a story about the exaltation of Jesus! For this reason, the Markan ending refers to a resurrection in Galilee three days away (Josephus, *Life* 269 on three days travel between Galilee and Jerusalem). The "Son of Man" Elijah role must arise again and again until the great and terrible Day of the LORD comes. Nonetheless, Mark 9:1 points to the real and present power (God's anointing Spirit) that most certainly defeats all demonic evil and death in the end.

Just as Q has neither Passion Narrative nor resurrection, Mark most likely originally lacked a resurrection story. Can it be assumed that for Q scribes the righteous man Jesus was thought to have been "assumed into heaven" like Enoch or Elijah?[26] For Mark, however, the lack of a resurrection appearance is not really about Jesus' postmortem state, but about the reappearance of his cause in the resumption of the Elijah-task of preparing the Way again from Galilee (Mark 16:7).

EXCURSUS: ENOCH AND ELIJAH

Enoch and Elijah come into play in the eschatological imaginations of Q and Mark since in biblical tradition both were assumed alive into heaven. Both were, in their respective ways, honored as representatives of righteousness and justice and shown the special favor of avoiding death (Enoch, Gen 5:24; Elijah, 2 Kgs 2:11). Both then became associated with the term "Son of Man."

Scholars generally agree that the figure of "One Like a Son of Man" (Dan 7:13, ca. 164 BCE) stands behind much of the imagination and eschatological speculation in the turn-of-the-eras Judean writings and New Testament gospels. *Bar 'enasha* (Aramaic: "the Son of Man") is a Semitic construction or idiom depicting a single human being (in view of the definite article); the wooden translation in Greek always has the definite article *ho huios tou anthrōpou*, which then seems to make it a title. The divine figure in Dan 7 appears to be earlier than other pseudepigraphic references (the Hebrew usage *ben 'Adam* in Ezekiel *passim* refers simply to the prophet's human status). It is also widely believed that the Danielic figure gave rise to a variety of messianic depictions after the middle of the second century BCE. Prominent among those pseudepigraphic depictions is the Son of Man in the Parables (Similitudes) of 1 Enoch. It is much discussed, however, whether the figure of the "Son of Man" in the Parables of chapters 37–71 bears any relationship to the term in Q and Mark. The debate about

---

26. Kloppenborg, *Q, the Earliest Gospel*, 80–84, discussing an idea of Daniel Smith.

the date of the Parables has not been settled, though it is now generally considered to be within either the earlier or the later first century CE.[27]

If the Son of Man sits upon a glorious throne to judge humanity (1 Enoch 62, kings and mighty; see 71:29; Matt 25:31), then there is clearly an ideological affinity of 1 Enoch with the references in Q and some in Mark. The future Son of Man sayings in Mark (8:38; 13:26; 14:62) and Q (12:8, 40; 17:24) can well connect with the notions of 1 Enoch if the Parables originated in the early first century. However, given what has been said about Elijah in the previous sections, does Mark understand the Son of Man as Enoch or as Elijah? The future references there are surely present in both the Synoptic Apocalypse (ch. 13) and in the Passion Narrative scene before the high priest.

Notably 1 Enoch shows a concern for temple and priestly issues (e.g., 1 Enoch 89:73–74).[28] These are also issues known from the Qumran library. In the later second century BCE, a disaffected group of priests removed to Qumran near the Dead Sea. Central to the group's ideology and organization were a Damascus Covenant and Community Rule, and the group continued until the destruction of their community by the Romans in 68 CE. Since copies of 1 Enoch (though all lacking the Parables) were found among the Qumran library texts, and that many other writings attest eschatological expectations, there would seem to have been at least a community of interest between the Enoch scribes and the Qumran scribes. Scholarship has identified this interest in at least two ways—a highly critical stance toward the Jerusalem temple and its priests, viewed as corrupt, and a palpable concern for ritual purity. Significantly, the Qumran literature does not emphasize the figure of the Son of Man at all, as the Parables of 1 Enoch do. In contrast, Qumran speculations refer to Melchizedek or the two messiahs of Israel and Aaron. Apart from the question of the provenance of Daniel, interest in the Son of Man looks to be a northern Palestinian scribal interest (Q and Markan material in Galilee, 1 Enoch near Mount Hermon). Lack of awareness of these scribal traditions may explain why Paul's letters never refer to the Son of Man.

One question arises for this Markan Elijah scenario in view of the future Son of Man sayings in Mark 8:38; 13:26; and 14:62. As in Q2 (17:24, 30), none of these references explicitly identify Jesus with this figure. Mark

27. Nickelsburg, "Enoch," 513; Nickelsburg, "Son of Man," 138–40; Suter, "Enoch in Sheol," 415–43.

28. Nickelsburg, 1 Enoch, 54; Nickelsburg, "Enoch," 515.

8:38a is entirely consistent with this Elijah identification. However, Mark 8:38b and the other two references are more consistent with 1 Enoch's conflation of God's judgment (1 Enoch 1:9; cited later by Jude, possibly, like the Letter of James, a later scribe [or scribes] kindred to the Q group) and the judgment *by Enoch* "that righteous Son of Man" (69:29; 71:13–17). The final form of Mark, it seems, conflated Elijah and Enoch expectations (Elijah in Galilean materials; Enoch reference in the Synoptic Apocalypse and the Passion Narrative, both arguably Jerusalem products). For Mark's Galilee materials, Elijah has already returned before the great and terrible Day of the LORD. Mark 8:38b in this view is a later gloss added (by Mark's Jerusalem editor?) to Jesus' saying, now concerning honor or shame before the future Son of Man. Note that there is a Mark–Q overlap here and again that Q's Son of Man is consistently the figure of the Enochic traditions.

If this reading of Mark is correct, that Elijah redivivus is humanly re-incarnated in the activities of John, Jesus, and his delegates, then Mark's us-age stands apart from that of 1 Enoch, Q, and later first-century depictions like Matt 25:31 (which clearly identifies Jesus and the Enochic Son of Man and Judge to come). As just mentioned, Jude alone in the New Testament quotes from the first chapter of 1 Enoch (1:9 in Jude 14-15), but unlike Q does not explicitly link Jesus with a last judgment.

EXCURSUS: THE SCRIBES OF MATTHEW AND LUKE— Q^3 AND Q^4?

As mentioned above, Kloppenborg discerned a further redactional layer in Q in the Temptation story, involving explicit references to Deuteronomy and Judean Torah. This layer might be discerned in a number of glosses elsewhere in Q (e.g., 11:42; 16:17). Without much effort, it is easy to see Matthew's extension of Q concerns in this direction. Luke best retains the order of Q, but revises it in a moralistic way, a point that cannot be pursued here. One important observation is that any essential mention or interest in *telōnai* related to Jesus disappears from early Christian literature after the Synoptic Gospels. References to *telōnai* supply a very important index in evaluating the social contexts of the earliest Jesus-scribes.[29]

---

29. Kloppenborg [Verbin], *Excavating Q*, 212–13.

A Social-Scientific Perspective on the Earliest Jesus Traditions

The focus of the discussion now turns more to social questions and tries to move beyond literary indices and interests into the exploration of implied scribal social contexts. In general geographic terms, it can be noted initially that the scribes of Enoch traditions clearly were located in the vicinity of Dan and Mount Hermon.[30] Jerusalem scribes were attached to the temple, and in that social location appear identifiable Pharisaic and Sadducean scribes. Jerusalem interests involved Galilee, so scribes representing priestly and temple interests could be expected to be found there. To the south, the Qumran scribes are well known from their library and the Dead Sea Scrolls.[31] How then did the scribes of the earliest Jesus traditions fit in? What were their social locations and interests? And how at the beginning did their interests intersect with and come to match those of Jesus of Nazareth? These social questions occupy the final section of this chapter. Some answers have already been anticipated above.

Q1 and the Telōnai

The key assumption of this exploration is that *the interests* of the oral sage Jesus of Nazareth somehow matched those of his earliest scribal tradents. If initially Q scribes were providing intelligence to the Herodian administration, then Jesus' interests would have been viewed as inimical to the Crown's interests. As we have Q today, its scribes appear more as sympathetic to Jesus.

It is important in this to stress that Jesus moved in an oral village or town culture and that he was for the most part illiterate. This judgment that Jesus was illiterate rests upon several considerations. Recall again that ancient literacy rates for Roman Palestine were low—somewhere around 3 percent. That a manual laborer like Jesus would have opportunity for learning to write at the sophisticated level of Q would have been close to zero.[32] Further, nothing has come down from antiquity in writing that could credibly be attributed to Jesus; conversely, he is known in the early written Jesus

---

30. Suter, "Why Galilee?," 167–212.

31. Scribes in Samaria served similar functions, e.g., as evidenced by the Samaritan Pentateuch. Samaria will be left out of the present analysis.

32. Mark 6:3; as a *tektōn*, Jesus worked in wood or stone; see Oakman, *The Political Aims of Jesus*, 69, 75–76; Hezser, *Jewish Literacy*, 173.

traditions through persuasive oral speech forms such as the proverb, the aphorism, and the parable.

A good deal of work has already been done to locate the Q tradents temporally and geographically. To some extent, analogies of Egyptian *kōmogrammateis* have been fruitful—both in identifying their functions at the village and town levels and in seeing their interests in various forms of worldly wisdom. Especially important have been the efforts of John Kloppenborg, his former student William Arnal, and his colleague Giovanni Bazzana.[33] What follows builds upon their work and hopefully deepens social insights into the first inscriptions about Jesus of Nazareth.

As just stipulated, Jesus was an illiterate peasant who comes into history through oral speech forms (proverbs, aphorisms, parables) subsequently written down. Moreover, as a building or construction laborer in wood or stone (*tektōn*), he traveled to find work.[34] This travel broadened his experience beyond that of the typical villager, and his wisdom consequently reflects a range of social settings in Galilee, the Decapolis, the villages of Caesarea Philippi, Syro-Phoenicia, and perhaps Jerusalem. His home base, from the evidence of the gospels, was Capernaum and the northern towns of the Galilean lake. His prominent associates at home were fishers. Some of them seem to have traveled with him, perhaps to find supplemental work. Jesus also seems to have had numerous associations with and sympathies for marginal or landless people, such as, lepers, prostitutes, and those considered demon possessed. He had a reputation as a healer, and this picture is likely grounded in his large social credit as a broker—both of material goods and connections with sympathetic patrons.[35]

Among those Jesus notably associated with were *telōnai*. The meaning of the word *telōnēs* has been long discussed in relation to the imperial and provincial taxation systems in first-century Palestine. If responsibility for imperial taxation was laid upon the provincial (royal and city) elites, these direct taxes were collected by their agents or slaves. For towns and cities, prominent men were entrusted with collection (Josephus, *War* 2.405,

---

33. Kloppenborg [Verbin], *Excavating Q*, 200–201; Arnal, *Jesus and the Village Scribes*; Bazzana, *Kingdom of Bureaucracy*.

34. See the evidence presented in Oakman, *The Political Aims of Jesus*, 69, 83 and by Fiensy, *Jesus the Galilean*, 74–76.

35. Social credit means that Jesus could promise benefits and deliver reliably, or at least had the reputation for being able to do so. On the notion of Jesus as a broker and his "social credit" see Malina, *The Social World of Jesus and the Gospels*, 151–57.

407).[36] *Telōnai*, however, are best understood as the contractors for indirect taxes.[37] "Tax farmers" paid a fixed sum for the rights to collect certain taxes (e.g., market taxes or road tolls). Their collection activities required scribes and accountants to record the "take." The take had to meet without fail the sum specified in the tax contract, and so the *telōnai* supplied collateral, but collection could always be over and above what was contracted for. For this reason, *telōnai* were notoriously hated by the commoners and despised by the elites for whom they worked.[38]

In light of this summary, it is important to observe (a significant index) that the collocation of the phrase *telōnai kai hamartōloi* is found only in Q2 and Mark, namely, Q 7:29, 34 and Mark 2:15–16. Further, both Matthew and Luke supply additional references to *telōnai*, but each with unique accents. For instance, Matthew, with high concern for Torah righteousness tellingly draws a synonymous parallelism between *telōnai* and *ethnikoi* (5:46–47; 18:17; cf. Luke 18:10–13); this association implies the commonplace about the unethical transactions of tax collectors. Luke, following a strong social justice theme, focuses in special material (3:12; 19:1–10) on the fact that *telōnai* were typically known for exploitative exactions on top of their tax contracts.

It is uncertain whether the word *telōnēs* appears at all in Q1 unless at Q 6:32, which raises an important question for the argument that follows. Was Matthew's *telōnēs* or Luke's *hamartōlos* original to Q1? *The Critical Edition of Q* flags the uncertainty.[39] This ambiguity of reconstruction can be resolved through a reading of Q1 from the standpoint also of the *telōnai* or their subservient scribes. Further, special traditions like Luke's parable of the Pharisee and the Publican also play a role in identifying the interests and context of Q1.

It is claimed here that the crucial interface of Jesus' interests and the interests of the Q1 scribes can best be found in Jesus' brokering-activity on

36. Schürer, *History*, 2:180 on the *dekaprotoi* of Tiberias. While this task could be seen as a high honor, it involved significant backing of wealth and risk.

37. Donahue, "Tax Collectors and Sinners," 39–61; Wuellner, *The Meaning of "Fishers of Men,"* 23–24.

38. Luke 18:11; 19:7; Hanson calls attention to the story of Joseph the Tobiad (Josephus, *Ant.* 12.175–178), "The Galilean Fishing Economy," 104. MacMullen, *Roman Social Relations*, 140, provides additional Greco-Roman references to the negative honor rating of *telōnai*.

39. Robinson, Hoffmann, and Kloppenborg, editors, *Critical Edition of Q*, 68–69; Kloppenborg, *Q Parallels*, 28–31.

behalf of indebted, marginalized, and ostracized people. As the analogies with Egyptian *kōmogramateis* ("village scribes") suggest, Galilean village and town accountants responsible for a variety of writing functions would have been in a position to be first to take note of what Jesus of Nazareth was doing and saying.[40] The Gospel of Mark 2:14–16 mentions Jesus' association with Levi the *telōnēs*, and, in the same breath, that Jesus ate with *telōnai* and *hamartōloi*. The Pharisees stood nearby as critics. What makes this notice credible as historical recollection is that Levi is related to the Alphaeus family, and this family seems to have been particularly close to the historical Jesus (cf. Mark 3:18 and Acts 1:13, James the son of Alphaeus; Mark 16:1, possibly Mary the mother of James). It is not clear whether Levi should be understood as a toll collector on the Via Maris or as a collector-accountant for fishing contracts.

If Q1 is approached as the initial assemblage of Jesus-words, then what meanings does it contain for the assumed village and town scribes (and their clients)? A previous attempt to sketch out this approach appeared in my 2008 essay "Jesus the Tax Resister."[41] The results can be summarized briefly: in Q 6:20b–23 the Beatitudes are an early form of the introduction to the Passover Haggadah, the story of Israel's liberation from slavery (a very important point, as will be seen); Q 6:27–28 enjoins the *telōnēs* to love those who hate his arrival (love here meaning, to mitigate especially their tax and debt situation); Q 6:29–30 metaphorically encourages generosity of the collector toward the debtor even if abused; Q 6:31, based upon the Golden Rule, appeals to self-interest in a just treatment of the indebted; Q 6:32 refers to the behavior of *hamartōloi*—the debtors—that although they too operate on a balanced reciprocity basis, now a generalized reciprocity with the "enemies" is the new standard (Q 6:34 loan with the expectation of a return, but 6:35 without expectation of a return); Q 6:36–38 enjoins, with appeal to God's mercy, the *telōnēs* not to execute against the indebted person by imprisonment (cf. Q 12:58–59); further on in Q, the so-called Mission Discourse, beginning with the political allegory in Q 9:58 in reference to the Galilean elites, refers to the behaviors expected of the tax-enforcers and tax-collectors to provide relief on their village rounds; the Prayer of Jesus ('*Abba*' Address + Second Table) links debt forgiveness, deliverance

40. Kloppenborg [Verbin], *Excavating Q*, 201.

41. Oakman, "Jesus the Tax Resister"; drawn upon subsequently in Oakman, *The Political Aims of Jesus*, 97–102 and reprinted with slight modifications in Oakman, *Jesus, Debt, and the Lord's Prayer*, 92–118.

from creditor-favorable courts (perhaps along the lines of Hillel's *prozbul*), and food security; the final materials in Q 12–14 imagine the danger of delation by spies and even crucifixion for tax subversion (Q 14:26).[42] In sum, one significant interest linking Jesus to Q scribes at least initially were the activities of tax-collecting agents and the impact of those activities upon the *ptōchoi* of Galilee.

Q2 and Mark

In addition to the conjunction of *telōnai* and *hamartōloi* in Q2 and Mark, as spelled out above, other secondary evidence for Jesus' involvement with subversion of tax and debt collection comes from a number of Jesus' stories and parables. Here conflicts with Pharisees also enter the picture. While Q1 makes no overt reference to temple or Torah or Pharisees, Q2 (11) expresses disagreement with Pharisees and their scribes. These core issues are: tithing (11:42), purity matters (11:39), burdensome demands (11:46), and preventing entry into the kingdom of God (11:52). Mark likewise stresses conflicts around "forgiveness of sins" (2:3–12, note that scribes demur), what is permitted on the sabbath (2:27; 3:1–6), and purity (7:1–8). Anthony Saldarini has argued that the Pharisaic scribes in Galilee were temple retainers, there to look after temple interests and revenues.[43] Saldarini's work supports the picture here. Further, if release from "sins" required a payment to the temple (Mark 1:44–45; 2:5–6, scribes of the temple), then sins were debts and "forgiveness" meant depriving the temple of income! Jesus' sympathy with *telōnai* and conflict with Pharisees again appears in Luke 18:10–13. The conflict also marks the tension between the elite's interests in taxes and the interests of their accountants.

While Q1 can attest knowledge of urban life, e.g., in the appearance of the word *hypokritēs* and the theater (both Sepphoris and Tiberias seem to have had theaters in Jesus' day), at the redactional level of Q (Q2), more critical comments on elements of urban life come into the picture. For instance, the *agora* is mentioned twice (Q2 7:32; 11:43). This suggests that scribes of Q2 were either situated in a city context or at least had to deal more frequently with an urban setting. And while Sepphoris and Tiberias are never named explicitly in Q, Q throughout is highly critical of urban

---

42. Original form of the Prayer of Jesus, see Oakman, "The Lord's Prayer in Social Perspective"; Oakman, *Jesus, Debt, and the Lord's Prayer*.

43. Saldarini, *Pharisees, Scribes and Sadducees*, 296.

realities (examples: Q 7:25: Herod Antipas had a palace in Tiberias; Q 9:58: oblique reference to Sepphoris/Zippori; Q 12:58–59: creditor's court and debtor's prison).

John Kloppenborg summarizes the social location of Q thus: "Q's discourse on the kingdom of God represents resistance to the imposition of a political and economic culture that would benefit urban elites at the expense of the small producers." Kloppenborg also draws upon Robert Redfield's distinction of the Great and Little Traditions.[44] This allows him to call attention to these facts about the ideology of Q: The Q1 tradents seem to have little direct knowledge of "specific agriculture practices" (following Jonathan Reed), but produce a sophisticated literary collection of wisdom based upon observation of natural and social processes. Q2 incorporates more biblical allusions, even a biblical citation at Q 7:27, and shows knowledge of the literary arrangement of TaNaK at Q 11:51. Of course, this accords with Q2's preoccupation with the deuteronomic theme of the fate of the prophets.[45]

Not until Q3 is Torah cited, tellingly from Deuteronomy. By contrast, Q is critical of the temple's Pharisaic representatives in Galilee and their tithing and purity demands. Mark too accords with this critical perspective on representatives of Israel's Great Tradition. Interestingly, the words *Ioudaios* and *Ioudaioi* do not appear in Q; their appearances in Mark 7:3 (polemical gloss) or Mark 15 (the mocking *titulus*) are not with a positive sense of self-identification. Conversely, the word "Israel" appears with a positive valuation in both Q (7:9; 22:30) and Mark (12:29; 15:32). Properly understood, the scribes of Q and Mark seem to have distinguished their identity as "Israelites" from the Judean bearers of the Great Tradition in Jerusalem. Indeed, Elijah was a champion of the little people of Israel over against the royal establishment of Ahab. In both Q2 and Mark, references to Elijah are over against the kingdom of Herod Antipas.[46]

---

44. Kloppenborg [Verbin], *Excavating Q*, Great/Little Traditions (206–7), Q's negative depiction of urban reality (210), summary quote on (260). Kloppenborg does not see the Q tradents as among the urban retainer class (210).

45. Kloppenborg [Verbin], *Excavating Q*, 206–11.

46. Interestingly, the notion of a larger Israel over against the ethnic identity defined by Jerusalem and Judean elites and the temple also appears in the letters of Paul (e.g., Gal 1:13–14; 6:16; 2 Cor 11:22; Phil 3:5; Rom 11:1, 26). Also, Q2 (3:8) and Paul (e.g., Gal 3:14) are concerned about descent from or relation to Abraham. "Great Tradition," see Redfield, *Peasant Society and Culture*, 41–42.

Scribal Interests and Jesus of Nazareth: A Concluding Model

What the foregoing indicates is that scribes of the early Jesus traditions manifested both points of ideological contact with other known scribal groups in first-century Palestine as well as significant differences. The abductive Ideological Profile Model developed here incorporates the foregoing analyses as well as previous sociological discussions of Louis Finkelstein and Zvi Zahavy. Finkelstein, for example, describes major concerns of priestly elites and "Patricians" to defuse some of the political implications of the Passover. Further, elite priests consider it possible to see an anthropomorphic God (thus, the High Priest enters the Holy of Holies with incense alight for fear of the vision).[47] And priestly ideology incorporates the high concern for purity associated with the Second Temple from Ezekiel to 1 Enoch and Qumran, and Revelation within the New Testament. While there can appear also concern for injustice, holiness is also a hallmark of the community honored by God. Ezekiel (e.g., 36:22–36), 1 Enoch (corruption brought on by the Watchers, 10:4–9; judgment against angels and also injustice, 62–63), the Dead Sea literature (1QS 1:2, 8, concern for justice and perfection), and Revelation (21:27, also judgment on the mighty)—all associate divine judgment with eliminating impurity and corruption. Finkelstein contrasts scribes lower in the social order by their emphasis on God's invisibility, concomitantly on the prophetic Word and the political implications of the Exodus. In very broad view, then, there can be two tradition streams: Ezekiel-Temple scribes and Deuteronomy scribes (with admixtures). This assertion dovetails with Robinson's notion of trajectories in New Testament traditions.

Zahavy makes a similar distinction, associating late Second Temple "*Shema'* scribes" with the Exodus in contrast to priestly-patriarchal scribal groups with the Amidah (Eighteen Benedictions): "The primary motifs of the national cult in Jerusalem are noticeably missing from both the *Shema'* and from the frame of blessings that surrounds it. Such ideas and institutions as the temple, the priesthood, Jerusalem, and Davidic lineage, all prominent motifs in the Amidah, the Prayer of Eighteen Blessings, are of

---

47. On visible theophanies, also see comments of Hanson, "How Honorable! How Shameful!" 100. In a private communication, Hanson has suggested that this may be reflected in the makarism in Matt 5:5: "How honorable are the pure in heart, for they shall see God." This would be an implicit critique of the high priest's monopoly of seeing God as well as an implicit critique of Pharisaic concerns for high purity concerns for hands, body, etc.

no concern to the framers of the *Shema*."[48] This view suggests that, with the exception of scribes near Dan and Mount Hermon, outlying scribes in the Galilee were more colored as it were by Northern Israelite interests while those of Jerusalem largely held to the tradition of Southern Judahite interests. Figure 6.1 depicts graphically how a number of social factors came together in this historical profile of early Roman scribalism in Palestine.

FIGURE 6.1

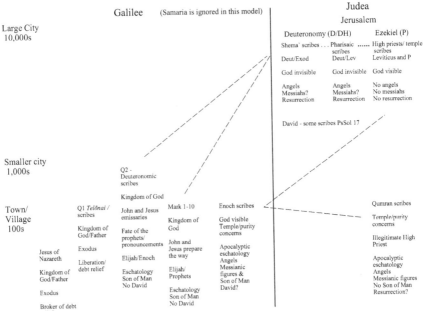

Ideological Profiles of Pre-70 Scribes in Roman Palestine

The scribes who first took notice of Jesus were close to the towns and villages of Galilee near the Lake, arguably in the service of Herod Antipas or other local elites in Tiberias. These town and village scribes, by analogy with Greco-Roman Egypt, wrote various documents both for the crown and for the peasantry. They stood under the boot of the powerful and were enforcers for various social expectations. For instance, scribes would have been needed by the *telōnai*—tax contractors—to record estimates of revenue and collection amounts for the farmed indirect taxes. Conversely,

48. Zahavy, *Studies in Jewish Prayer*, 13, 89–94.

scribes could produce marriage contracts, loans, and land deeds. Some specialized scribes would have served the courts as recorders of proceedings. These can be seen easily in Jerusalem in the temple's service; the scribes of the Pharisees and the scribes of the Sadducees come to mind (Mark 2:16; 14:1).

The tradents of the formative layer of Q noticed Jesus' emphasis on the kingdom of God and his frequent appeal to natural and social phenomena through aphorisms and parables—often in service of a praxis of generosity and benefaction. None of this betrays the apocalyptic interests of other scribes in Palestine. The latter interest first appears clearly in the redactional level of Q (Q2) and Mark—both written between 60 and 75 CE.

Significantly, the first inscription of Jesus' words in Q1 opened with inaugural words similar to those found today in the Aramaic introduction to the Passover Seder. This is the core interest connecting Jesus' table praxis (eating with *telōnai kai hamartōloi*) with the earliest Q scribes. While Q has no Passion Narrative, it seems incontrovertible that Jesus identified with the liberation meaning of the Passover story in view of his central Kingdom message and reputation for brokering on behalf of the outcast and the ostracized (his reputation as a healer and a broker). Israel's central story of liberation from Egypt would naturally appeal to the Galilean commoner. Very often in agrarian settings, the Little Tradition focuses on freedom stories.[49] Jesus' central interest in the Passover, as the probable legitimation and reason for the activities for which he was "written up," is attested in hindsight in Q2 in a place like 11:20 (in controversy with temple representatives) and in Mark's Last Supper represented as a Passover meal. Josephus and New Testament gospels alike attest Galilean interest in the Passover pilgrimage.[50] Passover was the time of the first grain harvest, and as such a focal interest of hungry peasants. However, it was not in elite priestly interests for commoners to connect this major feast with any different sociopolitical order surmised under the political tensor of a kingdom of God.

---

49. As I have previously written, "A special category of [typical peasant] tales referred to hidden treasures and benevolent robbers, who aided the poor in acts of revenge against the cruel nobles. The unusual popularity of these legends probably reflected the deep peasant desire to improve their lot, to compensate for their grief and humiliations suffered in real life" (Oakman, *Jesus and the Peasants*, 120, quoting Kazimierz Dobrowolski). More generally, see Hobsbawm, *Primitive Rebels*; Scott, "Making Social Space for Dissident Subculture," in *Domination*, 108–35.

50. For Passover interest attested in Josephus, see Oakman, *Jesus and the Peasants*, 273.

Finkelstein shows how (in his historical analysis of Passover Seders) elite Jerusalem interests toned down the freedom accent and tied Passover to the temple (Deut 26 midrash).[51] Likewise, Josephus's account of the Exodus leads straight to Jerusalem's temple (*Ag. Ap.* 1.228). Mark's gospel as it has come down to us confirms this link with his reference to Jesus' identification with the bread and wine elements of Passover at the Last Supper and his critique of the temple as a "den of robbers" (Mark 11:17; cf. 12:40). Paul also identifies Jesus' supper on the night he was betrayed as a communion meal, as God's communion with the people of Israel (1 Cor 11:23–29; cf. 5:7).

The later stage of Q shows the interests of Zahavy's *Shema'* scribes. While Q does not directly cite *Shema'* or Lev 19:18, the Kingdom-focus and the radical "love for enemies" of the Q sermon sit within the same orbit. It is not too far from Jesus' Kingdom message to the interests of the *Shema'* (i.e., the Oneness and Lordship of God), and enemy-love links closely to Lev 19:18 (Mark 12:29–31).

The *Shema'* scribes in Galilee shift to stronger interests tied to Judea and the temple—the fate of the prophets, creation, the Patriarchs of Israel, and especially apocalyptic. Q's Son of Man references show affinities with the figure of 1 Enoch's Parables (identified there as Enoch). This future Son of Man wielding judgment also makes appearances in Mark 3:38, Mark 13, and Mark's Passion Narrative. However, Mark's Galilean material seems to place more emphasis on Elijah redivivus. The apparent self-references (Mark 2:10, 28; 10:45) and references to the suffering of the Son of Man (8:31; 9:9, 12, 31; 10:33) bring this figure down to earth. What is notable in both Q and Mark is a lack of concern with ritual purity and of course a conflict with the representatives of the temple elites in Galilee, the Pharisees.

As figure 6.1 shows, Jesus and Q1 are representatives of town/village interests. Q2 moves more into an urban sphere or even places its scribes in an urban domicile. A credible possibility for this shift of perspective was the move of the Tiberian archives to Sepphoris during the tenure of Nero. The view here (initially in agreement with Kloppenborg and Arnal) is that the formative Q1 "secular" scribes belonged to the royal administration within the sphere of Tiberias and the Lake. However, with the archival shift a new set of scribes within the sphere of Sepphoris inherited the original

---

51. Finkelstein traces how the Hellenistic origins and scribal recensions of the Passover Haggadah traditions were intended to control and even defuse the political implications of the Exodus story ("The Oldest Midrash," 304; and "Pre-Maccabean Documents," 292–94).

Jesus inscriptions. Consequently, interaction with Judean interests became more prevalent at the redactional level of document Q.

Again following Zahavy, the scribal representatives of the Amidah prayer pursued priestly-patriarchal interests. The scribes of the Pharisees were intent on temple taxation issues and purity. Their presence in Galilee, then, would introduce temple interests into the earliest Jesus scribal traditions, evidencing conflicts especially around tithing, purity, and public honor and authority.

From figure 6.1, it can be grasped that Kingdom concern was consonant with *Shema'* concern, and that Exodus motifs link Galilean and lower-level Jerusalem scribes. The Q3 Temptation story introduces direct quotation from Deuteronomy. In addition to Mark's citation of the "Two Chief Commandments" of the law in chapter 12, Mark's Galilean section refers to five of the Ten Commandments in chapter 10 (adding a spurious command not to defraud, but not exactly in the order of Deut 5:16–20). Mark 10:18 provides a version of the *Shema'*, and the one thing the rich man is lacking is a concern for the *ptōchoi*—the destitute (v. 21)—precisely the concern of the Q Beatitudes. While there is a community of interest in the future Son of Man between Q2, Mark, and the Enoch scribes to the north near Mount Hermon, geographic proximity does not explain everything. The Enoch community is far more concerned about corruption among the Jerusalem priests than Q or Mark. So also is the Qumran community. Among both Galilee and Jerusalem Jesus-scribes, there seems little interest in purity, but more concern about social corruption and justice for those dispossessed of honor, power, and wealth. And as already stressed, temple taxation was part of the conflict at issue with those sympathetic to Jesus.

Clearly the Jesus-scribes in the pre-70 period stood within the political-economic tensions of royal and priestly-temple interests, as well as those of cities and landlords. It remains for another occasion to trace out in more detail the further development of those initial scribal interests outlined above in the Gospels of Matthew and Luke. Likewise, the trajectories of the Gospels of John and Thomas need further articulation with the earliest scribal interests and concerns. The explorations to this point have shown that scribal interests deserve more study. Attempts to clarify not only temporal and geographic provenances or redactional themes but also the social location and interests of scribes will be essential for a deeper understanding of early Christian and Jewish origins.[52]

---

52. I am deeply grateful to K. C. Hanson and Donovan Johnson for their perceptive editorial suggestions. Of course, I alone am responsible for the errors.

PART TWO

*The Radical Jesus, the Bible,
and the Great Transformation:
The Search for Hermeneutical Bridges*

CHAPTER 7

Culture, Society, and Embedded Religion in Antiquity

T HIS CHAPTER IS ABOUT the place of religion in society as the question
pertains to Jewish and Christian origins. Perhaps it will also make a
small contribution, in the memorable phrase of Karl Polanyi (relative to
another such social placement), "to enlarge our freedom of creative adjustment, and thereby improve our chances of survival."[1] We can only truly
survive, indeed thrive, if we do so together in mutual understanding and
appreciation by recognizing the common challenges that face us all.

Culture and Society

Since the foundation of modern social science, the relationship between
culture and society has been central within the discussion though extraordinarily difficult to define. The place of religion has also been difficult to
characterize, though it clearly participates in both culture and society.[2]
Durkheim essentially investigated the meaning of "society" in his great
dissertation *The Division of Labor in Society*. There, Durkheim explored
through a study of law the organization of "collective consciousness," and
its relative strength and weakness within societies based in mechanical or
organic solidarity. For Durkheim, "society" is a shared mental reality. If this
sharing is strong, and the social parts become interchangeable, as it were,
then a society of mechanical solidarity is in view. If this sharing is weak, and

---

1. Polanyi, *The Livelihood of Man*, xliii.
2. Bellah, "Sociology of Religion"; Bellah, "Religious Evolution."

the social parts are unique and interdependent, then a society of organic solidarity is in view:

> The [mechanical] solidarity that derives from similarities is at its *maximum* when the collective consciousness completely envelops our total consciousness, coinciding with it at every point. At that moment our individuality is zero . . . [Organic] solidarity resembles that observed in the higher animals. In fact each organ has its own special characteristics and autonomy, yet the greater the unity of the organism, the more marked the individualisation of the parts. Using this analogy, we propose to call 'organic' the solidarity that is due to the division of labour.[3]

When Durkheim came to write his last great work, *The Elementary Forms of Religious Life*, he focused on the collective representations of society. These "categories," Durkheim believed, make human life possible at all; they are assumptions about life.[4] Durkheim here revises Kant in a social direction. Collective representations are created and sustained in periods of "collective effervescence," among the simpler social arrangements of Australian tribes usually at the time of periodic group rituals. Durkheim believed such rituals are a universal social phenomenon. The collective representations exist "outside" the heads of the participants; hence, they do not refer simply to uniformity of thought, feeling, and action.

"Collective consciousness" and "collective representations," then, seem to represent in Durkheim's terminology respectively society and culture. Society refers to uniformity of thought, feeling, and action; culture provides opportunities to confirm uniformity (which is usually what happens) but also the possibility of new actions coming out of new interpretations of the collective representations.

Max Weber also struggled with this society–culture distinction. His traditional and legal types of authority confirm the basic values and norms of social action; however, the charismatic type of authority helps to understand when action might take new turns. Society is compounded of all kinds of interests and meanings involved with social action. The interests and meanings of the few may sometimes or often dominate the actions of the many:

> Not ideas, but material and ideal interests, directly govern men's conduct. Yet very frequently the "world images" that have been

---

3. Durkheim, *The Division of Labor in Society*, 84–85.
4. Durkheim, *The Elementary Forms of Religious Life*, 321.

created by "ideas" have, like switchmen, determined the tracks along which action has been pushed by the dynamic of interest. "From what" and "for what" one wished to be redeemed and, let us not forget, "could be" redeemed, depended upon one's image of the world.[5]

In Weber's great discussions of religion, the exemplary and emissary prophetic types often stand at the heart of religious innovation. In the former case, Gautama Siddhartha within Indian religion; in the latter case, Socrates within Greek tradition or Moses and Jesus within Israelite tradition. Each type, however, affects action in the world differently. The exemplary prophet, in an otherworldly mode, withdraws into contemplation or idealistic pursuits; the emissary prophet, committed to ascetic, inner-worldly action, effects disciplined action as a "tool" of the god. These charismatic figures undertake innovations, usually in periods of dramatic change or crisis, by drawing creatively upon the resources of their respective cultures.[6]

From these classic social analyses of religion, it is likely that the term religion encompasses both cultural forms present in the collective representations (myth) and social practices formative of collective consciousness (ritual). These forms "ground" both society and culture, are constitutional, so that religion is present in varying degrees in both.[7] Yet religion may both legitimate social order and call it into question. Religion is not simply or merely the reflex of interests, as Marx thought, but interacts with various interests pertaining to human reproduction, production, collective action, and social coordination. As both Durkheim and Weber saw, religion is that part of culture that "reflects" upon society, either confirming or disconfirming. Such preliminary theoretical reflections suggest that religion might be embedded sometimes more within social matrices (captive to powerful interests) and sometimes more within cultural matrices (freely interpreted).

Culture, then, is a reservoir of representations of society; society refers to the habits and institutions of behavior implementing culture. The two

---

5. Weber, "Social Psychology," 280.

6. Weber, "Social Psychology," 285; Weber, *Economy and Society*, 439–51.

7. Definitions of the word "religion" are highly debated; see Smith, "Religion, Religions, Religious," in Taylor, *Critical Terms*, 269–84. Given the obvious Latin root, two major etymologies have been suggested. Both would make sense if *religare*, "to bind back" or "ground," is linked to ritual, and *religere*, "to recount," designates myth. Ritual and myth, of course, are central concerns in religious studies.

spheres overlap and interact but are not identical. Religion stands within both as a constitutional element.

Embeddedness

Embedded journalists in the Iraqi war have given a striking illustration of the meaning of another central term in this discussion. Journalists have the obligation to ferret out the truth and to report it fairly and accurately to the public. However in the Iraqi war, journalists have been embedded within the ranks, and for strategic reasons denied the right to convey information about location, movement, or casualties. It would seem, the veracity of the old statement "truth is the first casualty of war" is affirmed in a new way, and the idea that truth can become subservient to power is illustrated in powerful fashion. These embedded reporters have illustrated what happens when important cultural forms, norms, and tasks are embedded in the sphere of military power—their ideal role and function is compromised and distorted. It may be that all of culture is so implicated, at least some or even most of the time.

The scholarly use of the notion of "embeddedness" seems to derive from Karl Polanyi. In attempting to account for why the ancients had no explicit concept of economy, Polanyi wrote, "The prime reason for the absence of any concept of the economy [for the ancients] is the difficulty of identifying the economic process under conditions where it is embedded in noneconomic institutions."[8] Though applied originally to "embedded economy," embeddedness can help to understand the relationship of other social spheres or domains. Religion, then, may be embedded within family, politics, or economics; and these can become embedded in religion as a cultural radical as well. Since religion inheres also in culture, the group's collective representations, it may support innovations in action within various social contexts.[9]

Max Weber too was well aware of the interaction of religion with the various human "spheres" (family, economic, political, esthetic, erotic, intellectual). Along similar lines, Robert N. Bellah has analyzed Islam's

8. Polanyi, "Aristotle Discovers the Economy," 71.

9. Oakman, "Models and Archaeology," 272–79; Hanson and Oakman, *Palestine in the Time of Jesus*, 13–14.

historical relationships within the "dramatistic contexts" of world, polity, family, and self.[10]

The functioning of Mediterranean culture, society, and religion has been analyzed within certain constraints—especially core variables of honor and shame, strong-group orientation, agonistic intergroup relations, dyadic personality, and the like. These sociocultural constraints seem to be a consequence of adaptive pressures within the historical-geographic situation of Mediterranean societies (common constraints that explain uniform cultural features at a high level of abstraction).[11] Recognizing these constraints is necessary to avoid anachronistic and ethnocentric interpretations. For instance, it is anachronistic to use postindustrial economic experience to understand preindustrial agrarian economies; it is ethnocentric to expect to find individualism within group-oriented biblical texts.

Related to the problems of anachronism and ethnocentrism is the distinction between emic and etic terms. "Emic" terms incorporate the natives' point of view; "etic" terms represent the view of the outsider or the perspectives of comparative experience. Social models and theories must incorporate both emic and etic dimensions, but the emic only take on significance as "data" when "put into perspective" by models and theory.

Based on Polanyi's work, and incorporating also comparative insights of Gerhard Lenski (1984) and John Kautsky (1982), the general functioning of "embeddedness" in antiquity might be understood according to this simple contrasting model:[12]

- Religion, politics, and economics embedded within elite interests can be predicted to serve organization and legitimation of a social system to benefit those elites. Order is the primary social goal and value. Religion is shaped significantly in the direction of what Weber called a "theodicy of good fortune," a justification of the status of the elite group.[13] Order is seen as rooted in a natural or cosmic pattern, and expressed in impersonal arrangements of political-economy. This situation is well described through a systems approach.

- Non-elite interests (including both declassed elites and non-elites) embedded within elite religion, politics, and economics will either adapt to suffering through religion (Weber's "theodicy of suffering") or attempt to access collective representations without elite

---

10. Weber, "Religious Rejections," 323–59; Bellah, "Islamic Tradition," 146–67.

11. See Malina, *The New Testament World*.

12. Lenski, *Power and Privilege*; Kautsky, *The Politics of Aristocratic Empires*.

13. Weber, "Social Psychology of the World Religions," 271.

authorization in order to resist and even overthrow that order. Finding meaning in suffering or seeking a reordering are primary social goals and values. Reordering is legitimated through an appeal to a higher religious court, and carried through in familistic or quasi-familistic arrangements. This situation is better understood through lenses of conflict theory.

Figure 7.1: Differing Interests and Sociocultural Orientations

The following table suggests that a nonreductive approach, i.e., one which does not simply collapse the distinction of society and culture, requires consideration of how both have been imagined in the two, major theoretical streams of modern social science:[14]

	Systems Approach	Conflict Approach
Interests	Uniting	Dividing
Social relations	Advantageous	Exploitative
Social unity	Consensus	Coercion
Society	System with needs	Stage for class struggle
Human nature	Requires restraining institutions	Institutions distort human nature
Inequality	Social necessity	Promotes conflict, unnecessary
State	Promotes common good	Instrument of oppression
Class	Heuristic device	Social groups with different interests

Table 7.1: Two Social-Theoretical Streams

It is important to keep the concerns of both systems and conflict approaches in play in the discussion. All of the foregoing theoretical considerations are now applied to several controverted issues pertaining to Jewish and Christian origins.

The Jerusalem Temple as System of Political Economy and Social Archetype

In the scholarship of Jewish and Christian origins today, Torah and temple (perhaps also Land), synagogue and "church" (assembly), and "Jew" and "Christian" are focal interests. Interrelated social institutions and cultural terms are in view; also important is that the destruction of the second

---

14. Adapted from Sanders, *Rural Society*, 9, based on work of A. Eugene Havens.

temple in 70 CE led to a significant restructuring of the Pharisaic and Jesus movements as they emerged during the postwar situation respectively as rabbinic Judaism and Christianity. This whole area of discussion is bedeviled by analytical unclarities about culture, society, and embeddedness, for instance when Judaism and Christianity are thought of as groups merely divided over theology and sealed off from ethnic or political realities, or when synagogue, assembly, and temple are seen as "purely religious" institutions.

The central status and role of the Jerusalem temple within late-Israelite tradition stems in important respects from the Josianic Reform and Deuteronomy.[15] It would seem that Josiah embraced Israelite religion as a bulwark of his kingdom (2 Kgs 23). The centralization of the cult was an expression of the embedding of Israelite religion within the political interests of the late-Davidides (Deut 12:5). The Deuteronomists also achieved power through this reform (e.g., Deut 17:8).

In the postexilic period, of course, Judahite priests of the family of Jedaia (Ezra 2:36) assumed status and power in the rebuilt temple. The temple took on a central political function under the Persian Empire, Hellenistic kingdoms, and early Roman Empire. Its economic requirements increased over the centuries. This can be seen not only in terms of the priestly dues but also in terms of the sacrificial requirements of the Hasmonean and Herodian temples.

The priestly dues in the postexilic period can be shown to have increased significantly. Not only is this clear from the growth of the temple tax from one-third shekel annually in Nehemiah's day (Neh 10:32) to one-half shekel annually in Josephus's time (*Ant.* 18.312; Matt 17:24); it is also clear from the various dues inferred from priestly traditions. Schürer shows that sacrifices, regular dues, and irregular dues became quite onerous.[16] The Priestly Code of the Pentateuch connected sins with sacrificial obligations or vows, so that moral sins became material debts.[17] The resulting temple sacrificial system itself organized the production of Judea and depended even on neighboring regions.[18] Diaspora Judeans also sent their temple taxes on a regular basis, but the Qumran group (at least according to 4Q159)

---

15. Althann, "Josiah," 1016.

16. Schürer, *History*, 2:257–74.

17. Belo, *Materialist Reading*, 39, 44, 47, 56.

18. Oakman, "Cursing Fig Trees," 259–60.

resisted annual payment. The temple was therefore a center of taxation, illustrating religion embedded in political-economy.[19]

In the mind of priestly elites and most Judean villagers, the temple held not only enormous prestige but also numinous awe. Not only was the Herodian temple physically imposing, but it represented in physical construction and ritual activity the entire cosmos. The vestments of the high priest were bejeweled and adorned with colors that literally mapped the world.[20]

Despite this powerful history and magic, the "central place" of the Jerusalem temple and its controlling priests were not accepted without demur. A Persian-period temple of Yahweh existed at Elephantine in Egypt. In the late Hellenistic period, the Tobiad family usurped the high priest's role in respect to direct taxation (Josephus, *Ant.* 12.161, 178). In the struggles around Hellenization, Onias IV founded another Egyptian temple of Yahweh in Leontopolis (Josephus, *Ant.* 13.63). And, of course, the Samaritans and the Qumran group challenged Judean supremacy.

The situation of Passover also illustrates the importance of the distinction between society and culture. After the Deuteronomists, the Passover festival was mandated to take place in Jerusalem (Deut 16:5–6; 2 Kgs 23:21–23). The Judean garrison at Elephantine had to have its Passover celebration authorized by Darius.[21] However, Passover was a collective representation in Israel, not entirely under the control of the centralized priestly establishment. It involved the memory of Israel's liberation, and lay Israelites continued to conduct the sacrifice of the Passover lambs (*m. Pesaḥim* 5:5–6; Josephus, *War* 6.423; *Ant.* 3.248). Finkelstein long ago, with refined social sensibilities, traced some of the implications of this for the development of the Passover midrash.[22] According to Finkelstein, important parts of the Haggadah are Ptolemaic. Most significantly, Finkelstein noted that elements of the service could be edited by Jerusalem scribes to mollify Egyptian rulers and that elements could also be interpreted so as to incite crowds to rebellion.[23] Even if the Haggadah is late, it is clear from

---

19. Hanson and Oakman, *Palestine in the Time of Jesus*, 124–45.

20. For the cosmic symbolism of the Solomonic temple, see Meyers, "Temple," 359–60; for the cosmic significance of priestly vestments, Josephus, *Ant.* 3.179.

21. Cowley, *Aramaic Documents*, 60–65.

22. Finkelstein "Oldest Midrash" and "Pre-Maccabean Documents"; more recent scholarship dates the Seder to the post-70 CE period, but clearly core elements were pre-70. See also Saldarini, *Jesus and Passover*.

23. Finkelstein, "Pre-Maccabean Documents," 293.

Josephus that Passover gatherings under the early empire could become occasions of riot and violence.[24]

Saldarini can assert without further ado that first-century Judeans only celebrated Passover by pilgrimage to Jerusalem.[25] Certainly, there is evidence that Judeans made the pilgrimage for this purpose. But it does not follow that Judeans far from Jerusalem would not have observed the Passover meal (recall the Elephantine garrison). A case can be made that the meal-tradition associated with Jesus of Nazareth was a Passover meal-tradition. To restate briefly what has been argued elsewhere, Jesus of Nazareth seems to have shared with Judas of Gamala and Zaddok a passion for liberty in the name of God alone, demonstrated interest in the Passover as evident in the Q-beatitudes of Luke 6:20–22, which probably echo themes of the Passover Haggadah, and which of course are identified with the bread and wine of Passover, as in the Last Supper words.[26]

Synagogue and *Ekklēsia* as Centers of Order and Discontent

In scholarship on early Judaism and Christianity, synagogue and "church" are frequently (and anachronistically) discussed as freestanding religious centers. Perhaps also they are considered along the lines of community centers or voluntary associations. The latter approach at least begins to reckon with the emic meaning of the social realities of the terms. Certainly, synagogue and *ekklēsia* derive from the needs of diaspora Judaism and the burgeoning Jesus movement. And both are grounded in Israelite cultural traditions.

Greater clarity, however, could be achieved regarding the function of these social centers when they are understood as embedded within familistic or political relations—Judean, urban, imperial.

The Hellenistic period unfolded generally as a story of successive kingdoms and empires (Ptolemies, Seleucids, Hasmoneans, Romans). The classical *polis* or city-state became embedded within the households of monarchs or the city-territory of Rome, i.e., was embedded within powerful families (royal or imperial). In this sense, the classical city-state was *derated* as a center of power by incorporation into larger power-spheres. However, the organizing principle of the largest power-sphere remained

24. Oakman "Models and Archaeology," 273–75.

25. Saldarini, *Jesus and Passover*, 16.

26. Oakman, "Models and Archaeology."

an expression of a powerful family. So in the ancient Mediterranean world, politics was how the most powerful family or families treated everyone else. (The *polis* and the *amphictyony* also originated in extended family networks—mutual-aid networks based on real or imagined kinship.) Moreover, the institutional language of the *polis* (*ekklēsia* or assembly of free citizens, *gerousia*, and the like) was also *inflated* through employment in the organization of villages or small towns and even Greco-Roman voluntary associations. So even villages arrogated to themselves the honorific offices of the Hellenistic cities; and voluntary associations, as much about honor as anything else, were purely local affairs.[27]

Likewise, ancient economy was organized within the family. Peasant and village formed the backbone of agrarian societies; large landlords controlled the energies and product of peasants. The elite value of leisure—for war, politics, or culture—was only possible because agrarian taxation siphoned off any surplus in the village.

Religion might occupy a domestic (family) or political (city, royal, imperial, temple state) location. As previously stated, the collective representations rooted in powerful historical traditions and experiences were carefully controlled and manipulated by powerful interests, but also (because available through corporate rituals) were "beyond control" and might be reinterpreted by charismatic figures in relation to agrarian discontent. As Weber puts it, "Wherever the promises of the prophet or the redeemer have not sufficiently met the needs of the socially less-favored strata, a secondary salvation religion of the masses has regularly developed beneath the official doctrine."[28] Robert Redfield, along similar lines, distinguished between "great traditions" and "little traditions": "In a civilization there is a great tradition of the reflective few, and there is a little tradition of the largely unreflective many. The great tradition is cultivated in schools or temples; the little tradition works itself out and keeps itself going in the lives of the unlettered in their village communities."[29]

With these conceptual distinctions in mind, then, we can turn to thinking about synagogue and *ekklēsia* of Jesus-followers as centers of order and discontent.

---

27. On organization of villages or small towns in Syria, see Harper, "Village Administration," 116–45; voluntary associations, Wilson, "Voluntary Associations," 3.

28. Weber, "Social Psychology," 274.

29. Redfield, *Pesant Society and Culture*, 41–42.

What can be known archaeologically about pre-70 Palestinian synagogues is still under vigorous discussion.[30] Hoenig is of the opinion that
the post-70 CE synagogue emerged out of the "public square" (*r'hov*) of
the Israelite town (*'ir*), and not the *bet-ha-kenesset*, which was the place
of administration before 70 CE.[31] He does not see synagogues as places of
religious service in Judea or Jerusalem before 70; synagogues as "houses
of prayer" seem only to have existed outside of Judea: "It may therefore be
inferred that in Judea before 70 CE there were no synagogues (houses of
prayer) similar to our modern concept nor was there a synagogue in the
Temple precincts."[32] What is clear is that synagogues, i.e. places of gather-
ing, had more general social purposes and functions before 70 CE.

Thus, the structures identified as synagogues at Gamala, Magdala,
and Masada seem designed to facilitate face-to-face meetings. It is probable
that such structures were multipurpose community buildings. Nothing to
date has been found in them to indicate ritual space such as the *bema* of
the Byzantine-period synagogues. Certainly, the Theodotus inscription
from Jerusalem indicates ancillary uses of synagogues as pilgrim centers.[33]
These inferences of function denote "order." Institutional innovation rests
on preexisting patterns (public square, administrative house) embedded in
Judean ethnic or political arrangements.

Though many of the appearances of Jesus in synagogues in the canonical gospels are likely fictional, issues of social order and especially
discontent come into view. The synagogue (as well the temple) is a place
of conflict in the Gospel of Mark. The conflict in Mark is largely around
purity issues (Mark 2:16), what may be done on the sabbath (Mark 2:24),
and what may be claimed apart from the temple (Mark 2:7). The Pharisees
in Mark represent interests embedded in Judean politics; Jesus' activities
come into conflict with those interests both in Galilee and Jerusalem. It is
likely that these Markan conflicts, along with the data in the Q woes against
the Pharisees (Luke 11:42–44) and Josephus's *Life*, reflect the Galilean
politics of the late Second Temple period (Mark 3:6). Hence, they reflect
embedded religion.

---

30. Levine, "Synagogues," 1421–24; Magen, "Samaritan Synagogues," 1424–27;
Riesner, "Synagogues in Jerusalem, 179–211.

31. Hoenig, "Ancient City-Square," 452.

32. Hoenig, "Ancient City-Square," 448–52.

33. See Hanson, "Theodotus Inscription."

Turning to the Jesus movement in the context of the Greco-Roman world, the term *ekklēsia* as a designation for the meeting of Jesus-followers recalls the assemblies governing the Greek *poleis*. Its relationship to the *qahal* at Qumran is also possible. Here orderly assembly is in view. This is true of both Paul's *ekklēsiai* and those of Acts. Stegemann and Stegemann discuss the political meanings of *ekklēsiai*; however, the term is inconsistently rendered by "churches" or "assemblies."[34] And though the political significance is considered, an apolitical meaning in the end seems stressed.

Yet it is increasingly recognized that the Pauline apostolate or commission was conducted within an imperial context. As Neil Elliott comments:

> Richard Horsley and Neil Silberman have contended that the *Iudaismos* in which Paul says he had advanced (Gal 1:14) was "not merely a matter of religious observance but a movement of political activism and autonomy by diaspora Jews." Thus Saul's "zeal" was directed toward "the end of ensuring community solidarity and security in Damascus" against "the specific political threat" posed to the larger Jewish community by the Jesus movement.[35]

Moreover, Paul's proclamation of the cross promoted a movement that the authorities must only have seen as subversive of Roman order.

Horsley says of Paul's assemblies, "However vague he was about social forms in 'the kingdom of God' which was presumably coming at the 'day of the Lord' and (the completion of) the resurrection, in his mission Paul was building an international alternative society (the 'assembly') based in local egalitarian communities ('assemblies')."[36] Perhaps the Pauline usage also had the undertone of "citizen assemblies" of the *basileia tou theou*, i.e. as embedded in God's power. First Corinthians 2:6 is suggestive of political tensions between Roman imperium and the *ekklēsiai* as outposts or colonies of the royal center. Paul, as a native of Asia Minor, would have been familiar with the Hellenistic colony-cities of Judean mercenaries founded by the Seleucids to control the local inhabitants. *Ekklēsia* does not appear in 1 Peter, the writer of which tends to think in household terms (1 Pet 4:17). This terminology may stem from either Judean ethnic foundations or the Asian temple-state (1 Pet 2:9; cf. Rev 1:6; 2:12; 21:22; Ezek 47–48). Elliott rejects the link between household and temple state.[37]

---

34. Stegemann and Stegemann, *Jesus Movement*, 188, 263.

35. Elliott, "The Politics of Empire," 23.

36. Horsley, *Paul and Empire*, 8.

37. Elliott, *1 Peter*, 414–17; see to the contrary Oakman, "The Ancient Economy and

Whether the "household of God" as in 1 Peter or the *ekklēsia* of the royal colony, the Jesus-group reflects religion embedded in kinship or politics. Moreover, embeddedness does not strictly entail reductionistic conclusions since (especially in Asia Minor) cultural innovations begin to appear particularly in the Pauline tradition. For instance, the cosmic symbolism of Colossians functions to keep imperial realities in perspective while enjoining new moral behaviors within family and local community and supporting a locally-transcendent vision of human being in the universal *ekklēsia* (Col 1:18, in a way similar to Stoicism).

"Jew" and "Christian" in the First Century

The difficulty of emic and etic perspectives, and the distinction between culture and society, is perhaps most apparent in the scholarly debate about the terms *Ioudaios* (in the New Testament, *passim*), *Ioudaismos* (Gal 1:13), and *Christianos* (1 Peter, Acts) as these appear in the first-century documents. Are these equally insider and outsider labels? Does *Ioudaios* denote "Jew" (in a cultural sense) or "Judean" (in a social sense)? Or can the two dimensions be so neatly distinguished? Certainly with respect to these terms, we are most aware of the cultural transitions since the first century.

Cohen has given a persuasive recent account of the ancient meanings of the term *Ioudaios*.[38] He analyzes the term under the headings of birth/geography, religion/culture, and politics.[39] It is not difficult here to see that he struggles with the Mediterranean organization of society (birth and politics) and culture (religion). The important question, if "Jew" denotes religiocultural identification, is how far Jews existed (in either emic or etic terms) before the Talmudic period. Cohen understands Jew as a function of religion or culture as "someone who believes (or is supposed to believe) certain distinctive tenets, and/or follows (or is supposed to follow) certain distinctive practices; in other words, a *Ioudaios* is a Jew, someone who worships the God whose temple is in Jerusalem and who follows the way of life of the Jews."[40] He thinks this definition is met in the cases of Izates (Josephus, *Ant.* 20.38–39) and Atomos (Josephus, *Ant.* 20.142). In each case, however, the definition still does not recognize the ethnic and political

---

St. John's Apocalypse," 76, 82.

38. Cohen, "Jew in Susanna"; Cohen, "Ioudaios."

39. Cohen, "Ioudaios," 70.

40. Cohen, "Ioudaios," 78–79.

dimensions of "worship" and "following the way of life." For Izates is not free to define what this means, but must adhere to the counsel of the Galilean Eleazar ("you ought not merely to read the law but also, and even more, to do what is commanded in it," Josephus, *Ant.* 20.44, LCL), and must also fear the political consequences of *to metathesthai* in terms of loss of throne (Josephus, *Ant.* 20.38, 47). Atomos is a Cyprian by birth, but is said to be among the friends of Felix and a Judean. By inference, Atomos is present in Palestine as a client of the Roman governor. Hence the meaning of *Ioudaios* is intertwined with imperial politics and ethnic relations. How otherwise is Atomos free to become a "go-between" and Felix is not?

Cohen thinks that ethnic Judeans "in the course of time," certainly by the turn of the eras, are reconceptualized as "religious associations" (and recognized both by insiders and outsiders as such). So, he sees significance in the use of terms like *thiasos* and *synagōgē*, designating religious association and congregation, as well as parallels with other associations ("Egyptians" become Isiasts).[41] What needs further consideration here is not so much the emic terminology but its social significance. These transitions took place in the last two centuries BCE under the impact of royal wars, Roman expansionism, and intensive "Hellenization" (which after Hengel's work needs to be seen as political-cultural transformation). The terminology reflects not only the reordering of ethnic life but also the resistance-against-royal/imperial-power of "ethnics" appealing to a higher court (the God of the Judeans, Isis, and the like). The Jesus movement also began in this way—with an appeal to a higher court ("the kingdom of God") under a client ruler of Rome.

Christianos, as is well known, appears historically for the first time in the New Testament in only three places (1 Pet 4:16; Acts 11:26; 26:28). Elliott is certainly correct that the term was originally used by outsiders, non-Judeans, as a term of derision.[42] This accords with what is known about Latin words with the *-ianus* ending: "This indicates its origin within Latin-speaking circles . . . where 'Christ' was regarded as a proper name (not a title . . .)."[43] The earliest instance in 1 Peter also shows that "this name" is associated with suffering. Here, *Christianos* is clearly seen to have been embedded in the social relations of the imperial culture, i.e., not as a freestanding, freely chosen, self-referential term for the early Christian movement. Acts

41. Cohen, "Ioudaios," 80.

42. Elliott, *1 Peter*, 789–96.

43. Elliott, *1 Peter*, 789.

26:28, where the label appears on the lips of Herod Agrippa II, confirms this as well. The social experience related to the label *Christianos* was also embedded within the central Mediterranean cultural values of honor and shame, since 1 Pet 4:5, 13 promises the suffering *Christianoi* compensatory honor in the final judgment.

Conclusions

While difficult to distinguish both conceptually and in reality, culture and society must be seen as referring to different but interpenetrating dimensions in human action. Culture remains a repository of ideas and archetypes—written in texts, customs, rituals, and stones—that have a certain wildness in relation to convention and habitual action. Elites depend on normative interpretations of cultural forms to promote docile and tractable underlings; non-elites reinterpret the great traditions in order to meet their own social needs. Society refers to the well-worn paths of habit, custom, interests, and institutions. Elites control these as well; but as Weber saw, innovations emerge (through charismatic and frequently non-elite figures) with sociocultural reinterpretations.

Religion has historically been close to the constitutional center of both culture and society. In the ancient world, religion was intertwined with kinship (ethnicity) and politics (cities, kingdoms, empires). Religion embedded in kinship signifies domestic cult and domestic metaphors (God/gods/goddesses as father/mother; adherents as brothers or sisters). Politics refers to how elite families treat everyone else. Religion embedded in politics signifies political religion (taxation, enforced customs) and political central metaphors (God/gods/goddesses as king/queen; adherents as citizens or subjects). In all of the archaic and historical religions this was so.

In the end, the ancient terms and issues of Jewish and Christian origins discussed in this essay cannot immediately be assumed to be our own. In some ways, the social and cultural distances between modern Christians and their origins are greater than between contemporary Christians and Jews! The social study of the beginnings of these two great world religions, however, can offer helpful perspectives in a world in which there are even greater challenges of analysis, understanding, and moral judgment ahead. Signposts regarding the challenges ahead can be found in numerous works: Armstrong 2001, Juergensmeyer 2001, Taylor 1998, to name a few.[44] How

---

44. Armstrong, *The Battle for God*; Juergensmeyer, *Terror in the Mind of God*; Taylor,

society and culture will interact, how religion will appear, and what role religion will play, remain open and enduring questions. Since the Reformation in the West, and throughout the globalizing modern period, religion's place has become a matter of order, contest, and choice in very distinctive ways. Stephen Toulmin (1992) gives a powerful account of the role religion played in the emergence of the "second phase" of modernity in the seventeenth century.[45] The wars of religion led to a "quest for certainty" that belied the spirit of Renaissance openness and tolerance in modernity's first phase. The quest for certainty effectively addressed religiously fueled ethnic and political conflicts on the one hand but introduced new problems through the Enlightenment marriage of cosmology and politics on the other. Our challenges lie not only in accurate historical self-knowledge or contemporary Jewish-Christian dialogue but in helping these great faith communities to live in peace among the global religions and contribute constructively to a hopeful future for all our children. To this end, distinguishing society and culture, and religion's place in both, will be an extraordinarily important task indeed.[46]

Critical Terms.

45. Toulmin, *Cosmopolis.*

46. This chapter was originally given in English as a paper for the International Symposium: "Was begegnet sich im christlich-jüdischen Dialog? Who Is Encountering Whom in the Christian-Jewish Dialog?" Augst, Switzerland, April 2003. It appeared first in German translation as *Das Verhältnis von Kultur, Gesellschaft und 'eingebetteter' Religion in der Antike*, in *Was Begegnet Sich im Christlich-jüdischen Dialog?*, edited by Gabriella Gelardini and Peter Schmid, 13–33. Translated by Andrea Haüser. Judentum und Christentum Series. Verlag W. Kohlhammer, 2004. The original English version appeared subsequently in *BTB.*

CHAPTER 8

Biblical Economics in an Age of Greed

> Wherever technology and capital are at work, the spirit of Western
> bourgeois society is active.
>
> Its principle is the radical dissolution of all conditions, bonds,
> and forms related to the origin into elements that are to be ratio-
> nally mastered, and the rational assemblage of these elements into
> structures serving the aims of thought and action. Goal setting
> takes the place of concern for being, the creation of tools replaces
> the contemplation of intrinsic values. —Paul Tillich[1]

THE BIBLICAL VALUES OF economic justice were forged in the agrarian
age, when most people were tied in family units to agricultural
production and the soil.[2] Agrarian production required primarily land and
labor (human and animal energy); however, transit commerce in Palestine
also ensured that commercial capital accrued to the powerful, who
controlled transit trade routes (for instance, from Arabia to Mediterranean
seaports).

For most people in the biblical periods, economic life was oriented to
need; only the relatively few could afford to contemplate greed. The very
word "economic," from the two Greek words *oikos* and *nomos*, means management of the household. Commercial cities like Tyre and commercial
agents were willing to take the risks for gain, but most elite culture looked
down on commercial people (although aristocrats were always willing to
benefit from trade).

Modern economists talk about factors of production—land, labor,
and capital. In the biblical periods, the relatively few ruling elites controlled

1. Tillich, *The Socialist Decision*, 47–48.

2. For characteristics of the "agrarian age," see Christian, *Maps of Time*, 24–26, 31–32;
Christian, *This Fleeting World*, 23–57.

135

land and capital, and whenever possible peasant labor. Such elites valued leisure in order to pursue a variety of non-agricultural goals; conversely, most people had only their own labor in order to pursue the provisioning of life.

Peasants, that is, farmers subject to state power and taxation, valued self-sufficiency and adequate subsistence. Peasants worked to produce and hopefully to consume what was produced. They resented taxes, debts, and elite storehouses, which could drive their food stores close to the subsistence margin. Droughts and pestilence would quickly lead to famine because most substantial stores were in the cities of the ruling elites (1 Kgs 8:35–40; see Joel 1).

Peter Brown has recently commented on the typical plight of the primary agricultural producers in the Roman Empire; this plight seems to have been typical throughout most of Mediterranean antiquity, including in the ancient Levant:

> Wealth came mainly from labor on the land. This means that, every year, over 60 percent of the wealth of the Roman empire was gathered at harvest time by a labor force that amounted to over 80 percent of the overall population . . .
> In the eyes of contemporaries, the primary cause of social stratification was the crushing imbalance in exposure to the risk of harvest shocks between the rich (who were cushioned against such shocks) and the poor farmers, whose sole resources lay dangerously open to the weather. It was these harvest shocks that all too often tipped the balance toward misery, debt, and dependence in a rural population that had to produce enough to raise the money needed to pay their rents and taxes.[3]

In order to establish a reference point in biblical economics for purposes of critique of modern market capitalism, state-provisioning must be distinguished from family economic values in the Bible. This two-pronged discussion hopefully then will provide a critical viewpoint for considering the age of global greed in which we find ourselves.

The Economy of the Israelite State in the Bible

Historically, Israelite tribalism preceded the era of the monarchy, and family economy persisted throughout the monarchic period. The Exodus is dated

3. Brown, *Through the Eye of a Needle*, 11–13.

roughly to 1250 BCE, and Israel emerged in highland Canaan toward the end of the thirteenth century BCE. The Egyptian Merneptah Stele contains the first mention of the people of Israel outside of the Bible.[4]

It is easily demonstrated that the earliest legal code in Israel, the Book of the Covenant found in Exod 20:22—23:33, has venerable ancestors in the ancient Near East. This is shown through a comparison between the Code of Hammurabi (ca. 1750 BCE) and the laws in the Covenant Code. Both assume settled agriculture and slave-based labor, although the precise proportion between slave and free peasant labor cannot be determined any longer. Whatever the proportion, most people will have been subject to rents and taxes, in kind and in labor—and after about 600 BCE also in money (Persian darics are mentioned in 1 Chronicles; Ezra; Nehemiah; but see Neh 5:15). The Covenant Code also assumes what is now called the Secondary Products Revolution, the use of animal energy and products to supplement agricultural produce and human labor.[5]

The Covenant Code was probably framed in the early days of the Israelite monarchy. As such, it is a royal product. Early Israelite tradition was highly ambivalent about the formation of the monarchy. The account in 1 Samuel 8 is telling: Yahweh says to Samuel that by requesting a king, the Israelites are rejecting Yahweh as their king. This is in stark tension with the promise to David through Nathan in 2 Samuel 7. Southern Judahite traditions were much more sympathetic to a royal house than Northern Israelite traditions. First Samuel 8 records clearly what the Israelites experienced with the monarchy.

Conscription of sons for the chariot corps	8:11
Labor corvee for plowing and harvesting	8:12
Labor corvee for manufacturing military equipment	8:12
Conscript women perfumers, cooks, bakers	8:13
Prebends (grain, grapes, olives) for members of the court	8:14
Taxation of grain and vine (tithes for officers)	8:15
Conscription of slaves, cattle, donkeys for royal work	8:16
Taxation of flocks	8:17
Israelites will be enslaved	8:17

Table 8.1 Samuel's Warning about the Social Dangers of Kingship

4. The reign of Pharaoh Merneptah is dated to 1233–1203 BCE.

5. Christian, *This Fleeting World*, 33–34; see Exod 21:28—22:15.

This picture comes from an early antiroyal tradition in Israel, but it matches well the description of the Solomonic monarchy in the Deuteronomistic History.

Just to select a few details, the criterion of embarrassment makes it clear that Solomon enslaved the Israelites in his kingdom. This can be seen by comparing 1 Kgs 5:13–18 (Israelites supply forced labor) and 1 Kgs 9:15–22 (Israelites do not supply forced labor). The definitive proof lies in the fact that forced labor was a major cause in the division of the monarchy after Solomon (1 Kgs 12:14, 16).

Solomon's provisions give another index of royal economics (1 Kgs 4:22–23). Table 8.2 provides one estimate of the magnitude of this food supply.[6]

Per day	Annual total	Annual food for this number of common people
Flour, 30 cors	10,950 cors	13,850 approx.
Meal, 60 cors	21,900 cors	27,700 approx.
10 oxen	3,650	1,016,000 approx. [combining oxen, cattle, sheep, see note 6]
20 pasture-fed cattle	7300	—
100 sheep	36,500	—

6. The biblical cor was about 7 bu or 253 kg. Flour or meal was extracted at about a 75 percent rate. The beggar's annual subsistence has been pegged at 200 kgs of grain per year, which would be without any margin for maintaining health or productive energy (Hamel, *Poverty and Charity*, 136 n242, 138–39, 247–48). Nehemiah's account of the daily need for his administration (5:14–19) helps to provide information about sustenance from animals—if 7 animals will supply 150 for one day, then 130 will feed about 2800 per day. Commoners of course would require far less, and most probably ate very little meat. A daily fraction of Nehemiah's provisions provide adequately for many more than 150, as shown here.

Per day for 150 people	Annual total of animals required
1 ox	365
6 sheep	2190
Fowls	Unknown
Every 10 days wine in abundance	36 installments
Total	over 2555

Table 8.3 Nehemiah's Food Ration

Deer, gazelles, roebucks, fowl	Unknown	Unknown
Total	—	more than 1,050,000

Table 8.2 Solomon's Provisions

Solomon also involved himself in commerce, especially through treaty arrangements with Tyre (1 Kgs 9:26–28). Transit trade from Arabia and sea trade from Tarshish in Spain brought spices and gold (1 Kgs 10:10–22). Ezekiel 27 provides a lengthy account of the market-reach of Tyre. For later Israel, Solomon's wealth became proverbial (1 Kgs 10:23–29).

The Hebrew word r' ḥov can mean any central square. Words for "price market" otherwise are not found in the Hebrew Bible, and long-distance markets controlled by elite interests should be distinguished from local markets for exchanges of necessities.[7] The New Testament also mentions marketplaces, but these passages do not give detailed accounts of trading.[8] The biblical critique of market capitalism, thus, must come from a different quarter.

Biblical Economics for the Israelite Commoner

Solomon's kingdom supposedly brought prosperity for everyone (1 Kgs 4:20, 25), but this idea is belied by the forced labor and consequently divided monarchy. In addition to the analysis of 1 Samuel 8, the social tensions in the state are dramatized in the story of Naboth's vineyard, illustrating the dangers posed by the ruler and expropriation of commoner property (1 Kgs 21:1–16). The enmity between the king and the prophet Elijah, champion of the commoner Naboth, cannot be more strongly expressed, "Ahab said to Elijah, 'Have you found me, O my enemy?'" (21:20).

The writing prophets will only briefly be mentioned here as their concerns are largely incorporated into the final shape of Torah. The classical prophets explicitly condemn economic injustices, such as Amos 2:6–7 or 5:24 in northern Israel or Isa 1:17, 21–23 in Judah. They have a keen critique of the elites and often a deep compassion for the plight of the lowly.

Most people in biblical Israel provisioned their households through agricultural labor. Here can only be discussed a select body of texts that

7. Dupertius, "Marketplace," 812; Snell, "Trade and Commerce (ANE)," 625–29.
8. Sidebotham, "Trade and Commerce (Roman)," 629–33.

indicate central concerns in the biblical economics of ordinary people (of course, still under the press of the Israelite state).

Family reciprocity and hospitality are ingrained in Israelite traditions. For instance, in the wisdom traditions of Israel can be found traditions depicting economic life closer to the town or village. Illustrating both industry and generosity is the poem in Prov 31:10–31. The wife of the honorable man manages the household well. Here must be a house of some wealth, since the wife can provision the house from afar (14), possesses house servants (15), buys fields and tends vineyards (16), weaves linen garments (19, 22), and engages in cloth business (24). More likely, most biblical commoners were like the description in Sir 38:24–34. The leisure of the scribe (38:24) is contrasted with those who work (38:25–34). The first mentioned is the peasant who plows and handles cattle. Various artisans are then mentioned (seal maker, smith, potter). "All these rely on their hands, and all are skillful in their own work" (38:31). The view of Sirach is from the leisured elites of the city (38:32).

Agriculture, arboriculture, and animal husbandry were the pursuits of most common Israelites. Deuteronomy 8:8 mentions the "seven kinds" of subsistence staples—wheat, barley, grapes, figs, pomegranates, olives, and honey. The vine and fig tree then become symbols of subsistence adequacy in times of peace (1 Kgs 4:25; see John 1:48); conversely, destruction of vine and fig tree are considered signs of social catastrophe (for Egypt, Ps 105:33; for Israel, Hos 2:12; Jer 5:17).

Wisdom and priestly writers then give some insight into ordinary economic life. Proverbs and the Wisdom of Jesus ben Sira, Deuteronomy (levitical priests), and the Holiness Code (Aaronide priestly material in Lev 17—26) encode many typical biblical economic values.

Proverbs shows much ambivalence about wealth and poverty. Wealth can be seen as a sign of divine favor (Prov 10:15, 22; 14:20) and poverty a sign of folly (6:10–11; 10:15; 24:33–34). Yet, God is honored by generosity to the poor (14:31); it is wise to be generous to the poor (28:27). Usury is looked down upon (28:8). Still, power and wealth delineate social stratification; debt typically provides a control mechanism (22:7; see Eccl 4:1–3).[9]

Sirach at a much later date seems to express more developed ideas about almsgiving and regularly counsels generosity to the poor. For him,

---

9. Hamel has remarked, "From the point of view of the landowner, the existence of debt was a sign that the correct degree of extraction was being applied to his tenants" (*Poverty and Charity*, 157).

"Good things and bad, life and death, poverty and wealth, come from the Lord" (11:14). Nevertheless, the wealthy are to treat the poor well. Alms atone for sin (3:30), the poor are not to be cheated of their living (4:1), the needy are not to be ignored (4:4–5), and the poor are to be greeted politely (4:8). Given that the sage will sit in judgment, he is not to deny justice to the poor man (4:9; 38:33). As is customary in Israel, the LORD shows great care for the widow and the orphan (4:10; 35:17; see Exod 22:22; Deut 10:18). Sirach (29:21–22) is clear that the basics of life are to be protected:

> The necessities of life are water, bread, and clothing,
>   and also a house to assure privacy.
> Better is the life of the poor under their own crude roof
>   than sumptuous food in the house of others.

Sirach is also clearly set against an acquisitive ethic and the pursuit of gold (8:2; 31:5–6). In fact, Sir 31:8 suggests that wealth is landed rather than derived from commerce. The merchant in Sirach's eyes is clearly corrupt (26:29), and greed is bad (37:11). These were the views of almost all agrarian elites, although again they were usually happy to benefit from trade and commerce.

The early Book of the Covenant already shows concern to prevent economic injustices. This can be seen, for instance, in Exod 22:25–27 (forbidding loans at interest) or 23:6–8 (warning against false charges and bribes). The developed legal traditions of Israel in Deuteronomy and Leviticus give a fuller picture of the concerns and stress points of "commoner's economics." Deuteronomy 24:6 concerns the seriousness of taking a millstone (for grinding grain) in pledge, "for that would be taking a life in pledge." Compare Sirach, who writes (34:24), "The bread of the needy is the life of the poor; whoever deprives them of it is a murderer." Deuteronomy 24:10–13 shows that clothing taken in pledge must be returned by nightfall so as not to deny the debtor use of a necessity. Wages are to be paid by the day (24:14–15). Aliens, orphans, and widows are not to be denied justice (24:17–18). And leftovers from the harvests of grain, grapes, and olives, are to be left to be gleaned by alien, orphan, widow (24:19–22). The Deuteronomists remind Israel that this accords with their own liberation from slavery in Egypt (Deut 24:22; cf. Exod 23:9).

For all of this, Deut 15:7 acknowledges that there will be those in need (in great tension with 15:4 "there will, however, be no one in need"). The provision for debt release every seven years (Deut 15:1) indicates the prevalence of the problem of agrarian debt and the attempt of levitical law to remediate it. In the ancient world, the revolutionary cry of peasants was often debt-release and land redistribution.[10] That these two problems—debt and denial of land access—threaten peasant subsistence is easily understood. Land and labor are the only factors of production fundamentally relevant to the peasant producer, and labor is the only factor really under the producer's control. Not surprisingly, the priestly law in Leviticus addresses both debt and land with the idealistic Jubilee legislation. The Jubilee envisions land redistribution and redemption from debt slavery (Lev 25:10, 13, 25, 41); however, foreign slaves are not accorded this liberation (Lev 25:44–46). This legislation is clearly for insiders only!

The picture developed so far of common biblical economics is sustained with Jesus of Nazareth. Jesus obtained a reputation as an effective broker of the kingdom of God, through his ability to connect those in need with those in possession.[11] This could be food or debt relief (Q 11:3–4). His politics consequently were focused upon adequate subsistence and the tyranny of Mammon (Q 6:20–21; L/Luke 12:16–21; Q 16:13; see Sir 5:1, 8). While Jesus can speak with sympathy about the traveling Samaritan, he does not appear to have appreciated elite commerce or commercialization (Q 19:12–26; Gos. Thom. 64). In agrarian settings, commercial agriculture or trade can provide capital that further indentures the ordinary producer.

Robert Bellah, discussing the work of Max Weber, suggests the insight that the ethic of Jesus had upended the norm of "love family and friends—do harm to enemies" by erasing the boundary between family and stranger (L/Luke 10:30–35) and offering generalized reciprocity (i.e., family-like exchanges) to strangers (Q 6:32–36). Bellah perceptively writes, "What has happened to the two principles of the ancient ethic of neighborliness is that the principle of the contrast between in-group and out-group has been abandoned and the principle of reciprocity has been absolutized."[12]

Ironically, with the transition of the message about Jesus to the major cities of the eastern Roman Empire, the carriers of the Christian message become traveling tradesmen and commercial people. Transformations of economic attitudes within the movement can be traced in part with respect to money: While Jesus made God and Mammon (trust in money on loan or deposit, or the estate storehouse) a strict either–or, the later New Testament writers simply warn against the "love of money" (1 Tim 3:3; 6:10; 2 Tim 3:2;

---

10. Oakman, *The Political Aims of Jesus*, 102.

11. Oakman, *The Political Aims of Jesus*, 70.

12. Bellah, "Max Weber and World-Denying Love," 283.

Heb 13:5; see Luke 16:14 and Eccl 5:10). After all, they have to deal with money in the regular course of business.[13] For all of this, the writer of Acts could claim that the Jerusalem Jesus-followers held everything in common (Acts 2:44–45; 4:32–35); indeed, the one word of Jesus recalled in the New Testament outside of the gospels is, "It is more honorable to give than to receive" (Acts 20:35). Economic reciprocity and familial community were hallmarks of the earliest Christians of the New Testament period.

In sum, biblical economics largely promotes a need-based under-standing and charitable relations between rich and poor but opposes the exploitation of debt or the greed of commerce. What then might biblical economics or economic values have to contribute in an age of greed and global capitalism?

Biblical Economic Values in an Age of Greed

The work of Karl Polanyi (1886–1964) can help to formulate a critical proposal. Polanyi contributed many works in economic history, including his posthumous *The Livelihood of Man*. Perhaps his most significant work for this conversation is his book *The Great Transformation*. Polanyi's basic argument there is that in preindustrial and premodern times, the economy was *embedded* in prior social and cultural relations such that econom-ics were subservient to ends other than pure rationalization of economic means-ends or market relations. Markets did not operate freely but were subordinated to other social interests and ends. With the coming of the Commercial and especially Industrial Revolutions, first in the Atlantic re-gions, then in other parts of the world, the market and economic relations were *disembedded*.[14] In fact, in twenty-first-century global civilization, eco-nomic life is the primary domain, and family, government, education, social relations, and culture are subject to the absolutization of market relations. Moreover, everything is for sale, particularly land, labor, and capital. There are no outcries for Naboth here, and few institutions seem able to acquire any real leverage against the pressure of "market forces." Adam Smith's "in-visible hand" has become an "act of God," and the Market is God.[15]

13. Oakman, *The Political Aims of Jesus*, 84–94, 114–18.

14. Polanyi, *The Great Transformation*; Polanyi, *The Livelihood of Man*; see chapter 6 in this volume.

15. Cox, "The Market is God"; see Sandel, "What Isn't For Sale"; also, his *What Money Can't Buy*.

The recent economic crises (2007–2008) in housing in the United States or monetary relations in Europe indicate the power of global market forces. It is truly the case that a small fiscal crisis somewhere can threaten the entire economic edifice everywhere. Money buys money, and technology-enhanced trading endangers money value almost moment by moment. The debasing of currency in China or Japan can garner the ire of the US. Congress that can do little about it. Retirement nest eggs are lost in almost one day!

The impact of outsourcing of labor has been a matter of comment for several decades. Now, jobs related to transhipping coal to China are colliding with very real concerns about further degradation of the atmosphere by burning hydrocarbons. Market forces in a variety of forms are shaping social questions of enormous human importance. Free trade agreements are everywhere in place. In the United States, at least, Ayn Rand and libertarian ideas have taken hold without effective counter from those who promote federal programs or ideas about the common good.[16] Strong antitax sentiments are promoted without any consideration apparently as to how they will affect transportation or education or safety nets for the poor.

Whether the actions of market players are purely motivated by greed, rational interest, or individual prudence, a conversation with biblical economics and biblical values can raise serious questions about economic motivations and the reduction of all human action to rational choice theory or human greed. Polanyi's idea of a substantive economy engaged with human needs and a rich variety of human ends can take support from biblical economics. A reductionism that leaves people without secure housing, jobs, or medical care can be nothing but an idolatrous practice in the light of the biblical witness.

Further help in this conversation can come from Herman Daly and John Cobb. In their 1994 book *For the Common Good*, a sympathetic critique of capitalism is offered while an analysis of what Alfred North Whitehead called "fallacies of misplaced concreteness" is undertaken. Abstractions from reality can prove very dangerous. Money is good when it is accurately indexed to real wealth, but too much money or too little can be very harmful in real value terms. GDPs and other production indices can be valuable as limited measures of wealth, but without consideration of their worth and distribution to real human beings such measures are

16. For a very effective contemporary representation of these libertarian views, see Michael Shermer, *The Mind of the Market*.

inadequate.[17] "Market relations" themselves become colossal abstractions, and often lead away from sound social policies and capitalization for the common good. Perhaps the most egregious demonstration of Whitehead's fallacy is the notion of "externalities," such as environmental issues pertinent to economic activity. Damage to the environment from mining, burning fossil fuels, and now fracking have not sufficiently been taken into economic calculations. We and our children will all live to pay the penalty for this shortsighted and foolish behavior.[18]

Even when productive resources worldwide are enormous, their maldistribution and the inordinate inequities of global power and wealth can only hinder the search for a satisfactory, need-based society. A few years ago, the United Nations reported that 1 percent of the world's adults owned 40 percent of the world's wealth. Further, "The report found the richest 10 percent of adults accounted for 85 percent of the world total of global assets. Half the world's adult population, however, owned barely 1 percent of global wealth. Near the bottom of the list were India, with per capita wealth of $1,100, and Indonesia with assets per head of $1,400."[19] Indeed, some corporations control more wealth than entire nations, while many people on the globe suffer exceedingly poor qualities of life and limited life-chances.[20]

What values and principles do biblical economics offer for the conversation? Here is a possible list:

1. The biblical witness against idolatry would challenge the Market as God or fetishizing of capital (for instance, the unrighteous Mammon of offshore accounts). Here the work of Lutheran theologians and theologians of secularity such as Harvey Cox can join in tandem. Cox's critique of the market has already been mentioned. Samuel Torvend reminds us that the Reformation was in a significant way born out

---

17. Daly and Cobb, *For the Common Good*, 35–43.

18. Daly and Cobb, *For the Common Good*, 37, 164.

19. Randerson, "World's Richest 1 Percent." Since Randerson's 2006 article, Oxfam in 2020 reports that world inequality is far worse—the 1 percent own at least more than 50 percent: See https://www.oxfam.org/en/5-shocking-facts-about-extreme-global-inequality-and-how-even-it.

20. For other grim details about maldistribution, see Smith, *State of the World Atlas*, 36–41.

of Luther's cry for economic justice and trust in the pricelessness of grace.[21]

2. The biblical witness points to the discussion, identification, or restoration of a variety of economic motives and ends. Here is the importance of the views of someone like Karl Polanyi or Paul Tillich. Rediscovering the early Tillich's ideas about religious socialism might be salutary for a world Christianity increasingly located in poor countries:

> Religious socialism was always interested in human life as a whole and never in its economic basis exclusively. In this it was sharply distinguished from economic materialism, as well as from all forms of "economism." It did not consider the economic factor as an independent one on which all social reality is dependent. It recognized the dependence of economy itself on all other social, intellectual, and spiritual factors, and it created a picture of the total, interdependent structure of our present existence. We understood socialism as a problem not of wages but of a new theonomy in which the question of wages, of social security, is treated in unity with the question of truth, of spiritual security.[22]

3. The concern for basic needs in biblical law would enjoin work toward minimum standards of life and qualities of life. These standards would include housing, food and nutrition, secure and meaningful employment, medical care, and the like. Here the work of Amartya Sen and Martha Nussbaum can be salutary.[23]

4. Biblical concerns for remediating injustices and restoring economic well-being can be clues to alternate distributive or redistributive mechanisms in society. So works like those of Roman Catholic Albino Barrera, trained as both Christian ethicist and economist, can lead the way toward identifying biblical themes that "still speak" to mitigate the "negative pecuniary externalities" of markets as well as a revitalized concern for economic welfare and human flourishing apart from market relations.[24]

21. Torvend, *Luther and the Hungry Poor.*

22. Tillich, *The Protestant Era*, xiv; Tillich, *The Socialist Decision*. On characteristics of twenty-first-century Christianity: Jenkins, *The Next Christendom*.

23. Martha C. Nussbaum, *Creating Capabilities*; Sen, *Development as Freedom*.

24. Barrera, *Biblical Economic Ethics*; Barrera, *Economic Compulsion*; Barrera, *Market Complicity*.

5. Or the renewed interest in ethics at schools of business can lead to discussions about transforming management principles toward sustenance economics, such as proposed by Bruno Dyck.[25]

6. A stronger sense of the meaning of "social security" should be sought, as in Tillich's sense. This cannot merely be provided by the volatilities of a money market. For Lutherans, this is a quest to fulfill the fourth commandment, to honor father and mother.

7. Finally, the "externalities" of an earth damaged by thoughtless economic practices need to be folded back into all economic calculation. For, "The earth is the LORD's and all that is in it" (Ps 24:1).

The question still remains for us, for the foreseeable future, whether any clarity about need-oriented economic values, means, and ends can counteract tremendous global market forces. Can a global, greed-based economic order be transformed into a widely available and accessible need-based economic order? Can the practices of individuals and communities reverse what seem to be overwhelming principalities and powers? Here we must remind and encourage one another that biblical faith and action has always been the hope for things yet unseen (Rom 8:24–25; Heb 11:1) and the sure promise of things to come (Rev 21:2–7).

25. Bruno Dyck, *Management and the Gospel*.

CHAPTER 9

Marcion's Truth

Biblical Hermeneutics in Developmental Perspective

I expect traditional religious symbolism to be maintained and developed in new directions, but with growing awareness that it is symbolism and that man in the last analysis is responsible for the choice of . . . symbolism. Naturally, continuation of the symbolization characteristic of earlier stages without any reinterpretation is to be expected among many in the modern world, just as it has occurred in every previous period.[1]

The "Estranged New World" of the Bible

The tree is known by its fruits. Marcion applied this principle to the Old Testament god. Modern scholars of the effective history of the Bible are beginning to apply it to the book. One no longer concludes that there must be two or more gods; what one does conclude, inevitably, is that holy books can be dangerous—a curse as well as a blessing.

The example of Marcion and Harnack reminds us of the urgency of moral (or "ideological") criticism of the Bible. We have to be explicit in our criticism of the Old Testament—and of the New! For the New Testament in its canonical status can be just as dangerous as the Old Testament. There can be "sub-Christian"—or "sub-Jewish"—features in the New Testament as well.[2]

1. Bellah, "Religious Evolution," 42–43.

2. Räisänen, "Attacking the Book," 79. Concerning Marcion of Pontus, see Harnack, *Marcion*; Jonas, *The Gnostic Religion*, 137–46; or Frend, *The Rise of Christianity*, 212–18.

MARCION DESERVES CREDIT AS an early biblical critic and hermeneutical thinker—both for contributing to the proto–New Testament (an
early "canon within the canon") and for exercising reasoned moral judgment about biblical theology. His truth, however, as contemplated in this
chapter, is not the questionable specifics of his theological or canonical proposals. Marcion's truth, chiseled out of the sediment of church history and
recast more generally, is the insight that after the moral and cultural critique
of social-scientific criticism, not to speak of feminist, postmodern, or postcolonial criticisms, virtually none of the biblical images of deity remains
universally influential. They are all now aliens. Even the New Testament
"God of love and mercy" depicts a Mediterranean Patriarch, whose cultural
logic is that of ancient patronage.[3] And there is much internal canonical
inconsistency: The God of John's Apocalypse is hardly Universal Love, and
the God of Jonah is rather inconsistent with the God of Nahum.

The Bible was formulated within the preindustrial agrarian civilizations of the Middle East.[4] Every biblical understanding of God is situated
within the horizon of ancient cultural roles and expectations. Though centuries of biblical interpretation abstracted theology from cultural context,
social-scientific criticism has recovered the culturally conditioned meaning
of the biblical traditions. While biblical meanings are now understood in
much more culturally "incarnate" ways, they seem even more remote and
irrelevant to the twenty-first century. Karl Barth's once "strange new world"
of the Bible has nearly a century later become the "estranged new world" of
the Bible. Brevard Childs's crisis in biblical theology still remains, but canonical approaches offer no real exit.[5] What canon is innocent of ideological interest or cultural conditioning? How can the Bible continue to "mean"
for the twenty-first century?

The claim of this essay is that developmental theories from the social
sciences can be of help in building new hermeneutical bridges. Though the
social sciences alone will not render a biblical image of God universally

3. Thoroughly discussed in Malina, "Patron and Client"; and Neyrey, *Render to God*,
Appendix 1 and *passim*.

4. Rohrbaugh, *The Biblical Interpreter*; Rohrbaugh, *The New Testament in Cross-Cultural Perspective*; Malina, "Interpretation: Reading, Abduction, Metaphor," and Bossman,
"Canon and Culture"—all give perceptive formulations of the cultural problem.

5. Childs, *Biblical Theology in Crisis*; see Sheppard, "Childs, Brevard"; and Barr, *Biblical Theology*. Stuhlmacher's "hermeneutics of consent" (*Historical Criticism*, 38–39, 87)
still does not grasp the depth of the problem; neither does Brueggemann's rhetorical
strategy (*Theology of the Old Testament*).

influential, they must be a vital partner in future conversations about biblical hermeneutics.

Modeling Sociocultural Development

> Now, it is certainly true that in some sense each culture is unique—just as each individual, each blade of grass, and each atom in the universe is unique. But how can one ever know this unless one has first compared a given culture with other cultures? What is more, there are degrees of distinctiveness. If a phenomenon were wholly unique, we could not possibly comprehend it. We are able to understand any phenomenon only because it bears some similarities to things we already know.[6]

The construction of cross-cultural models indicates the possibility of meaningful general understandings. Indeed, some today urge that, as human sciences, the social sciences are more hermeneutic than scientific.[7] Though a daunting task, the deployment of social-scientifically informed developmental perspectives in biblical theology must take into account both psychosocial and sociocultural frameworks.[8]

Several social theorists can provide building blocks for suitable developmental models. Heinz Werner's comparative and organismic theory presents human development as the natural result of increasing differentiation integrated through higher control centers. The vivid perceptions of children mix senses and employ physiognomic descriptions; likewise, the cultures of "undeveloped" peoples evince such linguistic characteristics. Eventually, the self becomes distinguishable from the objective world, and maturation entails a process moving from sensori-motor-affective through perceptual to abstract conceptual stages. Different cultures effect these transitions in varying measures.[9]

6. Kaplan and Manners, *Culture Theory*, 5.

7. Regarding the "hermeneutical turn" in social science, see Grondin, *Introduction to Philosophical Hermeneutics*, 110; Skinner, *Return of Grand Theory*, 37–38; Craffert, "The Emic-Etic Distinction."

8. Crain, *Theories of Development*; Eichrodt and most twentieth-century biblical theologies rejected developmental approaches; the argument here is closer to Eissfeldt's historical approach: Barr, *Biblical Theology*, 24; Hasel, *Old Testament Theology*, 1–47.

9. Werner, *Comparative Psychology*; Werner and Kaplan, *Symbol Formation*.

Emile Durkheim's *The Division of Labor in Society* contrasts "mechanical solidarity" and "organic solidarity." Legal traditions (including ancient and Old Testament law) provide important reference points for developmental assessment. With mechanical solidarity of simple human societies, individuals are "interchangeable" and law is largely punitive; with organic solidarity in complex societies, individuals become interdependent and their relations are governed more by contract law.

Lawrence Kohlberg characterizes moral development in terms of six stages: Action governed by (1) concern for reward and punishment from authorities, (2) self-interest [1-2 preconventional]; (3) achieving goodness as a person, (4) obedience for the good of society as a whole [3-4 conventional]; (5) concern for due process (negative freedom), and (6) concern for equitable justice (positive freedom) [5-6 postconventional]. There is movement here from naive egoism and heteronomous authority to individual freedom within genuine society based upon rational principles.[10]

Finally, Robert N. Bellah proposes a fivefold typology of religious evolution—primitive, archaic, historic, early modern, and modern—each stage characterized in terms of symbol system, religious action, context of social action, and effects on general social action.[11] Most pertinent to discussion of the biblical cultures are his categories of archaic and historic religion. In archaic symbolization (as seen in Bronze and Early Iron Age religions), deities are more objectively defined within a single world horizon, become the objects of speculative mythologies, and must be dealt with primarily through sacrifice. The archaic world is a two-class social world (elites and peasants), with the elites monopolizing political and religious roles. By contrast, historic symbolization (as seen in Israelite prophets, Greek philosophers, other representatives of Karl Jaspers's Axial Age) depicts a deity or deities within another world of value set over against this world.[12] This symbolic dualism leads to political and moral critique, opening possibilities for historical change. Religious action is oriented to salvation, and the self becomes more defined over against the group. The historic world is now a four-class world (political-military elite, cultural-religious elite, urban low-status groups [merchants, artisans], peasants).

10. Kohlberg, *The Philosophy of Moral Development*.

11. Bellah, "Religious Evolution."

12. Jaspers, *The Origin and Goal of History*; Bellah, "Religious Evolution," 22.

These theorists and perspectives support the following synthetic model of developmental poles within the sociocultural horizon of the biblical periods.[13]

	Archaic Social Organization (Bronze, Early Iron Ages)	Historic Social Organization (Iron, Jaspers's Axial Age)
Implications for social change	Static orientation	More dynamic orientation
Worldview	One world	Two worlds
Theology	Tribal gods and humans within single world (poly-, henotheism), gods reward and punish	God(s) in another world, move toward universal deity (monotheism), dualistic theodicy
Self	Emotive, concrete orientation (perception)	Rational control of emotion, some abstract facilities (conception)
Typical religious personnel	King, Priest	Prophet, Poet, Philosopher
Solidarity	Mechanical, two-class	Somewhat more organic, four-class
Religious action	Sacrifice, cult, concern for divine communication and purity	Salvation, concern for group—or self-destiny and eschatology
Morality	Authority and punishment orientation (royal case law), Kohlberg's preconventional	Responsibility measured against Covenant or the Good (apodictic law), Kohlberg's postconventional

Table 9.1: Developmental Model for Biblical Cultures/Periods

Related to biblical theology, these model categories point to the need for developmental assessment of biblical images for God and eventual "interpretive judgment" about the cognitive, moral, and symbolic progress or capacities of various biblical periods and cultures. Only a suggestive sketch is offered here.

Biblical Theology in Developmental Perspective

The discovery of Yahweh was something like the discovery of America; it took several centuries before Israel really began to understand what it had discovered . . . Israel's response to Yahweh was habitually a response based on imperfect knowledge at best,

13. This and following models are understood as ideal typical.

on misunderstanding and nonrecognition at worst . . . The one whom Jesus called his father is the Yahweh of the Old Testament. It is here that the totality of the experience becomes vital; for the father is not the Yahweh of any single book or writer of the Old Testament . . . The theology of the Old Testament has to be a study of the reality of Yahweh.[14]

It is now a standard conception in social-scientific criticism of the Bible that ancient economy and religion were embedded within politics and family as key institutional domains. The ancients were usually dyadic personalities, and collectivism describes the situation better than individualism. These generalities are not in question in this discussion. However, the move from archaic to historic social organization implies that some ancients effectively deployed religious energy in critique of politics and/or family and moved closer to individual selves. Certainly, king, priest, and prophet are well known from the biblical traditions. The emergence of a more complex set of roles and statuses (a four-class system) implies more organic than mechanical solidarity. However, morality was most likely to be conventional if not preconventional.

Israel, upon Iron Age appearance, had begun to achieve a historic configuration of symbolization and social organization. Bellah thinks this depended upon the "rationalization of political change."[15] However, there were strong vestiges, "mortgages," of tribal and archaic conceptualization.[16] The world of early Israel was still very much engaged in struggle with fertility deities and mythologies of the ancient Near East. Only with the further rationalizations of the Exile does a universalist Yahweh become really thinkable (though never entirely realized: universal law, Isa 42:2b; but nations of unequal value, Isa 43:3).

Ancient cognition was colored heavily by collectivist perceptual modes (gossip, group-think, and political propaganda). Biblical language indeed is rich with examples of Werner's physiognomic perception: God, walking (Gen 3:8; Hab 3:6), possessing hands (Ps 95:4–5); Nature, singing or clapping (Ps 98:8; Isa 44:23; 55:12); Compassion located in the bowels, anger associated with the nose (Ps 78:38). Only a relatively few ancient philosophers managed to reach abstract and conceptual understandings of the world; predictably, these Hellenistic-period philosophical traditions

---

14. McKenzie, *Theology of the Old Testament*, 26, 28–29.

15. Bellah, "Religious Evolution," 31.

16. Eilberg-Schwartz, *The Savage in Judaism* is particularly helpful.

entered into a critical assessment of ancient mythologies and elaborated arguments about physics, metaphysics, and ethics.

Within both testaments, Israelite and Christian movement struggled between archaic and historic symbolizations of deity, between images of God that enshrine Kohlberg's preconventional (punishment, self-interest) or postconventional (universal law, hospitality to strangers) moral views, between tribal Tyrant and God of universal mercy and justice. Later, christologies would also share in this struggle.

It might be claimed that Amos, Second Isaiah, Job, and Jonah mark the high points of Old Testament symbolizations of deity. As early as the eighth century BCE, Amos conceived of a God whose justice, though still oriented to punishment based upon honor concerns rather than positive delineations of general principle, encompasses and incorporates the surrounding peoples. Deuteronomy and the Deuteronomists, however, seem archaic by comparison. The Second Isaiah envisions a Creator God, the holder and wielder of all power and authority. Interestingly, this step toward universal deity involves theodicy-problems that are difficult to reconcile with more complex moral conceptions. The emergence of apocalyptic in the postexilic period is the logical result. Job indeed wrestles with the notion of a Deuteronomistic God who hovers over the sinner ready to punish, but Job's wrestling with shame also drives him to seek a more comprehensive notion of God (who has other, or better, things to do than simply account covenant infractions—a possible meaning of Job 40). Jonah's God, as well, marks an interesting move toward empathy and even "love for enemies."

Likewise in the New Testament, the Jesus of wisdom Q (Q1 6:35) sees a gracious God at the heart of reality while deuteronomic Q is preoccupied with divine vengeance at the coming of the Son of Man (Q2 17:27). Indeed, the God of the Synoptic Apocalypse (Mark 13) or John's Apocalypse (Revelation) seems at a preconventional moral level, while wisdom Q expresses the postconventional.

The biblical material mostly does not generate abstract conceptualizations of the world and God, but largely expresses worlds of poetic perception or metaphor. Only texts like Qoheleth, under the impact of foreign culture, engage in more abstract ruminations. Not until the Enoch traditions, Wisdom of Solomon (e.g., chapter 13), Philo, or Paul does this impulse take more complete hold in Israelite tradition. Indeed, in referring to maturity in Christ (Gal 4:7; 1 Cor 13:11–12; Eph 4:13), the Pauline tradition glimpses a deeper movement within the biblical traditions.

The Hermeneutical Task in Developmental Perspective

The presupposition of every comprehending interpretation is a
previous living relationship to the subject, which directly or indirectly finds expression in the text and which guides the direction
of the enquiry. Without such a relationship to life in which text
and interpreter are bound together, enquiry and comprehension
are not possible, and an enquiry is not motivated at all. In saying
this we are also saying that every interpretation is necessarily sustained by a certain prior understanding of the subject which lies
under discussion or in question.[17]

Marcion recognized the presence in the Bible of differing notions of deity
but did not have access to the developmental theories of modern social
science. Moreover, he could not consider that there were archaic and historic elements intermixed within both testaments. The social configuration
of Christianity and Judaism remained at best historic throughout late antiquity and the Middle Ages. The Protestant Reformation marked a new
development, Bellah's early modern type, with simplification of historic
dualistic symbolization and heightened focus upon the individual before
God. This was based to a degree upon Luther's return to literalism and
insistence upon a biblical center in Christ. Lutheranism, though avoiding
Marcionism, conservatively retained both "law" and "gospel," and articulated them either dialectically or in the unidirectional "law drives to gospel."
However, Lutheranism in either its propositional or experiential forms has
not always wrestled with the ideological consequences of these paradoxical
views of God (hence, its propensity to conservative ethics). Indeed based
upon its limited social-symbolic repertoire, early Protestantism generally
tended toward "characterological rigidity."[18]

Modernity has wrought radical changes and new freedoms, together
with profound challenges to traditional (including biblical) religion. Yves
Lambert recently argues that the axial-age religions respond to the modern
crisis typically in four distinct ways. They (1) become extinct as relics of the
past, (2) undergo adaptation or reinterpretation, (3) adopt a repristinat-
ing or fundamentalist stance, or (4) mutate into novel forms (usually with

17. Bultmann, "The Problem of Hermeneutics," 252.
18. Bellah, "Religious Evolution," 44.

scientistic features). In this sense, modernity is a new "axial age" when old things "fade out" and new things "fade in."[19]

Persistent (post)modern cultural difficulties point to important recurring "religiocultural patterns" (RCPs) and the importance of developmental thinking. Notable among these difficulties are the following: the rejection of key aspects of modern culture (as in postmodernism or fundamentalism); the ready association of certain kinds of religion with racism, sexism, and homophobia; and the difficulty in formulating RCPs that provide persuasively liberating critical accounts of religion or reality, more tolerant attitudes toward the aspirations of people of color or women in contrast to paternalistic racist culture or patriarchy, and varieties of religious personality and faith that can embrace doubt, criticism, and ambiguity.

These difficulties seem rooted in human developmental issues and suggest need for further reflection about models. As indicated above, biblical images of God were formulated through symbolic perceptions moving between archaic and historic organizational patterns. Modern conceptualizations make clear the cultural mortgages upon ancient symbols as well as the symbolic nature of human reality itself.

Indeed, human development generally seems to move between two poles and two broad types of RCPs.[20] Humans survive little on the basis of instinct and adapt through symbolic apparatuses of culture; they always stand somewhere between determinacy and contingency, what is given and volition, nature and culture. These dimensions cannot be separated, but RCPs may focus more on one pole than the other. Humans thus are dependent upon but free relative to their many environments—the largest of which is cosmic. Talcott Parsons gives an account of the human condition as a laminate of inorganic, organic, action, and telic systems. This is represented at a highly abstract level in Figure 9.1.[21]

19. The analyses of Lambert, "Religion in Modernity" and Armstrong, *The Battle for God* depend upon Jaspers, *Origin and Goal of History.*

20. Parsons (*The System of Modern Societies*) refers to the organic and action systems; Bergson (*Two Sources of Morality and Religion*) to group and human morality or "static" and "dynamic" religion. These are other terms for the two poles I have in mind.

21. Parsons, "Paradigm of the Human Condition," 361; Collins, *Theoretical Sociology,* 58.

	Ends
Reproduction (Family)	Goal attainment (Politics, social system)
Means	*Ends*
Adaptation (Economic system)	Pattern maintenance (Cultural system)
	Means

Figure 9.1: Talcott Parsons's Model of the Human Condition

Adaptation and reproduction have to do with the means of species-survival; goal attainment and pattern maintenance (to some degree) have to do with achievement of group development and progress. As such, especially at the level of the cultural system, these categories are enshrined in a group's mythology through which comes essential identity and notions of ultimate purpose.

These poles—adaptation pressure and arrangements for goal-directed freedom brought about through culture—are recognized in other terms by Henri Bergson in his great discussion of two sources of morality and religion:

> Social life is thus immanent, like a vague ideal, in instinct as well as in intelligence: this ideal finds its most complete expression in the hive or the ant-hill on the one hand, in human societies on the other. Whether human or animal, a society is an organization; it implies a co-ordination and generally also a subordination of elements; it therefore exhibits, whether merely embodied in life or, in addition, specifically formulated, a collection of rules and laws. But in a hive or an ant-hill the individual is riveted to his task by his structure, and the organization is relatively invariable, whereas the human community is variable in form, open to every kind of progress.[22]

Drawing from these general considerations, the following table identifies elements that elucidate the thrust of each polar RCP (along with a

---

22. Bergson, *Two Sources of Morality and Religion*, 27–28; compare Reventlow ("Theology," 488) on biblical eschatology/nationalism or Galtung's ("Religions, Hard and Soft") distinction between "hard" and "soft" religion.

prominent pathology of that pole). Human beings ordinarily pass beyond the genetic stage, but realizations of the potentialities and capacities of the secondary stage are limited in actual cultural achievements (as is clear from the biblical traditions). Primary enculturation is never left entirely behind, and is necessary for species survival, but secondary enculturation must also be acquired to adapt to new situations and to direct action in the absence of clear instinctual direction (consider model in Table 9.2).

RCPs or Religiocultural Patterns	
(Absolutism) "Genetic" culture	Symbolic culture (Relativism)
Primary socialization	Secondary socialization[23]
Core reality: Species survival, adaptation	Core reality: Goal-directed freedom
Family, economy	Culture, politics
Core values: Survival, group-oriented obligation and conformity, identity consolidation	Core values: Openness to change, creative integration of individual and group goals
Theology: Tribal, premodern or archaic	Theology: Universal, historic or modern
Self and personality: Collectivist, self-despising attitudes	Self and personality: Individualist, self-revising attitudes
Religious action: salvation as exclusive group protection and survival, by vicarious sacrifice	Religious action: salvation as realization and redemption of meaningful action, by grace
Cognition: Consistency truth-criterion	Cognition: Correspondence truth-criterion
Ideological indoctrination, group perception	Search for truth, abstract conception
Solidarity: Mechanical	Solidarity: Organic
Leadership: Formal authority structures	Leadership: Substantive authority
Credentials, qualifications	Credibility, qualities
Education: Uncritical repristination	Education: Critical representation
Apologetics, scholastic sentences	Hermeneutics, creative retrieval
"Rationality"[24]	"Reasonableness"

23. The term "genetic" culture derives from Geertz, "Religion as a Cultural System," 93–94; "primary" and "secondary" socialization are discussed by Berger and Luckmann, *The Social Construction of Reality*, 129–47.

24. Nord distinguishes between rationality and reasonableness as follows: "the attempt to be reasonable is inevitably less a matter of being rigorously logical than of being deliberative; it requires that we be open to new patterns of meaning; and it will not yield certainty so much as insight and, perhaps, a measure of plausibility. *Rationality*, as I shall

Morality: Preconventional	Morality: Postconventional
Intergroup dynamics: Intolerant and uncritical	Intergroup dynamics: Tolerant and critical
disengagement with outsiders	engagement with outsiders
Negative reciprocal relations	Balanced or generalized reciprocal relations

Table 9.2: General Model of Human Development

Core reality: The tabular analysis recognizes that cultural patterns might be oriented either more closely to the biological-familial sphere and environmental adaptation or to broader cultural horizons beyond the primary reference group.

Core values: These values describe the driving environmental force in the RCP. RCPs formulated on group survival and "genetic culture" will tend to maximize the group's advantages and welfare at the expense of other groups. RCPs formulated within "symbolic culture" will recognize a valid, though relative place for other groups' RCPs.

Theology: Each theological pole is rooted in adaptive social or symbolic cultural concerns. Archaizing theology is oriented to social cohesion and survival; progressive theology is oriented to meaningful individual freedom and responsibility. Biblical theology, though premodern, moves away from one pole toward the other pole.

Self and personality: The personality encouraged within the primary group is collectivist, conformist, and submissive; the personality cultivated within the secondary group is individualist, creative, and exploratory (though not necessarily disrespectful of tradition or the primary group).

Religious action: Familistic value-emphasis points to sacrifice as the highest form of love, and group purity and survival as core objectives; individualist freedom-of-action aims at building culture, struggling against meaninglessness, and a salvation that can only be redemption through grace (reversal of entropy).

Cognition: Truth may express either relative consistency or representations adequately corresponding to reality (or a mixture). Ideological truth is truth reduced to group or individual consistency; adequate truth

---

use the term, is a matter of following rules, of being logical, within a system of accepted truths; *reasonableness* requires self-critical questioning of a system's most basic assumptions and an openness to alternative ways of making sense of the world" ((*Religion and American Education*, 180).

attempts to correspond faithfully to reality even when inconsistencies appear within the group's cultural map. Abstract conception is an index of advanced cognitive development (Werner).

Solidarity: Accords respectively with core reality and values.

Leadership: Leadership in the primary sphere tends to be formal and censorious, backed by group sanctions; leadership in the secondary sphere is interested in the cultivation of substantive authority through assent, rooted in individual and critical thought.

Education: Primary education is constantly under the "gravitational force" of familial or group expectation or tugged toward indoctrination; secondary education proceeds on critical grounds toward greater "truth-adequacy."

Morality and intergroup dynamics: As these various cultural patterns play out, group behaviors accord. The primary mode is preconventional, other groups are treated with suspicion or as religious infidels. Their truths are impugned and their absolutes considered demonic. Conversion is pursued over tolerance and understanding. The secondary mode is postconventional, the limited perceptions and false absolutes of the primary group as well as the relativity of cultures are recognized.

The model indicates why gender, race, and class become core issues within contemporary religious discussion or modern academy, especially in respect to biblical authority and morality, since these are issues precisely where primary and secondary spheres mesh concretely. Primary culture persists in the face of and even resists secondary RCPs for two main reasons: (1) Primary mythologies are seen as "natural" or rooted in natural order, and (2) primary thinking is reinforced consistency (i.e. "consistency truth" or "rationality" [Nord] constantly enforced by group-reference and groupthink).

Secondary culture, dedicated to "correspondence truth," evaluates through rich information sets and multiple frameworks. Secondary RCPs permit critical appraisal of the claims about gender, race, and class thrown up from the primary view. Recovery of women's voices and examination of power-relations under patriarchy show breaks in the claim for natural statuses. Homosexual people are discovered to have been present and creative participants all along. Pigmentation is recognized to be no more than skin-deep, and social inequality often the result of power-relations under a veneer of legal justification.

Turning to religion, a conservative type—based in the primary world—has frequently aligned itself with rigid patriarchal role-stereotypes, racist stereotyping, and a conservative politics that enforces social stratification. Even primary religions of the underclasses, though these have held liberating impulses, have not often moved beyond RCPs that promise indefinite transcendence of the situation, or utopia.[25]

Secondary culture discovers the symbolic nature of religion and its power to direct human action. Bellah, for instance, has pondered the correspondence truth of religion in "symbolic realist" terms, in contrast to the history of reductionistic treatments of religion by the social sciences (seen merely as legitimation of political regimes, ideological superstructure, projection).[26] Symbolic realism depicts religion as "the most general mechanism for integrating meaning and motivation in action systems" and "the most general model that [a group] has of itself and its world."[27] All cultures have such compact symbols, serving to relate participants to their most general environment. Werner notes that "primitive people use a single word to express a whole situation or action"; moreover, he says: "The difference between lower and more advanced societies does not consist of the fact that primitive forms of behavior are absent in the latter, but rather that the more primitive the society the greater the homogeneity and the consequent dominance of primitive behavior."[28] This strong realist position provides a basis for understanding general human truths without reducing cultures to univocal meaning.

Secondary cultural impulses, of course, undergird modern biblical criticism. Lower criticism calls into question the naive immediacy assumed between modern versions of the Bible and an original "divine word." The facts of text-variation and translation, not to mention the messy historical picture of manuscript copying and the politics of Bible translation over centuries, bring some degree of sobriety to discussions about inspiration. Higher criticism incorporates science, history, and now social science into exegetical work. The critical consequences are well known. For instance, science undermines magical thinking and belief in miracles. Historical

25. Cone, *The Spirituals and the Blues*, 95.

26. Bellah is inspired by Augustine's intellectual search for faith (or faithful search for understanding: *credo ut intelligam*) and Tillich's notions of the depth dimension of experience and religion at the heart of culture ("Between Religion and Social Science," esp. 251).

27. Bellah, "Sociology of Religion," 12, 16.

28. Werner, *Comparative Psychology*, 271 and 277.

and cultural judgments come into play, e.g., regarding the historicity of the Markan Passion Predictions or Jesus' betrayal by Judas. The gospels show Jesus as an obedient Mediterranean son ready to do the will of his father. Yet if Jesus predicted his passion (the Markan passion-predictions are adjudged secondary by almost all gospel scholars) and foreknew that he was going to be arrested in the garden, why then did he need Judas's betrayal? Is there not here information that succumbs to the criteria of both historical and cultural embarrassment—since the betrayal belies the obedience?

Conclusion: Seeking a God of Influence

> The adequacy of any ultimate perspective is its ability to transform human experience so that it yields life instead of death . . . [Tillich's] restless quest for the 'dimension of depth' . . . was his great contribution to breaking out of the institutional ghetto and seeing once more, as Augustine did, the figure of Christ in the whole world.[29]

The modeling of development indeed poses important questions for biblical hermeneutics: Why or how will ancient biblical culture remain part of modern religious conversation? What biblical understandings about God should endure?

To be sure, genetic options are strongly represented today in conservative, sectarian, or fundamentalist religious groups. In the primary worldview, the Bible becomes a pattern for building an exclusive society or culture of the pure. This regression is increasingly evident throughout global Christianity, even in mainline churches that historically have founded universities.[30] One is more likely to hear that "we should relearn all the stories" than that "we should submit our heritage to searching criticism." Thus the cultural-linguistic approach of Lindbeck seems potentially regressive, perhaps more an expression of rationality than of reasonableness.[31]

For those willing to live with the Bible after social-scientific criticism, reinterpretation may be the wiser option. If the biblical material is not simply to become irrelevant, highjacked by fundamentalism, or incorporated into some strange scientistic syncretism, its meaning must be persuasively

29. Bellah, "Between Religion and Social Science," 245, 255.

30. Jenkins, *The Next Christendom.*

31. Lindbeck, *The Nature of Doctrine*; Esler stresses Lindbeck's importance in relation to an "intercultural approach" (*Modelling Early Christianity*, 16–18; and *Galatians*, 26).

translated. A biblical hermeneutic informed by developmental perspectives embraces the secondary paradigm both in terms of its critically reflective culture and its search for meaningful human direction within the widest possible frame. An authoritarian literalism is sterile insofar as it is incapable of a dialog with the heritage that could eventuate in a creative development out of it. If the major objective in reading is a consistent repristination (genetic culture), then one cannot expect creativity. If the major objective is modeling reality in which Bible, history, science, and ongoing human experience are part of the benchmarks for correspondence, then a fruitful discussion is possible.

One must reckon, though, that the gains of secondary enculturation far outweigh the losses of primary security, if a truer picture of reality is acquired and richer human options are made available—for surviving the technological threat to higher culture; participating successfully in a multiethnic global context without a Sunday school mentality, and escaping ecological disaster contingent upon religion, economics, and politics increasingly underwritten by primary cultural concerns.

Developmental perspectives indeed offer a potentially new starting point for controlled hermeneutical discussion about the Bible and biblical theology. There is the possibility, of course, that the present sketch leaves pertinent detail out of the picture. However, these ideal-type models—as hopefully useful and incisive simplifications of reality—do have the virtue of calling attention to possible causes for the persistence of primary thinking in ancient or modern religion (rooted in adaptive survival needs and pressures) and consequent resistance to secondary enculturation (since more complex reality and creative freedom threaten the primary group). As well, developmental models reveal the naiveté of an overconfident age of technology ignorant of broader and deeper human wisdom. The terrors of the present, underwritten by defensive puritanisms and fearful fundamentalisms, make such enriched hermeneutical discussion urgent.

CHAPTER 10

The Perennial Relevance of Saint Paul

Paul's Understanding of Christ and a Time of Radical Pluralism

You shall love your neighbor as yourself. —Lev 19:18 (quoted by both Jesus and Saint Paul)

The god of this eon has blinded the minds of those without faith so that they do not see the brilliant ray of the good news about Christ's glory, who is the Image of God. —SAINT PAUL, 2 Cor 4:4

For any Christian it is uncomfortable to be reminded that the faith has had at times a constricting rather than an expansive effect on human horizons; for a New Testament scholar it also suggests an historical problem.[1] —WAYNE MEEKS

THE EDGAR GOODSPEED LECTURESHIP at Denison University is named after one of the most prestigious U.S. biblical scholars of the twentieth century. As some of you are aware, Edgar Johnson Goodspeed (1871–1962) graduated from Denison University in 1890 and pursued an illustrious career at The University of Chicago. Goodspeed was best known in the scholarly world as a text critic and editor of papyri, and by the public for his *The Story of the New Testament*, his *The New Testament: An American Translation*, or his work on the Revised Standard Version Committee. Also familiar to scholars, however, was Goodspeed's Ephesians hypothesis, which serves as the beginning point for this chapter.[2]

1. Meeks, "In One Body," 209.
2. Goodspeed, *The Story of the New Testament*; *The New Testament*; *The Meaning of*

The Goodspeed Hypothesis took initial shape over Goodspeed's puzzlement with the origin of the Ephesian letter in the New Testament. In barest outline, the hypothesis goes like this: The vocabulary and style of Ephesians has long been argued by critical scholarship to be un-Pauline. Moreover, the best manuscripts of Ephesians do not have the address "to the Ephesians." Further, a passage like Eph 1:15 makes no sense if Paul had spent three years there (Acts 20:31; see 1 Cor 16:8). And, there is an intimate connection between the content of Ephesians and that of Colossians, strongly suggesting interdependence. Ephesians shows knowledge of all the authentic Paul letters; thus, Ephesians is very Pauline, but there are serious doubts about the authorship.

Goodspeed also noted that the Acts of the Apostles, despite the press given to Paul from chapters 13 onward, seems unfamiliar with some of the most important terms of Paul's own letters. Evidence suggests that the writer of Acts did not know Paul's letters.

Perhaps prompted by publication of Acts in the late first century, which featured prominently only the legendary Paul, some unknown Christian who lived near Colossae and knew that letter of Paul collected the authentic letters we know today. Ephesians was written by this disciple as a cover letter for the entire collection. Goodspeed later went on to identify this unknown disciple as Onesimus, Paul's fellow prisoner in Philemon. This helped, for Goodspeed, to explain a number of other features.

Why, for instance, was Philemon in the canon? If Onesimus collected Paul's letters, this fact is easily explained. Moreover, Onesimus was bishop of Ephesus ca. 100 CE. This helps to explain the variant at Eph 1:1; while Onesimus wrote Ephesians as a general cover letter, the variant indirectly recalls the letter's origin.

The Goodspeed Hypothesis provides a fascinating exercise in historical imagination, but what is its import for this discussion? In Goodspeed's day, it could be taken at face value perhaps that Paul was one of the seminal figures not only in the nascent Christian movement, but also in Western culture and world history. The "apostle to the nations," while not single-handedly responsible for the spread of the message about Christ, assumed legendary stature in the account of Acts and later Christian art. Today, in an arguably post-Christian world, in a time of radical pluralism more convinced of Christianity's alliance with imperial power than with truth, when even Harvard does not require the study of religion in the core curriculum!

Ephesians; Cook, *Edgar Johnson Goodspeed*. This chapter originated as an Edgar Goodspeed Lecture at Denison University, Granville, Ohio, in 2007.

The matter might not be so self-evident. In the modern period in fact, as expressed for instance in Nikos Kazantzakis' *The Last Temptation of Christ*, it has become almost commonplace to suggest that Paul betrayed the simple gospel of Jesus to found the abomination of Christianity.

The central questions entertained in this essay are these: Should Paul's letters have been collected? Should Paul have had whatever influence in world affairs that he is thought to have exercised? What were Paul's motivations as scholars recover them in his surviving correspondence? And what especially was his understanding of Christ as the basis for his own mission and message? In short, can Paul be taken seriously any longer in a time of radical pluralism?

Paul's Christology

The irony of these transitional questions for a scholar of New Testament studies should not be overlooked. Most Pauline scholars consider that Paul's original ideas had limited influence during his own lifetime—and precious little influence during later centuries of Christendom. It was the Legendary Paul who appeared in Acts and Paul the Roman martyr upon the frescoes of Christian churches. Paul's understanding of Christ was little appreciated, and it has taken enormous critical labor over the last century to open up new perspectives on Paul's christology.

Modern scholarly study of christology in earliest Christianity has shown a remarkable diversity of theological perspectives on the significance of Jesus of Nazareth (some closer to Jewish conceptions, some closer to Greek conceptions). Paul, though an apostle to the gentiles, thinks about Jesus and Christ through Judean conceptions; yet, his ideas are pitched in a remarkably open way, in such a way that Paul can be seen to be a radical Hellenistic man, someone with a strong ethnic background and commitment, who struggles nevertheless to live (for the most part) nondefensively within first-century Mediterranean pluralism.

Paul's understanding of Jesus and Christ can be presented in outline through five theses. These theses allow us, based upon the limited correspondence that we have from Paul, to characterize his radical conceptions about Christ with some degree of clarity. To begin with, something needs to be said about our database for Paul's thought. In the New Testament, thirteen letters are attributed to Paul—in canonical order, Romans, 1 and 2 Corinthians, Galatians, Ephesians, Philippians, Colossians, 1 and 2

Thessalonians, 1 and 2 Timothy, Titus, and Philemon. Of these, no critical scholar today considers the Pastorals—1 and 2 Timothy and Titus—as written or dictated by Paul. Three letters—2 Thessalonians, Colossians, and Ephesians—are still seriously debated as to authorship. With a large majority of German and American scholars, I consider these three to come from second-generation disciples of Paul and to represent the earliest layer of Pauline interpretation. This leaves in approximate order of historical composition (composed between 50 and 58 CE)—1 Thessalonians, Galatians, 1 and 2 Corinthians, Philippians, Philemon, and Romans.

Now to present the five theses with amplifying comments: It is fruitful to begin with 1 Cor 15:20–28. This passage provides a precís of Paul's eschatology and of core ideas relevant to the present discussion. Especially noteworthy are the phrases "the first fruits of those who have fallen asleep" (1 Cor 15:20), and "For as in Adam all die, so also in Christ shall all be made alive" (1 Cor 15:22). Later in 1 Corinthians 15 (v. 45) we encounter: "Thus indeed it has been written, 'The first man Adam became a living being'; the last Adam a life-giving spirit" (to which may be compared Rom 5:12–21 where Paul again contrasts Adam and Christ). Most significant is the material of 1 Cor 15:47–49: "The first man was from the earth, a man of dust; the second man is from heaven. As was the man of dust, so are those who are of the dust; and as is the man of heaven, so are those who are of heaven. Just as we have borne the image of the man of dust, we shall also bear the image of the man of heaven."

These observations lead to the first two theses with further amplifications. So *Thesis Number One*: For Paul, Jesus is not God (this distinction is important), but the "Man from Heaven" who bears God's image.[3] As a Judean thinker, Paul was a pure monotheist who would not have confused anything else with God. Whenever in his authentic letters Paul discusses Christ, he always contrasts Adam and Christ (again, Rom 5). He is not intent, as in the later christological controversies of the Constantinian period, to state the relationship of Jesus Christ to divine being in Greek substantialist categories.

Thesis Number Two follows logically: For Paul, Jesus' reign is not eternal, but Jesus plays only a temporary role in the eschatological drama unfolding (in Paul's mind) in 1 Cor 15:20–28. In the end, Jesus also will be subjected to God, and all of God's enemies including death will have been defeated. At that point, *Kyrios Iēsous Christos* turns over the rule to God; God will be "everything to everyone" (v. 28).

---

3. 1 Cor 15:47–49.

Theses One and Two perhaps seem shocking to our ears because they contradict directly two express statements in the Nicene Creed of the fourth–fifth centuries CE, which is a key symbol of Christian belief. There, in the second article, Jesus Christ is "true God from true God, begotten not made, of one being with the Father," and "his kingdom shall have no end." The first two theses indicate that Paul's christology holds some surprises, but what is his christological conception in positive relief?

Probably the single most important Pauline christological statements are to be found in 2 Corinthians 4, and given the contrasts he draws between the Old Covenant and the New in chapters 3 and 4, those statements could easily be misinterpreted.[4] The *locus classicus* for Paul's understanding of Christ is found in 2 Cor 4:4, and leads to *Thesis Number Three*: For Paul, Christ is a synonym for God's Image and refers to God's original blueprint for humanity. Second Corinthians 4:4 can be rendered: "the brilliant ray of the good news about Christ's glory, who is the Image of God." The phrase in Greek *eikōn tou theou* has a long history of discussion in Christian theology under the Latin term *Imago Dei*. But what did Paul understand by it?

The Greek phrase recalls Gen 1:27. In Paul's Bible, the Septuagint or Greek Old Testament, this runs: "And God made humankind; according to God's image he made the human being; male and female he created them." This image had belonged to the original dignity of created humanity. Paul's statements, and thinking, show that his christology is germane to a discussion of the first article of the Christian creed (belief in God as Creator) rather than exclusively the second article of the Christian creed. There is no doubt that Paul's gospel expresses the justifying and saving significance of Christ, but anachronistic Christian conceptions do not entirely help us to understand Paul. Those conceptions often regard the saving work of Jesus Christ as a divine rescue operation *out of* creation and humanity. But Paul's christology suggests something else is in view.[5]

Consider the Christ Hymn of Phil 2:5–11. Almost all modern versions read verse 6 in Nicene terms. Jesus Christ has divinity by nature, but lays it aside, "empties himself," to enter flesh and redeem the world. Here are two of the most familiar modern renderings:

---

4. The ideas of 1 Corinthians 15 are continued in 2 Corinthians. 1 and 2 Corinthians do not comprise two discrete letters, but a larger correspondence over a period of time. 2 Corinthians has long been argued to be composite, with important elements to be seen in 2 Corinthians 1–7, 8, 9, and 10–13.

5. Scroggs, *Paul for a New Day*, 19.

The New International Version of 1973:
Christ Jesus: Who, being in very nature [a] God, did not consider equality with God something to be grasped, but made himself nothing

The New Revised Standard Version of 1991:
Christ Jesus, who, though he was in the form of God, did not regard equality with God as something to be exploited, but emptied himself

Even the great Goodspeed translation did not lead in a different direction:

The *New American Translation* of 1923:
Though [Christ Jesus] possessed the nature of God, he did not grasp at equality with God, but laid it aside to take on the nature of a slave and become like other men.

There are good reasons to think these are poor translations of Paul's meaning. First of all, the Greek is rather ambiguous, and this ambiguity is still left alone in what remains to date the best English version, The Revised Standard Version of 1946:

Christ Jesus, who, though he was in the form of God, did not count equality with God a thing to be grasped, but emptied himself.

Second, "to be grasped" does not fit the Nicene view. "Though Christ Jesus was in God's Image," he does not confuse this with divinity. To be sure, the Greek phrase *morphē theou* ("form of God") is not *eikōn tou theou*, and the Philippians may not have held Paul's understanding of the sense; but Paul seems intent in context to work again from the contrast with Adam. Especially difficult for the Nicene readings of the Christ Hymn is the Greek word *harpagmon*—"he did not think equality with God [i.e., God's divine nature] was something to be stolen" best gives the sense. If Jesus Christ already had something as a natural possession, that is, the divine nature, why would it be something to be stolen? As you can see from my translation in Figure 10.1, it is important to remember that Paul always contrasts Adam and Christ. Paul has in the Christ Hymn all of the reverse elements of the Genesis story. His understanding of Adam in Phil 2 is especially related to Gen 3:4–5 (Greek Old Testament): "And the serpent said to the woman, 'surely you will not die, for God knows that on the day you eat of it, your eyes will be opened and you will be like gods, knowing good and evil.'" For Paul, what sets Jesus apart is that he did not do what Adam did. Though Jesus had the Image from birth, he never lost it. In Paul's mind, Jesus obeyed God through his entire lifetime, in humble obscurity. He did not try to "be like God," and for this reason, Jesus is revealed as the Model Human, now the Anointed Bearer of New Humanity, as the Christ who is the Image of God in the New Creation. He is Lord, *Kyrios*, and every knee will bow to him.[6]

FIGURE 10.1

Phil. 2:5–11 — Douglas E. Oakman translation

Keep thinking that this pattern is in you which was also in
    Christ Jesus:
        who though being in God's image **did not think**
           "being like God" was something to be seized,
           [A Adam originally in God's image and sinless,
           disobeyed God by wanting to be more; Jesus did
           not disobey]
        but **emptied** himself [B Renunciation = not taking
           Adam's route]
        taking a slave's form; [C Servant of God]
        when he existed in the likeness of human beings*,
           and being found in human form*, [A Jesus sin-
           less as a human being]
        he **humbled** himself [B Renunciation = not taking
           Adam's route]
        remaining obedient unto death, even death on a
           cross. [C Servant of God]
    For this reason [A+B+C], God has **highly exalted**
        him and
    given him the name above every name,
    in order that at the name of Jesus every knee — heavenly,
        earthly, under the earth — **shall bend** and
    every tongue **shall confess** that Jesus is Lord and
        Christ, all for the glory of God the Father,
with the result, my beloved, that you are actually (in accordance
with your past pattern of obedience, not only when I
was present but also now much more in my absence) working
out your own salvation with fear and trembling, for God is the one
working in you both to will and to effect what is pleasing.

---

6. For an alternate analysis of the Hymn, see Murphy-O'Connor, "Christological Anthropology"; e.g., along with the exalted status of Jesus, the Hymn may also have emphasized God's sovereignty, cf. Phil 2:10 and Isa 45:23. How far Jesus himself is understood as "deity" in the Hymn is precisely the core concern of this chapter.

Translation notes

The parallel structures give a clue to Paul's meaning. Main verbs (from the original Greek) are **bolded**.

*Behind these references to Jesus existing in the likeness of human beings or being found in human form may stand Daniel 7:13 with its enigmatic reference to "one like a human being" or "one like a son of man"; as in Daniel (7:18, 27), so here, the one stands for the many, "Christ" is bigger than Jesus (as Phil. 2:5, 12 show). The Adam-Christ contrast appears also in 1 Cor 15 and in Romans 5. Notice Paul's language at 1 Cor 15:22 and 49 (the "image of the man of heaven" which all will come to share).

Notice also that for Paul, "Christ" is revealed definitively in Jesus' resurrection. This understanding is brought clearly to expression in Romans 1:3–4, but is also intimated in 2 Cor 5:16.

Recent Pauline scholarship senses that for Paul Jesus represents a different humanity, and so is understandably exploring Paul's thought also in social and political terms, and in relation to Roman Imperial power and Caesar, who was then called Lord.[7] Yet, even more general christological implications are worth exploring. Where the Nicene Creed had resolved the relationship of Jesus to God in terms of paradoxes—Father and Son as two persons in one substance, with Jesus apparently 100 percent human and 100 percent divine—Paul is clear in his view as saying Jesus' significance is precisely in that he did not do what Adam did, he did not attempt to become like God. For Paul, Jesus did not commit the primal idolatry (a motif Paul explores in Rom 1), and so Jesus was obedient as Adam was not. Jesus was 100 percent human and never left the Garden of Eden. For this obedience, he opens the way to a new humanity under which power is ultimately transmuted into mercy and not coercion or oppression as in Imperial Rome. This implies a whole different kind of political economy, a point to which we return briefly at the end.[8]

Paul goes on to make clear to the Philippians that just as in Jesus, so God is also at work in them. This leads to the interesting *Thesis Number Four*: For Paul, Christ is Bigger than Jesus; Christ is an inclusive term, and Jesus is not "Christ" exclusively. Paul often calls Jesus "Christ Jesus," but more rarely Jesus Christ. By prefixing the term, he indicates that it is adjectival, not nominal. Jesus is anointed with the New Humanity; he

---

7. For representative treatments see Elliott, "Paul and the Politics of Empire"; Horsley, *Paul and Empire*; Horsley, *Paul and Politics*.

8. Georgi, *Remembering the Poor*, opened a unique angle of vision on this theme.

wears God's New Creation Image. But Jesus will not do so alone. The Christ Hymn indicates that every knee shall bow before the New Human Being![9]

In the letter to the Romans, Paul makes further revealing statements along these lines. First, he makes clear in Rom 1:3–4 that Jesus' revelation as "the Christ" is confirmed in his resurrection from the dead. Later, in Rom 8:29, Paul states the following: "those whom [God] knew beforehand, he appointed to be conformed to the image of his Son, in order that he be the firstborn among many brothers and sisters" (compare 1 Cor 15:48). This can be translated into the notion that Christ will pertain to or modify each and every person "in Christ." Likewise in Gal 2, Paul can use the language of "Christ is in me," or "I am in Christ." Rom 8 also indicates the cosmic significance of Christ and God's Spirit. The Spirit, for Paul, is also a Genesis idea. Just as God's Spirit effected creation in Gen 1, so God's Spirit effects new creation. It is through God's Spirit that Paul and the Romans address God as 'Abba':

> For all who are led by the Spirit of God are [children] of God. For you did not receive the spirit of slavery to fall back into fear, but you have received the spirit of son[or daughter]ship. When we cry, "Abba! Father!" it is the Spirit himself bearing witness with our spirit that we are children of God, and if children, then heirs, heirs of God and fellow heirs with Christ, provided we suffer with him in order that we may also be glorified with him. (8:14–17)

Moreover, the whole creation groans until the revelation of God's children (Rom 8:21–23), indicating again Paul's understanding of justification and salvation as aimed at first-article/creation ends.

One more touch can be put onto this sketch of Paul's understanding of Christ. *Thesis Number Five*: For Paul, life "in Christ" is Jesus-like, in other words, life in Christ means sharing the life of Jesus. Paul leads from his equation "the Christ = the Image of God" in 2 Cor 4:4 directly to this idea in 2 Cor 4:6–12:

> For it is the God who said, "Let light shine out of darkness," who has shone in our hearts to give the light of the knowledge of the glory of God in the face of Christ. But we have this treasure in earthen vessels, to show that the transcendent power belongs to God and not to us. We are afflicted in every way, but not crushed; perplexed, but not driven to despair; persecuted, but not forsaken; struck down, but not destroyed; always carrying in the body the

---

9. Receiving God's honor (cf. Isa 45:23) from both heavenly beings and humanity.

death of Jesus, so that the life of Jesus may also be manifested in our bodies. For while we live we are always being given up to death for Jesus' sake, so that the life of Jesus may be manifested in our mortal flesh. So death is at work in us, but life in you.

Here is no "theology of glory," but a sober and humble understanding that the life according with God's will is that life which Paul believed had transpired in the life of Jesus. Surely in this passage the term "life of Jesus" is double-edged. It means on the one hand the obscure life of the Galilean sage and prophet; it means on the other hand the resurrected life of the New Adam.

Paul's Christology and the Exclusivistic Christologies of Later Christianity

Paul's christology inspired his vigorous historical activity as an "apostle to the nations." Paul's gospel or good news to the nations concerned the redemption of humanity and creation. His gospel, "God's power leading to salvation" as he puts it in Rom 1:16, was the basis for reenvigorated communities of care in various Greco-Roman cities uniting diverse cultural groups and social classes (as we receive glimpses of them in Paul's authentic letters). Let me be very clear: Paul's work of embracing pluralism was done under an inclusive symbol of salvation that could underwrite respect for difference while at the same time articulate a community within a common humanity. Since Paul is the earliest voice we have in the New Testament, and his the earliest christology (understanding of Jesus) we have access to in the Christian tradition, this inclusive perspective is a significant finding.

How then did the exclusivist christologies of later Christianity emerge? Exclusivism already begins to develop within the New Testament. For instance, we can trace evolution from Paul's two-stage christology of the Christ Hymn (Obedient Jesus crucified as a slave becomes *Kyrios*, Lord of all) to a three-stage christology (Preexistent Son of God—Incarnation—Postexistent Son of God) in the Second Christ Hymn of Col 1:15–18.[10] Since Colossians expresses the thought of a second-generation disciple of Paul, this moves a step beyond Paul. In this Sequel Hymn, Jesus Christ was present with God at the first creation of the world. A similar idea appears also in John 1, roughly contemporaneous with Colossians. Such developments

10. Fuller, *The Foundations of New Testament Christology* has noted these stages of development.

are due both to the impact of Israelite Wisdom speculations (for instance, Wisdom of Solomon 7:22—8:8) as well as to exaggerated honor-claims for Jesus made in early Christian worship.[11] At the same time, in early Christian literature of the last quarter of the first century, the status of Jesus as participant in divine being is increasingly asserted, such as in Colossians, Hebrews, or John.[12]

It is debated by New Testament scholarship whether there really are in the New Testament claims for Jesus of equal status with God. Some see such claims as expressions of devotion and worship of Jesus alongside of God; others see them as expressions of Greco-Roman syncretism, and the increasing worship of Jesus as a Hellenistic god along the lines of the mysteries or other Greco-Roman cults. What might it mean if the New Testament does claim that "Jesus is God"? Jerome Neyrey has shown that functionally, within Greco-Roman conceptions, a god would have Original (creative) and Final (judging) power; in other words, this would express Jesus' role in relation to comprehensive power to define ultimate identity and purpose (as clearly comes to expression in John's gospel, e.g., Thomas in John 20:28: "My Lord and my God.").[13]

Interestingly, only two places in the New Testament make explicit, exclusive claims for Jesus Christ, namely, John 14:6 and Acts 4:12. Once exclusivism takes hold in christology, statements about Christ will only pertain to Jesus; Christian belief in parallel alignment then makes exclusive claims upon its adherents, in contrast to pagan syncretisms. Again, these are post-Paul developments. The New Testament's christological moderation may be surprising in view of the exclusive claims for Jesus in much of contemporary Christianity. This is largely a post–New Testament emphasis, and it seems apparent after critical review that Paul did not intend an exclusivist Christianity built around christological claims.

11. 1 Cor 14: 26; 2 Cor 5:16; consider also this sequence: 1 Cor 15:20 "Jesus the first-fruits of the new creation"—Rev 1:5 "Jesus, the first-born of the dead"—Col 1:15–16 "the first-born of all creation"—Heb 1:2 where Jesus is "[a Son] through whom also [God] created the world." For pluralism in early christological beliefs, see Neyrey, *Christ Is Community*.

12. Col 1:19; 2:9; Heb 1:5–14; or John 1:1–2.

13. Neyrey, "'My Lord and My God'"; Neyrey, *Render to God*, 134–38, where Neyrey discusses God's two powers in St. Paul's thought; see also Hultgren, *Christ and His Benefits*.

The Perennial Relevance of Paul in a Radically Pluralistic Time

Does Paul's christology, and the international perspective it provided him, have anything to say to us today? The twenty-first century will be a solid testing ground for ideas about internationalism and pluralism. In a post-Christian world, it may be that most enlightened persons will not be much concerned about Paul or Pauline ideals. Yet already it is becoming evident that tribalisms, parochialisms, and fundamentalisms—often legitimated by religious claims—present significant stumbling blocks to a healthy internationalism. As well, the fostering of imperialist, crusader, or ethnic-purity ideologies, supported by destructive modern weaponry, could make for an extremely violent alternative future.

For those whose sensibilities are still significantly informed by elements of the Christian tradition, who ask about the radical meaning of Christianity, how one retrieves Christianity's core symbols might make a significant difference as to how one lives within this pluralistic, twenty-first-century world. How Christian symbols, or religious symbols generally, contribute to defensive or welcoming identity, or open or closed stances with respect to others or the future, should be topics of vital conversation.

Paul, the Hellenistic Judean in Christ, acted with remarkable freedom. As he expresses the matter paradoxically in 1 Cor 9:

> For though I am free from all ... I have made myself a slave to all, that I might win the more. To the Judeans I became as a Judean, in order to win Judeans; to those under the law I became as one under the law—though not being myself under the law—that I might win those under the law. To those outside the law I became as one outside the law—not being without law toward God but under the law of Christ—that I might win those outside the law. To the weak I became weak, that I might win the weak. I have become all things to all [people], that I might by all means save some. (vv. 19–22)

Paul's promise and vision reach even clearer expression in Ephesians, from the hand of a later disciple: God has revealed "his purpose which he set forth in Christ as a plan for the fullness of time, to unite all things in him, things in heaven and things on earth" (Eph 1:10). Christ means "one new [human being] in place of the two [sc. Judean and gentile], so making peace" (Eph 2:15), but this is a progressive vision, as Eph 4:13 makes clear:

until we all attain to the unity of the faith and of the knowledge
of the Son of God, to mature [adult]hood, to the measure of the
stature of the fulness of Christ.[14]

Yet it does not seem that the ideal of a universal humanity will be
well received in today's academy. Ironies abound in a pluralistic age! Even
though we are divided in every way from our neighbors and colleagues,
we are called to mutual respect notwithstanding that we apparently have
little in common. The dark forces of overarching metanarratives are the real
problem—not our differences![15]

Take the example of the biblical studies guild, that part of the academy I
know best. The postmodern situation of biblical interpretation has given rise
to a plethora of competing claims about the purposes and results of biblical
studies.[16] These have ranged from postcolonial claims that the Bible is simply
the instrument of the oppressor, to varieties of "ideologically committed"
biblical studies, whether feminist, liberationist, postcolonial, theological, or
the like, to the ironically universal claim of postmodernism that we cannot
know anything for certain based upon biblical studies. One reason for the
proliferation of methods since the mid-twentieth century is that we have
become much more aware of the "media" for religion—whether psychological, sociological, or cultural. The social, cultural, and human substrate of all
perception, thinking, and imagining is now clearly perceived.

There still remain legacies in biblical studies of the Enlightenment
project to lay a foundation for a common humanity. The social-scientific
criticism of the Bible, for instance, offers something of an offense within
the current ferment of biblical studies since it continues the Enlightenment
claim that objective, positive knowledge of world, self, other, and perhaps
ultimate conditions is possible, indeed even essential to our liberation and
fulfillment as human beings.[17] Such a universal claim crosses the various
committed provincial claims, universalizes the underlying assumption of
the postcolonial, and contests postmodern deconstruction.

Attention to cross-culturally informed models and theory is especially
important in all of this. For if cross-cultural understanding is possible, then
there is a universal basis for both understanding and human development.

14. See 1 Cor 13:11; 2 Cor 5:19.

15. But, see Skinner, *The Return of Grand Theory*.

16. Morgan and Barton, *Biblical Interpretation*, 15–42; Adam, *What Is Postmodern Biblical Criticism?*

17. Elliott, *What Is Social-Scientific Criticism?*

Early forms of cross-cultural study of the Bible, like ethnography in general, have stressed the ethnocentric and anachronistic in previous approaches. Nevertheless, the investigation of the socially peculiar in the New Testament, which has been at the heart of so much recent biblical investigation, must continue to be balanced and complemented by a hermeneutics informed through larger social-theoretical understandings of human interests and human values.

Here we confront questions of Truth and Method: Are biblical studies simply an antiquarian endeavor or merely ideological tools for emancipation of present-day thought and culture from the Bible? How conversely can biblical studies help us to connect to the past, to each other, or to the future? What are the cognitive and moral bridges? The universalist questions keep pressing in, increasingly as biblical studies become international and ecumenical.[18] Why continue this? What is biblical study's deepest significance?

Perhaps it *would* be better, on the one hand, to speak of some type of cultural localism or relativism as the final truth. After all, sacred categories build rather discriminatory social and cultural worlds (as first clearly argued by Emile Durkheim, then carried further by students like Mary Douglas or Peter Berger). In an extreme version of this view, Paul's christology remains a self-referential exercise, a dead letter to moderns, merely about disputes of first-century Judaism or unresolved social and cultural issues of the Hellenistic period. Considerations of New Testament christology describe, with no surplus of meaning, the contest of shame and honor around the historic figure of Jesus. Goodspeed's Hypothesis remains simply an interesting historical exercise. This is, as it were, a strong nominalist position: General categories exist in name only. Biblical culture offers only relative truth value, with perhaps some suggestive analogies. And our best contemporary hope lies within self-created spirituality, a skeptical tolerance, or stoic counsels of despair.

Yet such perspectives are not completely satisfactory in intellectual terms. They do not answer why in liberal arts places we study history, the Bible, or other cultures with interest. What draws us to history, to others, or to our world? Is it really disinterested interest? In contrast to the nominalist view, perhaps, stands a strong realist position. While not necessarily denying certain relative features, this position argues for a substantial truth content that communicates from particular cultures across cultures.

18. For Räisänen, *Marcion, Muhammad and the Mahatma*; generally, Gadamer, *Truth and Method*.

Robert Bellah, for instance, has pondered the truth of religion in "symbolic realist" terms.[19] Bellah works out this intuitive position in relation to the history of reductionistic treatments of religion by the social sciences (where religion is seen merely as legitimation of political regimes, or ideological superstructure, or psychological projection). He is inspired by Augustine's intellectual search for faith (or faithful search for understanding: *credo ut intelligam*, "I believe in order that I might understand") and Tillich's preoccupation with ontology and the depth dimension of experience.[20] Indeed, Pierre Grondin claims that the key to Gadamer's hermeneutic also goes back to Augustine's *verbum interius* (the "inner word").[21] This strong realism, however, does not mean that all cultures have univocal meaning. Serious concern with context and cultural relativities undoubtedly complicate any cross-cultural concern.[22] This realist position attempts to understand the depth of culturally constitutive symbols, and their ability to transcend local culture with broad appeal.

Paul in his day was aware of the question of the universal.[23] It pressed upon him from within his own tradition, especially in the hopes of the sixth-century prophet we now call the Second Isaiah, who saw Israel as a "light to the nations." It pressed upon Paul from Jeremiah, whose hope for a new covenant and a law written on the heart would enormously influence Paul. It pressed upon him from his own upbringing in Tarsus, home to Greek philosophies like Stoicism that yearned for world-citizens (cosmopolitans) and an orderly world spirit, the Logos. But it also pressed upon Paul through the memory of Jesus of Nazareth. Paul faced the scandalous idea that God had vindicated the outlaw Jesus by raising him from the dead. The ultimately Unjust Man, accursed by the Judean Torah, who had associated uncritically with the outcast and the sinner, was ultimately the Man of Deepest Justice and Divine Pleasure. He was the model of humanity in God's intention. In faith, the vindication of that one righteous man for Paul now would bring hope and redemption to the unrighteous everywhere.

Paul's struggle in essential ways *is* our contemporary struggle as we confront the destructive forces of exaggerated difference. Whether it is Iraq, Afghanistan, Pakistan, Darfur—human sacrifices everywhere are

19. Bellah, "Between Religion and Social Science," 251.

20. Bellah, "Between Religion and Social Science," 255.

21. Grondin, *Introduction to Philosophical Hermeneutics*, xiv, 119, 138.

22. Cf. Esler, *Modelling Early Christianity*, 1–20.

23. Hutchins, "Universal and Particular"; Meeks, "The Image of the Androgyne"; Meeks, "In One Body"; Boyarin, *A Radical Jew*, 7–12.

demanded for the sake of political and economic aggrandizement, ethnic purity, or national security. Indeed, the theme of dehumanizing hatred that brings only violence and grief has been explored profoundly in several recent films. Avner, the Mossad agent in Steven Spielberg's *Munich*, recognizes only after exacting terrible revenge upon Israel's enemies that "this road will not lead to peace." The road of ethnic revenge and purity never does. At the end of Spielberg's masterpiece of moral inquiry, we are left only (as the final vision of the film) with a haunting view of the Twin Towers in New York City, a warning of what is still to come.

The young suicide bombers studying at the Madrassa, in the film *Syriana*, are instructed by a cleric, "They will tell us the dispute is over economic resources or military domination and if we believe that we play right into their hands . . . Liberal societies have failed. Christian theology has failed. The West has failed."[24]

But the West is Judaism, Christianity, Islam!! Despite all the failures of exclusivism, the writers of scripture still provide a reservoir of imaginative faith and hope. Despite the deadly realities, they can if read critically encourage us on the way to love, justice, and peace. The great prophet of Isaiah 25 proclaimed:

> On this mountain the LORD of hosts will make for all peoples a feast of rich food, a feast of well-aged wines, of rich food filled with marrow, of well-aged wines strained clear. And he will destroy on this mountain the shroud that is cast over all peoples, the sheet that is spread over all nations; he will swallow up death forever. Then the LORD God will wipe away the tears from all faces, and the disgrace of his people he will take away from all the earth, for the LORD has spoken. It will be said on that day, Lo, this is our God; we have waited for him, so that he might save us. This is the LORD for whom we have waited; let us be glad and rejoice in his salvation.

The Holy Quran adds its second regarding the Mountain, in Surah 52:17–19: "Truly the reverent shall be in Gardens and bliss, . . . [Allah] will say, 'Eat and drink in enjoyment for that which you used to do.'" Spike Lee's *Malcolm X* recounts how the apostle of black nationalist separatism undertook a journey to Mecca. The Hajj is a duty of every Muslim. Through his experience, Malcolm came to realize that Allah, the God of Mohammad and Abraham, is the God of all people—black, brown, red, yellow, even white! Within months of his return to the US, in early 1965, Malcolm was

---

24. Gaghan, dir., *Syriana*.

gunned down in New York City, the home of immigrants, ethnic richness, and the place of the future Twin Towers. But at Malcolm's funeral, actor Ossie Davis offered these poignant words: "Consigning these mortal remains to earth, the common mother of all, secure in the knowledge that what we place in the ground is no more now a man—but a seed—which, after the winter of our discontent, will come forth again to meet us. And we will know him then for what he was and is—a Prince—our own black shining Prince!—who didn't hesitate to die, because he loved us so."[25] Davis spoke truer than he realized. For in these haunting words, lifting up hope in a time of despair, Davis and those who loved Malcolm saw as in a mirror at the end of history, or its real beginning, the Human Reality that Paul of Tarsus had also glimpsed under the name *Kyrios Iēsous Christos*.

If biblical studies is not simply antiquarian, then hermeneutical consciousness considers that transcendent meanings arise out of particular social systems, that is, are built ritually and symbolically out of peculiar experiences and cultural purity constructs, but also considers how they are *not* entirely constrained by them, how they have social and cultural resonance beyond their original contexts. New Testament christology, in this view, begins in the contest around Jesus' honor or dishonor, but is rooted in deeper questions about human dignity more broadly conceived—and perhaps the social and cultural arrangements, or the economic and political bases for such dignity.

Though there is estrangement from the biblical world today, as well as uncritical allegiance, critical scholars remain attracted to and fascinated by that world of traditions. The core symbols of the Bible (since not everything there is equally profound in a human or a divine sense) can continue to communicate as they give voice to "general human concerns."[26] In any case, reader and biblical text stand within the same continuum of possible experiences (despite differing interpretations) that not only make interhuman communication possible, but also give rise to profound religious symbols.[27]

The realist position I have depicted, coming to expression in Pauline christology, posits something in biblical symbols that speaks about the essentially human. This realism is both a constructive quality and a

25. Davis, Eulogy.

26. My former Pacific Lutheran University colleague Kathi Breazeale, for instance, once remarked that the environmental crisis is both a general human concern and "common ground"; for gender issues, see Meeks, "The Image of the Androgyne"; Bartchy, "Undermining Ancient Patriarchy"; Bartchy, "Who Should Be Called Father?"

27. See the discussion of Cassirer, *Language and Myth*; McFague, *Metaphorical Theology*.

standpoint for evaluation and conversation. A close colleague of mine in biblical studies, Philip Esler, helped to produce in 2001 an article titled "Talking to 'Terrorists.'"[28] Esler and his colleagues conclude that social identity theory could be helpful in resolving intergroup conflicts. One important idea in this theory is "re-categorization," whereby members of two categories are brought "together under an inclusive, superordinate one." It seems as though this realistic proposal is certainly appreciated by former UN Secretary-General and Nobel Peace Prize–winner Kofi Annan:

> In the 21st Century [he says] I believe the mission of the United Nations will be defined by a new, more profound, awareness of the sanctity and dignity of every human life, regardless of race or religion. This will require us to look beyond the framework of States, and beneath the surface of nations or communities. We must focus, as never before, on improving the conditions of the individual men and women who give the state or nation its richness and character. We must begin with the young Afghan girl, recognizing that saving that one life is to save humanity itself.[29]

And in another speech, Annan says:

> Although increasingly interdependent, our world continues to be divided—not only by economic differences, but also by religion and culture. That is not in itself a problem. Throughout history human life has been enriched by diversity, and different communities have learnt from each other. But if our different communities are to live together in peace we must stress also what unites us: our common humanity, and our shared belief that human dignity and rights should be protected by law.[30]

For its serious students today, there is something in the Bible that is not just relatively true, but true against the widest possible horizon. Bellah speaks of such "compact symbols" that orient people within the world. Indeed, we see within the New Testament precisely the expansion of the human and cosmic significance of "Christ"; but this procedure need not now be understood as a legitimation of Eurocentrism or grounds for ethnic cleansing or any exclusivistic statement of truth. It may be rather an invitation to an inclusive "gentle Truth" that welcomes and embraces the fullness of the human.

---

28. Brannan et al., "'Talking to Terrorists.'"
29. Annan, Nobel Peace Prize Address.
30. Annan, Truman Library Address.

CHAPTER 11

The Promise of Lutheran Biblical Studies

The one who does much 'work' is not the righteous one, but the one who, without 'work,' has much faith in Christ. The law says: "Do this!", and it is never done. Grace says: "Believe in this one!", and forthwith everything is done.[1]

This means that faith is security where no security can be seen; it is, as Luther said, the readiness to enter confidently into the darkness of the future.[2]

"The nerve of failure" and "the faith of loss" point to a situation in which the idols are broken and the gods are dead, but the darkness of negation turns out to be full of rich possibility. Out of the nothingness which has swallowed up all tradition there comes nihilism but also the possibility of a new ecstatic consciousness.[3]

MANY READERS OF THIS journal will recall with pleasure bygone days of conversation or study in St. Louis with the Christ-Seminary Seminex faculty. There, generations of students first glimpsed the promise of Lutheran biblical studies. That exiled faculty nurtured a promising tradition, and its great cloud of witnesses pointed to a "better hope" (Heb 7:19). Among them, Robert H. Smith has made consistently notable contributions. Always a popular teacher, Bob exercised much influence through the classroom. While I never had the privilege of a formal class with Bob (his

1. Luther, "Heidelberg Disputation," Theses 25–26, cited from *Martin Luther*, 503.
2. Bultmann, *Jesus Christ and Mythology*, 40–41.
3. Bellah, *Beyond Belief*, xi.

sections always closed early!), I have enjoyed a lengthy conversation with the honoree about the meaning of the New Testament. Bob has also contributed to church and academy over the years through valuable publications. The current writer cannot forget the excitement of reading *Easter Gospels* when it first appeared, a fine testament to the strength of the Seminex tradition of biblical scholarship.[4] May Bob and other readers find in this essay an equal dedication to the promise of that tradition.

Earliest Christologies

Christ stands at the center of scripture in a Lutheran understanding. Such a sensibility implies both inquiry into the earliest detectable understandings of the meaning of "Christ" and ongoing concern with christology as a basis for theology. Q, Mark, and Paul preserve perhaps the earliest theological understandings we have of Jesus of Nazareth.[5] The following paragraphs will focus especially on their understandings of Jesus, for these seem to agree in an essential way. This agreement will then provide the basis for christological and hermeneutical reflections in the second half of the article, viz., explorations of what Lutheran faith and commitment means today in dialog with earliest christologies and contemporary culture.

Jesus in Q

In recent years, there has been a major interest in the theology of Q.[6] Many dramatic claims have been made for this early tradition on the basis of only hypothetical formats. Because complex and not entirely compatible, these claims have not had adequate time for scholarly testing. Still, it is possible to say something about the Q community's understanding of Jesus.

The Q tradition has been analyzed into two major types: wisdom elements and apocalyptic elements. Various stratigraphies of these elements have been proposed, but a strong argument suggests that the wisdom elements preceded the apocalyptic. Paul's 1 Corinthians also shows a mixture

4. Smith, *Easter Gospels*.

5. While Paul antedates Mark by at least twenty years, Paul's christological thought seems more developed than either Q's or Mark's. Therefore, Paul is treated last.

6. See Kloppenborg, *The Formation of Q* and Kloppenborg [Verbin] *Excavating Q*; Jacobson, *The First Gospel*; Mack, *The Lost Gospel*; Allison, *Jesus Tradition in Q*. As noted previously, Q materials are cited according to location in Luke.

of these two elements. This fuller form of Q (with both wisdom and apocalyptic elements) is the basis for our discussion. Q may have attained this form by the time of Paul, because places like 1 Cor 6:2 seem to presuppose views found in Q (e.g., Q 22:29–30).[7]

Several "christological" aspects of Q (using the term loosely to refer to its views of Jesus) are important for the present reflections: The linked missions of John the Baptist and Jesus, their equality in the mind of the Q community, the focus of their messages on preparation for God's kingdom, the distinction between Jesus and the Son of Man, the absence of the word "Christ" in Q, and the lack of Passion Narrative and resurrection accounts in the Q gospel. This is not a comprehensive list, but it suffices for purposes of this discussion.

That the missions of John the Baptist and Jesus were firmly linked is ascertained by both formal and substantive analysis of Q. Formally, John's and Jesus' ministries are articulated already by the stage of Q2 (finished probably no earlier than 54 CE). In the understanding of Kloppenborg and Mack, Q1 (the earliest Q stratum) did not contain the preaching of John the Baptist. John's eschatological message marks it as a later articulation.[8] Q1 has no christological perspective, unless its framework lies within Judean wisdom speculation.

The equality of John and Jesus as messengers in the mind of the Q community is expressed substantively through passages like Q 11:49–50, which contextualize their work within the overall purposes of God. The content of their messages—repentance and preparation for the imminent arrival of God—is identical. There is, of course, chronological difference between the two figures. This is acknowledged by Q, as in Q 7:28, but Q 7:35 reminds of the larger context.

The focus on their messages as preparation for God's kingdom, then, is consistent with other early conceptions found in Mark (1:4, 15). This focus begins to shift already in Q with the unclear relationship between Jesus and the Son of Man. The problem is apparent through a comparison of Q 12:8 and Matt 10:32. Matthew's rendition, "So every one who acknowledges me before men, I also will acknowledge," identifies Jesus and the Son of Man; Luke's version does not. Since Luke is generally agreed to supply the

7. However, difficulties with this view are discussed in Oakman, "The Lord's Prayer in Social Perspective," 211–12.

8. Jacobson sees the "Deuteronomic" (apocalyptic) material in Q as generally earlier than the wisdom material; Allison develops a very different tradition history.

less edited text of Q, Luke simply hands on an earlier view that Jesus would be recognized and honored by the Son of Man.[9]

The word "Christ" did not appear in Q, as far as can be seen. Perhaps this reflects some of the ambivalence found in Mark 12:35. For Mark, as we shall see, the word refers to anointing by the Holy Spirit. Q is more interested in revelation than in spirit; in line with a wisdom orientation, Q sees Jesus as a revealer (Q 10:21–22). "Holy Spirit" in Luke 10:21a and in Luke 11:13 is redactional. Otherwise, identifying Jesus as Christ may have been a Judean preoccupation (though see Rom 1:3). The Q community shows little interest in a relationship to David.[10]

Most significantly, perhaps, Q lacked Passion Narrative and resurrection accounts. By focusing on Jesus' words exclusively, the center of gravity in this tradition was maintained quite differently than in Paul or the Synoptic Gospels. The theological ramifications of gospel structure have been discussed in numerous publications. This treatment will conclude by observing that Q's christology (if we should call it that) primarily underscores Jesus' importance for revealing God's eschatological wisdom and the true way to repentance. This way involves participation in God's eschatological reality by others (the Q sermon of Luke 6:20–49). The poor and dispossessed will be especially privileged in this new arrangement (Q Beatitudes). As I have tried to show elsewhere, these beatitudes likely come out of the hopes for liberation celebrated at Passover.[11] This insight needs to be explored with reference to a larger compass of Q material, and it cannot be done here.

Jesus in Mark

The key that unlocks the "good news of Jesus Christ" in Mark is surely John the Baptist's comment in Mark 1:8: "I have baptized you with water; but he will baptize you with the Holy Spirit."[12] Jesus' own experience crystallizes around the reception of the Spirit through his baptism.

---

9. Bultmann, *Theology of the New Testament*, 1:29; Crossan has an important analysis of the Son of Man traditions (e.g., *The Historical Jesus*, 238-47); see also treatment in chapter 6 in this volume. Those details are not repeated here.

10. Oakman, "The Lord's Prayer in Social Perspective," 211; "Models and Archaeology," 278–79.

11. Oakman, "Models and Archaeology," 275–79.

12. Waetjen, *A Reordering of Power*, 67–68; Myers, *Binding the Strong Man*, 127.

John's baptism takes place in the wilderness, on the fringe of Judean society. Unlike the other gospels, Mark does not tell us why Jesus comes for baptism. There is not a disclaimer here as in Matthew—Jesus really did not need it (Matt 3:14–15). For Mark, Jesus is wholly identified with the penitent. Yet his experience is different. As he comes up out of the water, the heavens are torn open, the voice comes, and the Spirit descends upon him (Mark 1:10–11). In his anointing with the Spirit, Jesus as the "Spirit-Baptizer" has been identified. This is how Mark understands the word "Christ": God's Anointed is at the same time an Anointer of others. Like Elijah of old, Jesus bestows God's Spirit upon others (1 Kgs 19:16; 2 Kgs 2:9–10; Mark 1:8; 6:15; 9:4, 11, 12, 13; 15:35, 36).

Mark's framework of thinking is dominated by Judean eschatology. The coming of the Spirit marks the beginning of eschatological struggle with evil. The Markan temptation story, brief though it is, announces that the campaign against Satan and the forces of evil has begun. It will continue in the narrative as Jesus is recognized by and casts out the demons. Its most insidious aspect is indicated when Jesus himself is accused by powerful Jerusalem scribes of being in league with Satan (3:22). The struggle for God's kingdom cannot be straightforward when powerful interests and leaders oppose it.

Jesus is particularly concerned with the outcast and powerless. He has a word of power for them. The Greek noun and verb forms for "power" (root *dyna-*), make significant appearance in this gospel. Especially noteworthy are the following instances: After the hemorrhaging woman is healed, "he perceived that power had gone out of him" (Mark 5:30); "such powers are coming about through his hands" (6:2); "until you see the kingdom having come in power" (9:1); "if you can! All things are possible to the one who believes" (9:23); "all things are possible with God" (10:27); and so on.

Jesus does not shoulder the work alone. He calls disciples and empowers them with the Spirit. Like Elijah, Jesus anoints others as well: "So they went out and proclaimed that all should repent. They cast out many demons, and anointed with oil many who were sick and cured them" (Mark 6:12–13). Even those who are not in Jesus' immediate entourage can join the struggle (Mark 9:39).

Summoned from a seemingly ordinary existence (Mark 6:3) by a God on the fringes, Jesus powerfully injects the Spirit of God's kingdom into the dynamics of his contemporary society. A new community dedicated to the coming of the kingdom is born.

Jesus in Paul

For Paul, as for Mark, the life of Jesus (as much as Paul knows of it) represents a distinctively new experience of God. For Paul also, the encounter with God leads to intensive involvement with the marginal—this time in Greco-Roman society. As Paul says, "not many of you were wise by human standards, not many were powerful, not many were of noble birth. But God chose the weak things of the world to put the strong to shame . . ." (1 Cor 1:26).[13] Paul's God remains unknown to the wise of the world; God's wisdom is foolishness to the world, because it is revealed in the preaching of the cross.

What was Paul's experience that led to this account of God? Paul's understanding of God undergoes a dramatic development through the revelation that comes to him about Jesus. The Damascus episode is not easily understood, because it tends to be read from the standpoint of the theology of the Acts of the Apostles. This procedure obscures the radical nature of Paul's insight into Jesus.

Before Damascus, it is essential to remember that Paul "as to the law" was a Pharisee (Phil 3:5). This statement suggests that Paul was rigorously concerned to observe the purity laws of Torah in daily life. Such observance meant respecting God's Sabbath, concern for cleanliness, abstention from certain foods, and so forth. Paul based his relationship to God on such observances.

As Paul himself tells it in Galatians, a point came when he realized his understanding of Torah was inadequate in the light of the Christ. How are we to understand this turning point?

Paul says in Galatians 1 that he received a "revelation of Jesus Christ" (1:12). In contrast to the dramatic and graphic account in Acts 9, Paul's own statement is muted: "God, who had set me apart before I was born and called me through his grace, was pleased to reveal his Son . . ." (1:15–16). At this moment, the exegete is faced with a decision. The Greek literally reads "in me," but English versions regularly substitute "to me." The matter is usually argued that the Greek preposition *en* can in Koine Greek also mean "to." This reading seems, therefore, to posit some sort of experience as is recounted in Acts. However, there are interesting grounds for not moving too quickly to vision or external experience. What is revolutionized for

13. See discussion in Meeks, *The First Urban Christians*, 51–73.

Paul through this revelation is his understanding of Christ, and thereby of the God who has called through grace.

Three incidentals in Galatians lead to the translation preference "in me." In Galatians 3:1 (cf. 6:17), Paul is regularly translated as saying, "It was before *your* eyes that Jesus Christ was publicly exhibited as crucified!" The Greek is ambiguous. *Kat' ophthalmous* could as well mean "eyeball by eyeball" (i.e., in respect to *Paul's* eyes). In chapter 4, Paul says in passing: "For I testify that, had it been possible, you would have torn out your eyes and given them to me" (4:15). Evidently, Paul's eyes had some affliction at that time. Perhaps this is the "thorn in the flesh" to which Paul refers in 2 Cor 12:7.[14] Finally, in Gal 6:11, Paul seems again to allude to his afflicted eyesight: "See what large letters I make when I am writing in my own hand!" What was it that Paul really "saw"? Our thesis is that Paul came through his affliction to an understanding of God's Christ, and thereby of God's purposes for the marginal generally. Keep in mind that for Paul this revelation was "gospel" and that it led directly to his mission to the uncircumcised.

The key to Paul's understanding of Christ lies in 2 Cor 4:4, "Christ, who is the image of God." Behind this brief statement is implied Paul's entire understanding of the significance of Jesus. For Paul undoubtedly alludes to Gen 1:26–27 and to the belief that Adam and Eve originally bore the "image of God." Paul calls this image (*Imago Dei*) "Christ." So in 1 Cor 15:49 he can say that "as we have borne the image of the man of dust, we will also bear the image of the man of heaven." Paul insists in 2 Cor 4:11 that suffering is necessary in order to make visible the "life of Jesus." While this phrase could refer to the resurrection, it is more likely a literal reference to the kind of life the earthly Jesus exhibited.

Philippians 2:5–11 brings these considerations into focus. Paul wants the Philippians to have Christ's mind or pattern in them. This mind or pattern was also in Jesus. When the Christ Hymn (vv. 6–11) is read through the Genesis story, here is the result:

> [Christ Jesus] who though being in God's image did not think being like God was something to be seized, but he emptied himself by assuming the image of a slave.[15]

14. See Borg and Crossan, *The First Paul*, 63–65, who identify Paul's chronic condition (based upon William Ramsay's information about the malarial plain of Tarsus) with recurring malarial fevers. Cerebral malaria can cause impairment of eyesight.

15. See details in previous chapter of this volume; for additional argument, see Neyrey, *Christ Is Community*, 219–27; Byrne, "Philippians," 794.

Jesus, unlike Adam, did not try to be like God. Because of this obedience, Jesus still bears the original *Imago Dei*. This exegetical result is corroborated by the fact that Paul consistently contrasts Adam and Christ (1 Cor 15; Rom 5).

As Paul continues his extrapolations, he comes to see that Jesus' life and image is what all will share (1 Cor 15:49). This idea is strikingly stated in Rom 8:

> When we cry, "Abba, Father!" it is that very Spirit bearing witness with our spirit that we are children of God, and if children, then heirs, heirs of God and joint heirs with Christ ... [God] also predestined [us] to be conformed to the image of his Son, in order that he might be the firstborn within a large family. (vv. 15–17, 29)

Jesus is the elder brother of the new family of Adam.

How did Paul come to this insight? Judean eschatology certainly played a role. However, Paul's own experience seems to have been decisive. While this is speculative, it makes sense of the evidence to hand: Paul's eye-affliction disqualified him within the Pharisaic understanding of right-relationship to God (Lev 21:20; 26:16).[16] Paul became impure, and in wrestling with this shame and veritable extinction, he came to see God's presence in the accursed Jesus (Gal 3:13). "For our sake [God] made him to be sin who knew no sin, so that in him we might become the righteousness of God" (2 Cor 5:21).

Paul finds a radical God of mercy, a God intent on showing mercy to the marginal and the lost, in the obscurity of Jesus' life. Paul's understanding of Jesus replicates in a number of respects the hidden Servant of Isaiah 52–53. It also bears uncanny resemblance to Plato's understanding of the perfect, just man:

> We must take away his reputation, for a reputation for justice would bring him honor and rewards, so that it wouldn't be clear whether he is just for the sake of justice itself or for the sake of those honors and rewards. We must strip him of everything except justice and make his situation the opposite of an unjust person's. Though he does no injustice, he must have the greatest reputation for it, so that his justice may be tested full-strength and not diluted

---

16. Pharisees would have taken purity stipulations related to Aaron and the priests seriously. This understanding of Paul's revelatory experience diverges from recent Lutheran approaches, such as Bornkamm, *Paul*, 23. It also casts an interesting light on Acts 9:8.

by wrong-doing and what comes from it. Let him stay like that unchanged until he dies—just, but all his life believed to be unjust. In this way, both will reach the extremes, the one of justice and the other of injustice, and we'll be able to judge which of them is happier.[17]

Jesus in Early Christological Perspective

These inquiries point to one evident thing: The earliest christologies that we can distinguish, in stating Jesus' ultimate significance, attempt to bring out the meaning of his person and work for human community in relation to God. They are not about saying how God was in Jesus. Earliest christologies pursued intuitions about the fullness of human being and community as perceived through the words, commitments, or life of Jesus of Nazareth. As such, they point to Jesus' true humanity and God's commitment to re- deem or restore it in others, and suggest ways that Jesus' followers might live in peace with others who are very different (Luke 7:35; Mark 9:38–39). Paul's view of Jesus (bearing the image of the Heavenly Human), perfectly intelligible within a first-century Judean framework, is perhaps the most advanced statement of first-generation christology: "God was in Christ reconciling the world to himself" (2 Cor 5:18); Paul's view of the Christ-life is equally Jesuanic: "always carrying in the body the death of Jesus, so that the life of Jesus may also be manifested in our bodies" (2 Cor 4:10). This reconciliation and life have enormous creative effect in this world, not just in the next.

As symbols, earliest christologies pointed to the reclamation of human being with God and "located" human beings within the redeemed com- munity. Later christological developments, under the influence of Judean wisdom speculation (for instance, John 1 or Col 1:15–17), would articulate Jesus' relationship to the larger cosmos and ultimately Being Itself. Unlike the earlier views, the later tended to separate Jesus from humanity. Earliest christologies, however, did not purport to inform about the absolute nature of God or the place of Jesus within the divine substance. They do tell about God relative to human identity and purpose.[18]

17. Plato, *Republic* II,361b–d, quoted from Reeve, *Republic*, 37.

18. For a similar conclusion, though based upon study of Jesus and the apocalyptic Son of Man figure, see Wink, *The Human Being*.

Contemporary Christian Faith, or
How Do We Live with Our Received Symbols?

It is evident within contemporary American churches that many Christians are practical docetists and monophysites. Such views have real consequences. Under the clear influence of a triumphalist dispensationalism, the fundamentalist Christian Right has seemingly consigned historical responsibility and the environment to the devil.[19] Supersessionist or absolutist christological claims, even in mainline denominations, profoundly separate Christians from Jews and Muslims (as well as other religious traditions). If the only real question for most Christians is whether "Jesus was God" (a heresy even in Nicene terms), would we not be well served by reexamining and restating the meaning of our central claims?

To complicate parochial matters, the globalization of culture and consciousness proceeds apace and like an imploding stellar mass imparts to us increasingly dense questions. Everything culturally and religiously is up for examination. Old socializations have broken down or been abandoned. What will come to replace them? In our globalizing, postmodern condition we face a pluralism of symbols. If all we have are broken symbols, after the analogy of Paul Tillich's "broken myths," how will we then live with our shattered fixtures?[20] Should we sweep them away utterly? Abandon them for new constructs? Or should we try to find within our heritage—as Lutherans and Christians generally—theological resources that will carry us into new experiences and toward new historical horizons? Such considerations, taken with the foregoing exegetical results, at least urge a rethinking of christology within contemporary Christianity. Some project of symbol criticism and reconceptualization seems called for. The remaining reflections suggest directions this project might take.

Paul Tillich's definition of symbol has become something of a classic reference point in contemporary theology.[21] His ideas can be brought

---

19. This is evident not only from the popularity of the "Left Behind" novel series by Tim LaHaye and Jerry B. Jenkins, but also from the apocalyptic turn in U.S. policy and the anti-environmentalism of the Bush Administration. For the historical roots of this development, see Boyer, *Prophecy Belief* or Armstrong, *The Battle for God*, 75–93, 167–82, 214–18, 309–16.

20. Tillich, *The Dynamics of Faith*, 50–51: "A myth which is understood as a myth, but not removed or replaced, can be called a 'broken myth.' Christianity denies by its very nature any unbroken myth, because its presupposition is the first commandment."

21. McFague, *Metaphorical Theology*, 96–97.

into fruitful connection with contemporary social-science views. Tillich distinguishes between "sign" and "symbol," though both point beyond themselves. He argues that symbols differ from signs in important respects: Signs "do not participate in the reality of that to which they point, while symbols do." Symbols refer to realities otherwise closed to humans. Symbols correlate human spiritual concerns with those otherwise inaccessible realities. Symbols are not created, but "given." Finally, symbols grow and die.[22] Tillich's "Protestant Principle," related to his understanding of religious language, coordinates theological criticism with the demand of the first commandment.[23] More generally, Tillich's Principle is iconoclastic in the search for organically more holistic symbols. Humans cannot live without symbols any more than they can live without air; however, symbols-as-airway-constriction can only lead to death. Tillich's iconoclasm stands in service of a larger iconography.

Work within the contemporary social sciences gives force to Tillich's insights.[24] For instance, Clifford Geertz sees symbols as having two qualities: (1) Serving as "models for" and (2) serving as "models of." As models for, symbols structure relationships in the physical world. Geertz thinks of genes as quintessential models for, but these are not symbols. As models of, symbols represent the world.[25] Culture is comprised of such models of. Geertz writes:

22. Tillich, *The Dynamics of Faith*, 42–43.

23. Tillich in his European incarnation was especially preoccupied with the relationship between bourgeois faith and the working class movements. Originally, he wanted to show how Protestantism's Principle, that "no aspect of human existence" is exempted from God's judgment about contradiction and hypocrisy and that "the whole man is the subject of the religious demand and promise," is relevant to the situation addressed by Marxism. Religious socialism, then, wanted to free Protestant tradition from its "antiproletarian past"; "The Protestant Principle," 167, 180; *Systematic Theology*, 1:3–6, 11–15; see also Tillich quote above in n. 20, and below on Tillich's later concern with "priestly" or "catholic substance."

24. It was in philosophy (Charles Peirce, Ernst Cassirer) and the social sciences (Emile Durkheim, Bronislaw Malinowski) that the study of symbol first reached theoretical sophistication. The Peirce-Cassirer approach examined symbols within some kind of classification scheme, e.g., index, sign, icon, and symbol. Smoke is an index of fire. A sign stands for something to someone in some respect. Icons are pictorial representations. Symbols are signs that involve some peculiar subjective attitude. Signs become symbols. The article by Heisig, "Symbolism," 14:198–208 has been very helpful here; Morris, *Anthropological Studies of Religion*, especially 218ff, underlies this discussion as well; also Casirer, *Language and Myth*, 7, 38, 56.

25. Geertz, "Religion as a Cultural System."

It is, in fact, this double aspect which sets true symbols off from other sorts of significative forms. Models *for* are found, as the gene example suggests, through the whole order of nature; for wherever there is a communication of pattern, such programs are, in simple logic, required . . . But models *of*—linguistic, graphic, mechanical, natural, etc., processes which function not to provide sources of information in terms of which other processes can be patterned, but to represent those patterned processes as such, to express their structure in an alternative medium—are much rarer and may perhaps be confined, among living animals, to man.[26]

The human being, then, is *homo symbolicus* (Ernst Cassirer's term).[27] Malinowski's view that symbols "modify the human organism in order to transform physiological drives into cultural values" finds important application and development in the work of Talcott Parsons.[28] Parsons's "action theory" has much to offer students of religion and theology, because it attempts to articulate all of the dimensions of human being, including the intrapsychic and extrasocial.[29] Parsons sees the physical realm as something distinctively different from the organic. The organic is "organized" at a higher level of information (in exchange for raw energy). Biological drives represent a different kind of "energy." Human beings stand within a third emergent sphere, the realm of action directed by symbolic understandings. Parsons's scheme respects both the complexity of life in terms of its organization and the reality of human freedom (symbolic meanings).[30]

With these conceptions of symbol in mind, we can appreciate the importance of social-scientific definitions of religion, such as Geertz's well-known proposal:

26. Geertz, "Religion as a Cultural System," 94.

27. Cassirer, *Essay on Man*, 44: "Hence, instead of defining man as an *animal rationale*, we should define him as an *animal symbolicum*."

28. Heisig, "Symbolism," 202.

29. Parsons, "A Paradigm of the Human Condition."

30. The social sciences have also explored the relationship between religion and ideology. Feuerbach and Marx long ago called attention to need-projection and false consciousness. It seems that groups justify their interests through such ideologies, and that theology expresses ideology as really as any other group rationalization. Criticism is necessary, therefore, because of our propensity to universalize our own interests, because of our ability to delude ourselves that others hold all of the values that we do, and because of our tendency to dispense cheap grace (to speak indiscriminately, as my grandfather used to say, about "what God loves").

(1) a system of symbols which acts to (2) establish powerful, pervasive, and long-lasting moods and motivations in men by (3) formulating conceptions of a general order of existence and (4) clothing these conceptions with such an aura of factuality that (5) the moods and motivations seem uniquely realistic.

Or the more parsimonious and derivative formulation by Robert Bellah, "a set of symbolic forms and acts that relate man to the ultimate conditions of his existence."[31] While these understandings underscore religion's/theology's cultural involvements and functional role, they are not entirely reductionistic: for while they focus on the function of symbols, seem to make them merely a reflex of human need, and make no judgment about their validity, they root religious symbols within levels of reality and human experience that remain "open." As expressive of ultimate conditions of existence or as conceptions of general order, religious symbols are experienced as participating in reality in the way that Tillich understands them.

The Promise of Lutheran Biblical Studies

What might all of this imply for contemporary christology and Lutheran biblical studies? For Christians, those for whom Jesus is the Christ, Jesus is a model for ultimate reality (a model for human being, "a model of the godly life") and a model of ultimate reality (what ultimate reality is all about, what its deepest principles are, how humans fit into that reality). Furthermore, Jesus becomes a criterion in dialog with other faiths and other symbols. The project of symbol criticism serves not only to ascertain what is really important within our own tradition, but also to evaluate other religious (symbol) traditions. In that dialog with difference, however, there are risks. Perhaps our symbols and traditions also need reconsideration. Jesus becomes an essential criterion for Christian claims about his ultimate significance, especially in terms of whether those claims provide adequate models for and of.

The project of symbol criticism may then proceed to considerations about reconceptualization and even innovation. Our sacred traditions are "broken" in any number of ways, though the acknowledgment of this among Christians is not very clear. We see that our creeds and sacred texts are not absolute perspectives, but perspectives on ultimate reality framed under very human conditions. Revelation must come through them, despite them

31. Geertz, "Religion as a Cultural System," 90; Bellah, "Religious Evolution," 21.

even, or not at all. They are not the ultimate revelation; at best, they point to it. Yet they remain indispensable, for as whole people it is clear we cannot live without a sense of identity and purpose or without core symbols. We cannot live without them, but how can we live with them? Should we restructure symbols to restore their life-giving power, or do we simply reinterpret them? If we must restructure, how will we do so? Sallie McFague, an important pioneer in raising such questions, has thus spoken of the idolatry and irrelevance generally of contemporary religious language and inquired as to the possibilities and grounds of its revitalization.[32]

Central to the promise of Lutheran biblical studies is the birthright of asking questions of our deepest convictions and traditions. This is closely related to a Lutheran sensibility about the importance of interpretation and the "central-message hermeneutic."[33] Christ is at the center; that has been our conviction. But for the future this hermeneutic will be challenged to address new questions.

Several tasks seem required as the central message engages the twenty-first-century context. The "meaning capacity" of Christian symbols, including "Christ," must be developed by (1) probing them radically, i.e., going as deeply into them as possible and (2) broadening them out to see their connections to other religious symbols (even non-Christian). Core meanings of Christian symbols should be clarified and restated in ways that leave things open to the ultimate symbols of others. Further, religious symbols should be questioned as to how they contribute to life and living constructively—to enable us, e.g., to see Christ in all the world or to bring life out of death.[34] Finally, religious symbols should be queried to provide criteria of health (as an expression of salvation), e.g., in psychic, social, political, economic, or cultural terms.

Biblical scholarship, as it uncovers and explores the original context and meaning of biblical texts, comes to see through cultural anthropology the culturally conditioned contour of biblical values, the compromise of biblical promise by biblical politics (as in the history of racism), or in our

32. McFague, *Metaphorical Theology*, 4–14.

33. I am indebted to former colleague Lyman Lundeen for the term "central-message hermeneutic."

34. Bellah claims, "The adequacy of any ultimate perspective is its ability to transform human experience so that it yields life instead of death." "[Tillich's] restless quest for the 'dimension of depth' . . . was his great contribution to breaking out of the institutional ghetto and seeing once more, as Augustine did, the figure of Christ in the whole world" ("Between Religion and Social Science," 245, 255).

times biblical involvement in perpetuating or justifying patriarchy and homophobia.[35] "Bible study" or biblical proclamation cannot simply consist of retracing or restating biblical images and stories, or drawing immediate analogies at whim, without more encompassing and systematic vision. Why we return to these texts, and how we will relate them to our own contemporary questions, requires substantial and intentional discussion.[36] The need for critical perspective and ongoing reflection is ever more pressing. This is not a distinctive Lutheran problem, but since the Lutheran common life is fed so much from biblical study and preaching, the problem for us is acute. The promise of Lutheran biblical studies is profoundly linked, then, with pursuing clarity about the central meaning of the biblical tradition.

Church leaders may be engaged for a long time in building convictional commitment in a pluralistic situation vastly complicated by globalization. We are in over our heads, as Robert Kegan says, with a postmodern, posttraditional, post-just-about-everything curriculum.[37] In the struggle to maintain commitment under conditions of globalization, chaotic pluralism, and cultural relativism, defense mechanisms can become strongly active. Despite knowledge that reality is complex and no one possesses the absolute truth, there is the constant temptation in the modern period by what Stephen Toulmin (after John Dewey) calls "the Quest for Certainty."[38] This quest manifests itself in religious confessionalism, fundamentalism, or traditionalisms of all kinds. Again and again, this quest has led Lutherans to succumb to their twin temptations—hypocritical moralism on the one hand or legalistic orthodoxy on the other. But it has also been a major theme in other cultural spheres as seen in scientism, various totalitarianisms, and increasingly in marketism (belief that the market, market relations, and economic forces are absolute). Other values are driven out and disappear; the richness of life surrenders to fatal reductionism; human being and the *Imago Dei* are debased once again.

Paul Tillich and others are surely right that doubt is as important in the contemporary theological scene as some presumed certainty. We must

35. Malina, *The New Testament World*, traces the cultural mortgages. Paul's writings are tightly coupled with contemporary Christian moral understandings and, consequently, not always very highly regarded by women because of his apparent misogyny or gays/lesbians because of Rom 1:26–27 and 1 Cor 6:9; not surprisingly, the ELCA's sexuality studies seem interminable.

36. Cf. Tillich's method of correlation; Parks, *Big Questions, Worthy Dreams*.

37. Kegan, *In Over Our Heads*.

38. Toulmin, *Cosmopolis*, 10, 35.

reclaim again Tillich's radical application of the Reformation doctrine of justification by faith to the intellect: "The step I myself made in these years was the insight that the principle of justification through faith refers not only to the religious-ethical but also to the religious-intellectual life. Not only [s]he who is in sin but also [s]he who is in doubt is justified through faith."[39] Equally important for the coming challenges—as constructive categories for the depth and breadth of God's involvement with creation and redemption—will be Tillich's notions of "Catholic Substance" and "Spiritual Community" or McFague's and others' discussions of theological language.[40] Tillich also said long ago with much prescience:

> Without trying to repristinate outworn symbols Protestantism must rediscover the realistic meaning of symbols, must denounce the misinterpretation of symbols as mere signs, must attempt to discover the germs of a new symbolism in our present life . . . The presence of the holy in the Catholic cult creates a continuous influx of priestly substance into Protestantism and humanism, directly and indirectly. The arts and literature of the last centuries are the main witnesses for this extremely significant process.[41]

Moreover, the community of God's concern, the Spiritual Community, is larger than the church: "We do not use the word 'church' for the Spiritual Community, because this word has been used, of necessity, in the frame of the ambiguities of religion. At this point we speak instead of that which is able to conquer the ambiguities of religion—the New Being . . ."[42] McFague has suggested the answer lies in developing a "metaphorical theology," in which the metaphors of religious language interact with the models of theological language. These sensibilities are also found in recent work of Lutheran colleagues who search for new resources to help us relate to changed circumstances. A "critical faith" keeps the meaning of christology and the center of the Christian tradition fresh, because our inherited certainties have become in some respects absurd, and yet we must still live

39. Tillich, *The Protestant Era*, x; Tillich links the Protestant Principle necessarily with doubt, "If faith is understood as belief that something is true, doubt is incompatible with the act of faith. If faith is understood as being ultimately concerned, doubt is a necessary element in it. It is a consequence of the risk of faith" (*The Dynamics of Faith*, 18).

40. Tillich, "Permanent Significance"; Tillich, *The Future of Religions*; Tillich, *Systematic Theology*, 3:149–61; McFague, *Metaphorical Theology*, 14–29; Borg, *The God We Never Knew*, 57–79.

41. Tillich, "Permanent Significance," 29.

42. Tillich, *Systematic Theology*, 3:149.

with them. Only through faithful criticism, searching, probing evaluation, can we ascertain with clarity what is really important. This is truly a central Lutheran commitment and contribution to Catholic life.[43]

Over fifteen years [since 1988], my Whiteheadian and feminist colleagues here at Pacific Lutheran University have stimulated me to think holistically about the fecundity of creation, its restless efflorescence, its propensity to throw up hundreds of half-baked solutions for every one fully cooked, its complex interrelationships. We are left within our provincial world view to interpret all of this. The Christian tradition has been equally fecund, as Ernst Troeltsch long ago showed, and we cannot ignore its temporally conditioned character. We inherit it, but mere iconoclasm does not seem to be the best way. Neither are we called to iconodulism. Our responsibility as thinking-doubting faithful is to live graciously out of that tradition without absolutizing it. It too is full of idolatries and new servitudes. As we come to appreciate other religious heritages, without our old idolatries or imperialistic assumptions, we will find ourselves again within criticism. What is really important in our own tradition? What is important in the traditions of others? Can we forge metafaith languages that do not betray our own faith? Can we achieve a global spiritual iconography? Can we find Christ among us and throughout the whole world? Martin Luther and the Seminex faculty, including Robert H. Smith, taught us to wrestle with the biblical texts until a word of grace and blessing should come for us. Whatever the twenty-first century may bring for Christianity, we can still count on that biblical promise.[44]

43. McFague, *Metaphorical Theology*, 4–14, 193–94; Lundeen, *Risk and Rhetoric in Religion*; Ingram, *Wrestling With the Ox*; Rasmussen, *Earth Community, Earth Ethics*; the term "critical faith" comes from Theissen, *A Critical Faith*; see also his, *Biblical Faith*.

44. I am grateful for critical responses to drafts of this essay by Gordon Pease and Samuel Torvend. Of course, they cannot be held responsible for my inept use or abuse of their wise critiques.

Epilogue

What Would We Do Now with Jesus and the Bible?

Gnōthi seauton, "Know yourself." —THE ORACLE OF DELPHI

During that twenty-year period [the age of Napoleon] an immense number of fields were left untilled, houses were burned, trade changed its direction, millions of men migrated, were impoverished, or were enriched, and millions of Christian men professing the law of love of their fellows slew one another.

What does all this mean? Why did it happen? What made those people burn houses and slay their fellow men? What were the causes of these events? What force made men act so? These are the instinctive, plain, and most legitimate questions humanity asks itself when it encounters the monuments and tradition of that period.

For a reply to these questions the common sense of mankind turns to the science of history, whose aim is to enable nations and humanity to know themselves. —LEO TOLSTOY, "Second Epilogue," *War and Peace* [tr. Maude]

THE PICTURE OF THE historical Jesus as a shrewd peasant, a village sage, whose heart and actions were against the Mammon-lords of Galilee, and whose focus on a different kind of political-economic order under the term the kingdom of God resulted in his political execution on the cross, should serve as a warning against a comfortable *Kultur-Christentum* devoid of sociocultural perspective and criticism. Not only Napoleon in the early nineteenth century, but also the ferocious struggles in the last century that demanded the industrial sacrifice of millions, memorialize the dark side of humanity. For Jesus, God's gracious election and patronage could redeem the dishonored for an honorable community. In Saint Paul's mind, humanity was enslaved to powers of sin and death in a primordial time, but now the object of God's gracious affection in Christ. For Rabbinic Judaism, the human being lives with two natures—the Good Nature, *yetzer hatov*, and the Evil Nature, *yetzer hara*—and the Mishnah is full of wise warning and prudence for the righteous life (e.g., *m. 'Aboth*, "The Fathers"). The Christian traditional notion of sin signifies the missing of the mark of God's intention for human being, but where sin abounds, grace abounds all the more (Rom 5:20). These traditions attest to the complexity of human nature and history *sub specie aeternitatis*.

In all of these responses to the God of Israel, furthermore, how the individual will relate to others is a key idea. The biblical traditions are deeply concerned with society, and they claim to reveal something about the Divine Intentions for humanity within community.

To Jesus are attributed three sayings about love: Love of neighbor as self (Mark 12:31, after Lev 11:19); love of enemies (Q 6:35); and love of others by the example of Jesus' own love (John 13:34). For St. Paul, only the resurrecting power of God can rescue from the enslaving powers and create a new humanity, but the new paradoxical freedom-obedience is empowered already now by God's creative Spirit within the new community of Christ's body. Coming closer to our own time, the Jewish person in 1934 can join the resistance against the Nazis in answer to the *yetzer hatov* or sell out his kin to save himself under the influence of the *yetzer hara*. The Christian likewise at that time was required to choose between the German Christians and the Confessing Church. Centrally, the Bible is opposed to dehumanization and social injustice; centrally, the Bible is concerned with human fulfillment in response to Israel's God within a community of justice, other-care, and harmony.

In the waning years of my teaching career, I was able to run a course called the Bible in History and the Modern World. For most students, this was a course wherein they learned that the Bible was a library and not a unified book. They learned to think about claims of inspiration in light of manuscripts, variant readings, and translations. They studied the rise of historical criticism and the enormous emotional impact of critical thought upon both pietism and orthodoxy. They considered the question of science and myth (geological history and biological evolution) in relation to Gen 1–2. They encountered social-scientific criticism through anthropological considerations of the patriarchal extended family of Mediterranean antiquity; through realization that the Bible was compiled within agrarian societies without many labor-saving devices; and through recognition that honor and collectivism (over against individual achievement) were values that shaped biblical perspectives of the world.

Among the largest questions of my course were these: Should the Bible continue to influence, say, American society? and if so, how? and if not, why? And if so, what "interpretive bridges" must be built to convey meaningful interactions and discourse with the people and traditions of the Bible?

Of course, through historical study, students became aware that very few knew much about the Bible before 1500; that the Renaissance (Erasmus) and the Reformation (Luther) both looked to the past for renewal, and built the linguistic foundations for modern vernacular Bibles; that English versions of the sixteenth century were all profoundly indebted to the work of William Tyndale; and that at least in the West the centrality of biblical authority was a largely Protestant idea, to be inherited by modern cultures with deep Protestant roots. Through surveys, students were also made well aware that most contemporary Bible translations read in the United States are very conservative and influenced by doctrinal concerns. Even the Revised Standard Version (later editions) and New Revised Standard Version, text critically considered, are in places less critical than the first Revised Standard Version of 1946 (e.g., in the handling of the variant at Luke 22:19–20, where the 1946 RSV follows good text-critical procedures to adjudge 19b–20 as not original to Luke's text; the variant comes from conflation later with 1 Cor 11:23–26 and obscures the literal focus of Jesus' oath in Luke 22:15–19, "I shall not eat/drink"). And of course, the NRSV came into being due to contemporary gender issues.

So in the new millennium, the United States at least continues to wrestle with the question, what does the Bible say about this or that? These are important questions if one assumes that the Bible has some kind of authority. Among numerous other critical issues, many simply academic, the course I taught was designed to enlighten students on the pervasive problem of "literalism" with respect to the Bible, namely, that a verse here or there, even if misunderstood in the light of historical and social-scientific criticism, could be invoked to determine a momentous issue of the day. Further, students in my course were made aware that biblical authority could become merely a fetish. For instance, nowhere in the Bible is there any clear word about medical abortion, but a large contingent of modern U.S. Bible readers are convinced that the Bible (and God) abhors abortion. Or a verse in Revelation could lead to an entire world conspiracy theory to go right along with QAnon. And now in time of pandemic, the antiscience propensity of many conservative U.S. Christians is underwriting a tragic opposition to the sound scientific advice of medical professionals.

The course did have a constructive agenda as well. What bridge could bring a positive influence into our twenty-first-century midst? For addressing this question, the model that K. C. Hanson and I devised in *Palestine in the Time of Jesus* was put to good use.[1] For if values are central in culture, and determinative of norms, statuses, and roles, then a bridge might be built out of dialog especially about biblical norms and values in the light of today's shaped after the Great Transformation. Values of democracy, equality, and individual freedom, for example, are inchoate within the Bible, but not fully formed. This dialogical approach would be similar to Rudolf Bultmann's famous proposal about demythologization, i.e., translating meaning from a prescientific myth then to a scientific age now.

Hanson and I also proposed a critical method for adjudicating this values-dialog, which in turn would involve considerations of norms, statuses, and roles. Drawing upon Krister Stendahl's famous 1962 *IDB* article "Biblical Theology," we amplified his two questions into four—from What did it mean? and What does it Mean? to:

> (1) What in the biblical record is culture-bound and outmoded (for example, women's roles)? (2) What values might we want to attempt to translate (for example, fictive kinship)? (3) What should we retain without question (for example, commitment to the God whom Jesus proclaimed)? and (4) What is "coming to expression" in the biblical traditions (for example, hopes, visions, dreams)?[2]

Given the interests of this present volume, a further illustrative example of (2) might consider the following.[3] A large tension stands within Deut 15:1, "Every seventh year you shall grant a remission of debts," already appears in 15:4, "There will, however, be no one in need among you" and 15:7, "If there is among you anyone in need." On the one hand, there should be no one in need of a release from debt; on the other hand, clearly Israelites could fall into financial difficulties (as also evident from the rules in Lev 25

---

1. Hanson and Oakman, *Palestine in the Time of Jesus*, 13.
2. Hanson and Oakman, *Palestine in the Time of Jesus*, 151.
3. Recall again the exposition of these themes in chapter 8 of this volume.

and the information in Neh 5). Further, usury among Israelites is prohib-
ited (Deut 15:37), but Deut 15:3 shows that debts (presumably loans with
interest) could be collected from non-Israelites.

Notably, these rules are familial or tribal, not extending to those considered foreigners. Protecting the interests of the family and family property
are essential. To transfer these strictures without further ado into modern
contexts would obviously be difficult given that capitalism requires, despite
the family's interests, impersonal loans at interest and contractual penalties
upon default. However, no worries. Literalist readings of such biblical texts
and arrangements ignore them almost entirely. No good conservative Bible
reader today, as far as I know, is seriously contesting the basis of capitalism
by appeals to Deuteronomy. By contrast, evangelical Bible readers are well
recognized for their central preoccupation with sexual morality and family
issues based upon frequent appeals to biblical texts (such as Gen 9:1–11
to oppose "sodomy" and homosexuality, or the Household Codes in the
Pauline tradition to enforce a modern nuclear family patriarchy).[4]

If the radical Jesus is taken as the reference point for the core meaning
of the Christian tradition (and this has been debated), then he becomes
the crucial criterion (*pace* Bultmann's mere "presupposition") for christology, Christian theology, and Christian ethics. And yet, the radical Jesus
seemingly makes things even more difficult with, for instance, the Q-saying
"lend without expecting anything in return" (Q 6:35), which if taken literally would abolish capitalism. The absolutization of such an uncritical
generosity would not only undermine charity but would hardly seem just
to those who worked for what they achieved. However, if such "hard sayings" are placed within a conversation about the radical aims of Jesus, then
perhaps he can be perceived as a wise promoter of a realistic alternative
to the Mammon-centric context of his day. If as Bellah claims (following
Max Weber), Jesus aimed to reverse the common first-century ethic of
"love your friends, hate your enemies" and to erase the line between family
insiders and strangers equally entitled to family generosity (Q 6:35), then
translation to a realistic value-set commensurate with modern conditions
might be possible.[5]

If the crucial hermeneutical bridge is a dialog about human values,
and it is acknowledged that both Israelite law and Jesus (especially in the Q
traditions) are sharply focused on economic issues that sunder community,

4. Borg, *Convictions*, 17–18.
5. Bellah, "Max Weber and World-denying Love."

then a clear critical case can be argued that both Judaism and Christianity have a central concern with economy as it supports the well-being of all societal members. By extension, this concern would advocate for fair wages, health and safety on the job, equal pay for equal work, fairness to women in the workplace, and the like. Values, thus, will consequently affect norms, statuses, and roles.

In the global scene today, exploitation of cheap labor by multinationals, vast inequalities resulting from financial machinations, the contributions of the internet to inequality and exploitation—all could be called the concerns of "biblical economics." And while in the U.S. the First Amendment guarantees separation of church and state and free exercise, the First Amendment clearly cannot rule that there is no cross-fertilization between political values and religious values informed by the biblical traditions. This is probably a too simplistic representation of numerous issues that might require a dialog in view of the Great Transformation, but so go all long-term dialogs.[6]

The reflections of this Epilogue *warrant* the continued critical social study of the Bible, and the ongoing effort to ask about its *warranted influence* today (even in global context). It is not enough simply to study biblical languages; biblical society and culture must also come under consideration. A literalist approach is unhelpful in a twenty-first-century world in which the aspirations of a global humanity ramify values and seek a constructive articulation.[7] A critical-dialogical approach, especially for communities that look to the Bible for warrant or authority for life, will be far more helpful, but require much more critical study, wise perspective, and responsibility in the handling of biblical texts.

---

6. Borg, *Convictions*, 31, referring to Kenneth Burke's "unending conversation," indeed reminds us that we all join the conversations that began before us and will continue long after we are gone!

7. See the helpful critiques of literalism in Borg, *Convictions*, 106–15; Rogerson, *Introduction to the Bible*, 134–49; consider as an exemplary alternative the careful study of biblical themes in Barrera, *Biblical Economic Ethics*.

Bibliography

Adam, A. K. M. *What Is Postmodern Biblical Criticism?* Guides to Biblical Scholarship. Minneapolis: Fortress, 1995.

Adan-Bayewitz, David, and Mordechai Aviam. "Iotapata, Josephus, and the Siege of 67: Preliminary Report of the 1992–94 Seasons." *Journal of Roman Archaeology* 10 (1997) 131–65.

Allison, Dale C., Jr. *Constructing Jesus: Memory, Imagination, and History.* Grand Rapids: Baker Academic, 2010.

———. *The Jesus Tradition in Q.* Harrisburg, PA: Trinity, 1997.

Althann, Robert. "Josiah." In *ABD*, 3:1015–18.

Annan, Kofi. Nobel Peace Prize Address, Oslo, Norway, December 10, 2001. https://www.nobelprize.org/prizes/peace/2001/annan/lecture/.

———. Truman Library Address, Independence, Missouri, December 11, 2006. https://www.un.org/sg/en/content/sg/speeches/2006-12-11/truman-library-speech-annan-says-un-remains-best-tool-achieve-key.

Applebaum, Shimon. "Economic Life in Palestine." In *The Jewish People in the First Century: Historical Geography, Political History, Social, Cultural and Religious Life and Institutions,* edited by S. Safrai and M. Stern, 2:631–700. Compendia Rerum Iudaicarum ad Novum Testamentum, section 1. Philadelphia: Fortress, 1976.

———. "Josephus and the Economic Causes of the Jewish War." In *Josephus, the Bible, and History,* edited by Louis H. Feldman and Gohei Hata, 237–64. Detroit: Wayne State University Press, 1989.

Arav, Rami, and Richard A. Freund, eds. *Bethsaida: A City by the North Shore of the Sea of Galilee.* 4 vols. Kirksville, MO: Truman University Press, 1995–2009.

Armstrong, Karen. *The Battle for God: A History of Fundamentalism.* New York: Ballantine, 2001.

Arnal, William E. *Jesus and the Village Scribes: Galilean Conflicts and the Setting of Q.* Minneapolis: Fortress, 2001.

———. "The Rhetoric of Marginality: Apocalypticism, Gnosticism and Sayings Gospels." *HTR* 88 (1995) 471–94.

Asgeirsson, Jon Ma., Kristin de Troyer, and Marvin W. Meyer, eds. *From Quest to Q: Festschrift James M. Robinson.* BETL 146. Leuven: Leuven University Press, 2000.

Attridge, Harold W., Dale B. Martin, and Jürgen Zangenberg, eds. *Religion, Ethnicity and Identity in Ancient Galilee.* WUNT 210. Tübingen: Mohr/Siebeck, 2007.

Augustine (Aurelius Augustinus Hipponensis). *A Select Library of the Nicene and Post-Nicene Fathers of the Christian Church.* Vol. 2, *City of God and Christian Doctrine.*

Edited by Philip Schaff. Translated by Marcus Dods and J. F. Shaw. Grand Rapids: Eerdmans, 1956.

Aviam, Mordechai. "Distribution Maps of Archaeological Data from the Galilee: An Attempt to Establish Zones Indicative of Ethnicity and Religious Affiliation." In *Religion, Ethnicity and Identity in Ancient Galilee*, edited by Harold W. Attridge, Dale B. Martin, and Jürgen Zangenberg, 115–32. WUNT 210. Tübingen: Mohr/Siebeck, 2007.

———. *Jews, Pagans and Christians in the Galilee*. Land of Galilee 1. Rochester, NY: University of Rochester Press, 2004.

———. "People, Land, Economy, and Belief in First-Century Galilee and Its Origins: A Comprehensive Archaeological Synthesis." In *The Galilean Economy in the Time of Jesus*, edited by David A. Fiensy and Ralph K. Hawkins, 5–48. Early Christianity and Its Literature 11. Atlanta: Society of Biblical Literature, 2013.

———. "Yodfat." In *The New Encyclopedia of Archaeological Excavations in the Holy Land*, edited by Ephraim Stern, 5:2076–78. 5 vols. New York: Simon & Shuster, 1993, 2008.

Banaji, Jairus. "Commercial Capitalism in the Mediteranean from the Late Republic to Late Byzantium." N.d. https://www.academia.edu/25257051/Commercial_Capitalism_in_the_Mediteranean_from_the_Late_Republic_to_Late_Byzantium.

Barag, Dan. "Tyrian Currency in Galilee." *INJ* 6–7 (1982–1983) 7–13.

Barr, James. *The Concept of Biblical Theology: An Old Testament Perspective*. Minneapolis: Fortress, 1999.

Barrera, Albino. *Biblical Economic Ethics: Sacred Scripture's Teachings on Economic Life*. Lanham, MD: Lexington, 2013.

———. *Economic Compulsion and Christian Ethics*. New Studies in Christian Ethics 24. Cambridge: Cambridge University Press, 2005.

———. *Market Complicity and Christian Ethics*. New Studies in Christian Ethics 31. Cambridge: Cambridge University Press, 2011.

Bartchy, S. Scott. "Undermining Ancient Patriarchy: The Apostle Paul's Vision of a Society of Siblings." *BTB* 29 (1999) 68–78.

———. "Who Should Be Called Father? Paul of Tarsus between the Jesus Tradition and *Patria Potestas*." *BTB* 33 (2003) 135–47.

Batten, Alicia. "The Degraded Poor and the Greedy Rich: Exploring the Language of Poverty and Wealth in James." In *The Social Sciences and Biblical Translation*, edited by Dietmar Neufeld, 66–77. SBL Symposium Series 41. Atlanta: Society of Biblical Literature, 2008.

Bauer, Walter, and Frederick W. Danker. *A Greek-English Lexicon of the New Testament and Other Early Christian Literature*. 3rd ed. Chicago and London: University of Chicago Press, 2000.

Bautch, Kelly Coblentz. "Enoch, First Book of." In *NIDB* 2:262–65.

Bazzana, Giovanni B. *Kingdom of Bureaucracy: The Political Theology of Village Scribes in the Sayings Gospel Q*. BETL 274. Leuven: Peeters, 2015.

Becker, Marc. "Peasant Identity, Worker Identity: Conflicting Modes of Rural Consciousness in Highland Ecuador." Special issue: "Historia y Sociedad en los Andes, Siglos XIX y XX." *Estudios Interdisciplinarios de América Latina y el Caribe (University of Tel Aviv)* 15.1 (2004) 115–39.

Bellah, Robert N. "Between Religion and Social Science." In *Beyond Belief*, 237–59.

———. *Beyond Belief: Essays on Religion in a Post-Traditional World*. Berkeley: University of California Press, 1991.

————. "Islamic Tradition and the Problems of Modernization." In *Beyond Belief*, 146–67.

————. "Max Weber and World-Denying Love: A Look at the Historical Sociology of Religion." *JAAR* 67 (1999) 277–304.

————. "Religious Evolution." In *Beyond Belief*, 20–50.

————. "The Sociology of Religion." In *Beyond Belief*, 3–17.

Bellah, Robert N. et al. *Habits of the Heart: Individualism and Commitment in American Life*. Updated ed. Berkeley: University of California Press, 1996.

Belo, Fernando. *A Materialist Reading of the Gospel of Mark*. Translated by Matthew J. O'Connell. Maryknoll, NY: Orbis, 1981.

Ben-David, A. *Jerusalem und Tyros: Ein Beitrag zur Palästinensischen Münz- und Wirtschaftsgeschichte (126 a.C.–57 p.C.)*. Basel: Kyklos, 1969.

Berger, Peter L. *The Sacred Canopy: Elements of a Sociological Theory of Religion*. New York: Doubleday, 1967.

Berger, Peter L., and Thomas Luckmann. *The Social Construction of Reality: A Treatise in the Sociology of Knowledge*. New York: Doubleday, 1966.

Bergson, Henri. *The Two Sources of Morality and Religion*. Translated by Audra, R. Ashley, Cloudesley Brereton, and with the assistance of W. Horsfall Carter. Notre Dame: University of Notre Dame Press, 1977. (Original French edition, 1932.)

Berlin, Andrea M. "Between Large Forces: Palestine in the Hellenistic Period." *BA* 60 (1997) 2–51.

————. "Household Judaism." In *Galilee in the Late Second Temple and Mishnaic Periods*. Vol. 1, *Life, Culture, and Society*, edited by David A. Fiensy and James Riley Strange, 208–15. Minneapolis: Fortress, 2014.

————. "Jewish Life before the Revolt: The Archaeological Evidence." *JSJ* 36 (2005) 417–70.

Bernstein, Henry, and Terence J. Byres. "From Peasant Studies to Agrarian Change." *Journal of Agrarian Change* 1 (2001) 1–56.

Black, Matthew. *An Aramaic Approach to the Gospels and Acts*. With an introduction by Craig A. Evans and an appendix by Geza Vermes. 3rd ed. Peabody, MA: Hendrickson, 1998.

Borg, Marcus J. *Convictions: How I Learned What Matters Most*. San Francisco: HarperOne, 2016.

————. *The God We Never Knew: Beyond Dogmatic Religion to a More Authentic Contemporary Faith*. San Francisco: HarperSanFrancisco, 1997.

Borg, Marcus, and John Dominic Crossan. *The First Paul: Reclaiming the Radical Visionary behind the Church's Conservative Icon*. New York: HarperOne, 2009.

Bornkamm, Günther. *Paul*. Translated by D. M. G. Stalker. New York: Harper & Row, 1971.

Borowski, Oded. *Agriculture in Iron Age Israel*. Winona Lake, IN: Eisenbrauns, 1987.

Bossman, David. "Canon and Culture: A Call for Biblical Theology in Context." *BTB* 23 (1993) 4–13.

Boyer, Paul S. *When Time Shall Be No More: Prophecy Belief in Modern American Culture*. Cambridge: Harvard University Press, 1992.

Boyarin, Daniel. *A Radical Jew: Paul and the Politics of Identity*. Contraversions 1. Berkeley: University of California Press, 1994.

Brannan, David W., Philip F. Esler, and N. T. Anders Strindberg. "Talking to 'Terrorists': Towards an Independent Analytical Framework for the Study of Violent Substate Activism." *Studies in Conflict and Terrorism* 24 (2001) 3–24.

Broshi, Magen. "Agriculture and Economy in Roman Palestine: Seven Notes on the Babatha Archive." *IEJ* 42 (1992) 230–40.

———. "The Population of Western Palestine in the Roman-Byzantine Period." *BASOR* 236 (1980) 1–10.

Brown, John Pairman. "The Foreign Vocabulary of Jesus' Aramaic." In *Israel and Hellas*, 3:203–73. 3 vols. Berlin and New York: Walter de Gruyter, 1995–2001.

———. "Prometheus, the Servant of Yahweh, Jesus: Legitimation and Repression in the Heritage of Persian Imperialism." In *The Bible and the Politics of Exegesis: Essays in Honor of Norman K. Gottwald on His Sixty-Fifth Birthday*, edited by David Jobling, Peggy L. Day, and Gerald T. Sheppard, 109–25. Cleveland, OH: Pilgrim, 1991.

Brown, Peter. *Through the Eye of a Needle: Wealth, the Fall of Rome, and the Making of Christianity in the West, 350–550 AD*. Princeton: Princeton University Press, 2012.

Brueggemann, Walter. *Theology of the Old Testament: Testimony, Dispute, Advocacy*. Minneapolis: Fortress, 1997.

Bultmann, Rudolf K. "Die Bedeutung der neuerschlossenen Mandäischen und Manichäischen Quellen für das Verständnis des Johannesevangeliums." *ZNW* 24 (1925) 100–46.

———. *History of the Synoptic Tradition*. Translated by John Marsh. Rev. ed. San Francisco: Harper & Row, 1963.

———. *Jesus and the Word*. Translated by E. H. Lantero. New York: Scribner, 1958.

———. *Jesus Christ and Mythology*. New York: Scribner, 1958.

———. "The Problem of Hermeneutics." In *Essays, Philosophical and Theological*, 234–61. Translated by James C. G. Greig. London: SCM, 1955.

———. *Theology of the New Testament*. Translated by Kendrick Grobel. 2 vols. New York: Scribner, 1951–1955.

Byrne, Brendan. "The Letter to the Philippians." In *The New Jerome Biblical Commentary*, edited by Raymond E. Brown, Joseph A. Fitzmyer, and Roland E. Murphy, 791–97. Englewood Cliffs, NJ: Prentice-Hall, 1990.

Cadbury, H. J. "Erastus of Corinth." *JBL* 502 (1931) 42–58.

Carney, Thomas F. *The Shape of the Past: Models and Antiquity*. Lawrence, KS: Coronado, 1975.

Case, Shirley Jackson. "Jesus and Sepphoris." *JBL* 45 (1926) 14–22.

Cassirer, Ernst. *An Essay on Man: An Introduction to a Philosophy of Human Culture*. 1944. Reprint, Doubleday Anchor Book 3. Garden City, NY: Doubleday, 1953.

———. *Language and Myth*. Translated by Susanne K. Langer. New York: Dover, 1946.

———. *The Philosophy of Symbolic Form*. Translated by Ralph Manheim. Preface and introduction by Charles W. Hendel. 4 vols. New Haven: Yale University Press, 1953–1996.

Cato, Marcus Porcius. *Marcus Porcius Cato, On Agriculture; Marcus Terentius Varro, On Agriculture*. Translated by William Davis Hooper and Harrison Boyd Ash. Rev. ed. LCL. Cambridge: Harvard University Press, 1935.

Chancey, Mark. A. "The Ethnicities of Galileans." In *Galilee in the Late Second Temple and Mishnaic Periods*. Vol. 1, *Life, Culture, and Society*, edited by David A. Fiensy and James Riley Strange, 112–28. Minneapolis: Fortress, 2014.

———. *Greco-Roman Culture and the Galilee of Jesus*. SNTSMS 134. Cambridge: Cambridge University Press, 2005.

Chancey, Mark A., and Eric M. Meyers. "How Jewish Was Sepphoris in Jesus' Time?" *BAR* 26.4 (July–August 2000) 18–33, 61.

Charles, R. H. *The Apocrypha and Pseudepigrapha of the Old Testament*. Vol. 2, *Pseudepigrapha*. Oxford: Clarendon, 1913.

———. *Eschatology: The Doctrine of a Future Life in Israel, Judaism and Christianity*. Introduction by George Wesley Buchanan. 1963. Reprint, Eugene, OR: Wipf & Stock, 1999.

Charlesworth, James H., ed. *The Old Testament Pseudepigrapha*. 2 vols. Garden City, NY: Doubleday, 1983–1985.

Childs, Brevard S. *Biblical Theology in Crisis*. Philadelphia: Westminster, 1970.

Christian, David. *Maps of Time: An Introduction to Big History*. Foreword by William H. McNeil. Berkeley: University of California Press, 2004.

———. *This Fleeting World: A Short History of Humanity*. Great Barrington, MA: Berkshire, 2008.

Cohen, Shaye J. D. "Ioudaios, Iudaeus, Judaean, Jew." In *The Beginnings of Jewishness: Boundaries, Varieties, Uncertainties*, 69–106. Hellenistic Culture and Society. Berkeley: University of California Press, 1999.

———. "Ioudaios: 'Judaean' and 'Jew' in Susanna, First Maccabees, and Second Maccabees." In *Geschichte—Tradition—Reflexion: Festschrift für Martin Hengel zum 70. Geburtstag*. Vol. 1, *Judentum*, edited by Hubert Cancik, Hermann Lichtenberger, and Peter Schäfer, 211–20. Tübingen: Mohr/Siebeck, 1996.

Collins, Randall. *Theoretical Sociology*. San Diego: Harcourt Brace Jovanovitch, 1988.

Cone, James. *The Spirituals and the Blues: An Interpretation*. New York: Seabury, 1972.

Cook, James I. *Edgar Johnson Goodspeed: Articulate Scholar*. Biblical Scholarship in America. Chico, CA: Scholars, 1981.

Cowley, A. E. *Aramaic Papyri of the Fifth Century B.C.* 1923. Reprint, Ancient Texts and Translations. Eugene, OR: Wipf & Stock, 2005.

Cox, Harvey. "The Market Is God: Living in the New Dispensation." *The Atlantic* 1 (March 1999). http://www.theatlantic.com/magazine/archive/1999/03/the-market-as-god/306397/?single_page=true.

Craffert, Pieter F. "Taking Stock of the Emic–Etic Distinction in Social-Scientific Interpretations of the New Testament." *Neotestamentica* 28.2 (1994) 1–21.

Crain, William. *Theories of Development: Concepts and Applications*. 3rd ed. Englewood Cliffs, NJ: Prentice-Hall, 1992.

Cromhout, Markus. *Jesus and Identity: Reconstructing Judean Ethnicity in Q*. Matrix 2. Eugene, OR: Cascade, 2007.

———. "Were the Galileans 'Religious Jews' or 'Ethnic Judeans?'" *HTS* 64 (2008) 1279–97.

Crossan, John Dominic. *The Birth of Christianity: Discovering What Happened in the Years Immediately after the Execution of Jesus*. San Francisco: HarperSanFrancisco, 1998.

———. *The Historical Jesus: The Life of a Mediterranean Jewish Peasant*. San Francisco: HarperSanFrancisco, 1991.

Crossan, John Dominic, and Jonathan L. Reed. *Excavating Jesus: Beneath the Stones, Behind the Texts*. New York: HarperSanFrancisco, 2001.

Dalman, Gustaf. *Arbeit und Sitte in Palästina*. 8 vols. Hildesheim: Olms, 1928–2001.

Daly, Herman, and John B. Cobb, Jr. *For the Common Good: Redirecting the Economy toward Community, the Environment, and a Sustainable Future*. 2nd ed. Boston: Beacon, 1994.

Dar, Shimon. "The Agrarian Economy in the Herodian Period." In *The World of the Herods*, edited by Nikos Kokkinos, 305–11. International Conference The World of the Herods and the Nabataeans Held at the British Museum, 17–19 April 2001. Stuttgart: Steiner, 2007.

———. *Landscape and Pattern: An Archaeological Survey of Samaria 800 B.C.E.—636 C.E.* With a historical commentary by Shimon Applebaum. BAR International Series 308. Oxford: BAR, 1986.

Davies, Philip R. *Scribes and Schools: The Canonization of the Hebrew Scriptures.* Library of Ancient Israel. Louisville: Westminster John Knox, 1998.

Davis, Ossie. Eulogy at the Funeral of Malcolm X, Faith Temple Church of God, February 27,1965. The Official Web Site of Malcolm X (Estate of Malcolm X): https://www.malcolmx.com/eulogy/.

DeMaris, Richard E. *The New Testament in Its Ritual World.* New York: Routledge, 2008.

Dietze, C., von. "Peasantry." In *Encyclopaedia of the Social Sciences,* edited by Edwin R. A. Seligman and Alvin Johnson, 12:48–53. 15 vols. New York: Macmillan, 1930–1935.

Donahue, John R. "Tax Collectors and Sinners: An Attempt at an Identification." *CBQ* 33 (1971) 39–61.

Douglas, Mary. *Purity and Danger: An Analysis of Concepts of Pollution and Taboo.* Second impression with corrections. London: Routledge & Kegan Paul, 1978.

Duling, Dennis C. *A Marginal Scribe: Studies in the Gospel of Matthew in a Social-Scientific Perspective.* Matrix 7. Eugene, OR: Cascade Books, 2012.

Dupertius, Rubén R. "Marketplace." In *NIDB* 3:812.

Durkheim, Emile. *The Division of Labor in Society.* Translated by W. D. Halls. With an introduction by Lewis Coser. New York: Free Press, 1984.

———. *The Elementary Forms of Religious Life.* Translated by Karen E. Fields. New York: Free Press, 1995.

Dyck, Bruno. *Management and the Gospel: Luke's Radical Message for the First and Twenty-First Centuries.* New York: Palgrave Macmillan, 2013.

Ebeling, Gerhard. "The Significance of the Critical Historical Method for Church and Theology in Protestantism." In *Word and Faith,* 17–61. Translated by James W. Leitch. Philadelphia: Fortress, 1963.

Edwards, Douglas R. "Identity and Social Location in Roman Galilean Villages." In *Religion, Ethnicity and Identity in Ancient Galilee,* edited by Harold W. Attridge, Dale B. Martin, and Jürgen Zangenberg, 357–74. WUNT 210. Tübingen: Mohr/Siebeck, 2007.

———. *Khirbet Qana: From Jewish Village to Christian Pilgrim Site,* edited by J. H. Humphrey, 101–32. The Roman and Byzantine Near East 3. Portsmouth: JRA, 2002.

———. "The Socio-Economic and Cultural Ethos of the Lower Galilee in the First Century: Implications for the Nascent Jesus Movement." In *The Galilee in Late Antiquity,* edited by Lee I. Levine, 53–73. New York: Jewish Theological Seminary of America, 1992.

Eilberg-Schwartz, Howard. *The Savage in Judaism: An Anthropology of Israelite Religion and Ancient Judaism.* Bloomington: Indiana University Press, 1990.

Eisenstadt, S. N. "Review of Wittfogel's *Oriental Despotism.*" *Journal of Asian Studies* 17 (1958) 435–46.

Elliott, John H. *1 Peter: A New Translation with Introduction and Commentary.* AB 37B. New York: Doubleday, 2001.

———. *Beware the Evil Eye: The Evil Eye in the Bible and the Ancient World.* 4 vols. Eugene, OR: Cascade Books, 2015–2017.

———. "The Evil Eye in the First Testament: The Ecology and Culture of a Pervasive Belief." In *The Bible and the Politics of Exegesis: Essays in Honor of Norman K. Gottwald on His Sixty-Fifth Birthday*, edited by David Jobling, 147–59. Cleveland: Pilgrim, 1991.

———. "The Fear of the Leer. The Evil Eye from the Bible to Li'l Abner." *Foundations and Facets Forum* 4,4 (1988) 42–71.

———. "From Social Description to Social-Scientific Criticism: The History of a Society of Biblical Literature Section 1973–2005." *BTB* 38 (2008) 26–36.

———. "Jesus the Israelite Was neither a 'Jew' nor a 'Christian': On Correcting Misleading Nomenclature." *Journal for the Study of the Historical Jesus* 5.2 (2007) 119–54.

———. "On Wooing Crocodiles for Fun and Profit: Confessions of an Intact Admirer." In *Social Scientific Models for Interpreting the Bible: Essays by the Context Group in Honor of Bruce J. Malina*, edited by John J. Pilch, 5–20. Biblical Interpretation Series 53. Leiden: Brill, 2001.

———. "Patronage and Clientage." In *The Social Sciences and New Testament Interpretation*, edited by Richard L. Rohrbaugh, 144–66. Peabody, MA: Hendrickson, 1996.

———. *What Is Social-Scientific Criticism?* Guides to Biblical Scholarship. Minneapolis: Fortress, 1993.

Elliott, Neil. "Paul and the Politics of Empire." In *Paul and Politics: Ekklesia, Israel, Imperium, Interpretation*, edited by Richard A. Horsley, 17–39. Harrisburg, PA: Trinity, 2000.

Engle, Anita. "An Amphorisk of the Second Temple Period." *PEQ* 109 (1977) 117–22.

Eppstein, Victor. "The Historicity of the Gospel Account of the Cleansing of the Temple." *ZNW* 55 (1964) 42–58.

Esler, Philip F., ed. *Ancient Israel: The Old Testament in Its Social Context*. Minneapolis: Fortress, 2006.

———. *Babatha's Orchard: The Yadin Papyri and an Ancient Jewish Family Tale Retold*. Oxford: Oxford University Press, 2017.

———. "The Context Group Project: An Autobiographical Account." In *Anthropology and Biblical Studies: Avenues of Research*, edited by Mario Aguilar and Louise Lawrence, 46–61. Blandford Forum, UK: DEO, 2004.

———. *The Early Christian World*. 2nd ed. London: Routledge, 2017.

———. *Galatians*. New Testament Readings. London: Routledge, 1998.

———. "Intergroup Conflict and Matthew 23: Towards Responsible Historical Interpretation of a Challenging Text." *BTB* 45 (2015) 38–59.

———, ed. *Modelling Early Christianity: Social-Scientific Studies of the New Testament in Its Context*. London: Routledge, 1995.

———. "An Outline of Social Identity Theory." In *T & T Clark Handbook to Social Identity in the New Testament*, edited by J. Brian Tucker and Coleman A. Baker, 13–40. T & T Clark Handbooks. London: Bloomsbury T. & T. Clark, 2014.

Feldman, Louis H. *Flavius Josephus: Translation and Commentary, Judean Antiquities, Books 1–4*. Leiden: Brill, 1999.

Fiensy, David A. *Christian Origins and the Ancient Economy*. Eugene, OR: Cascade Books, 2014.

———. "Did Large Estates Exist in Lower Galilee in the First Half of the First Century CE?" In *Christian Origins and the Ancient Economy*, 98–117.

———. *Jesus the Galilean: Soundings in a First Century Life*. Piscataway, NJ: Gorgias, 2007.

———. *The Social History of Palestine in the Herodian Period: The Land Is Mine*. Studies in the Bible and Early Christianity 20. Lewiston, NY: Mellen, 1991.

Fiensy, David A., and Ralph K. Hawkins, eds. *The Galilean Economy in the Time of Jesus*. Early Christianity and Its Literature 11. Atlanta: Society of Biblical Literature, 2013.

Fiensy, David A., and James Riley Strange, eds. *Galilee in the Late Second Temple and Mishnaic Periods*. Vol. 1, *Life, Culture, and Society*. Minneapolis: Fortress, 2014.

———, eds. *Galilee in the Late Second Temple and Mishnaic Periods*. Vol. 2, *Cities, Towns, and Villages*. Minneapolis: Fortress, 2015.

Finkelstein, Louis. "The Oldest Midrash: Pre-Rabbinic Ideals and Teachings in the Passover Haggadah." *HTR* 31 (1938) 291–317.

———. *The Pharisees: The Sociological Background of Their Faith*. 2 Vols. Philadelphia: Jewish Publication Society of America, 1940.

———. "Pre-Maccabean Documents in the Passover Haggadah." *HTR* 35 (1942) 291–332.

———. "Pre-Maccabean Documents in the Passover Haggadah." *HTR* 36 (1943) 1–38.

Finley, Moses I. *The Ancient Economy*. Updated ed. Berkeley: University of California Press, 1985.

———. *Ancient History: Evidence and Models*. American Council of Learned Societies. New York: Viking, 1986.

Firth, Raymond. *Symbols: Public and Private*. Ithaca, NY: Cornell University Press, 1973.

Foster, George M. "Peasant Society and the Image of Limited Good." In *Peasant Society: A Reader*, edited by Jack M. Potter, May N. Diaz, and George M. Foster, 300–23. Boston: Little, Brown, 1967.

———. "A Second Look at Limited Good." *Anthropological Quarterly* 45.2 (1972) 57–64.

———. "What Is a Peasant?" In *Peasant Society: A Reader*, edited by Jack M. Potter, et al., 2–14. [original article 1965]

Frankel, Rafael. "Some Oil Presses from Western Galilee." *BASOR* 286 (1992) 39–71.

Frankel, Rafael, and Seán Freyne. "Galilee." In *ABD* 2:879–99.

Fraser, P. M. "The DIOLKOS of Alexandria." *Journal of Egyptian Archaeology* 47 (1961) 134–38.

Frend, W. H. C. *The Rise of Christianity*. Philadelphia: Fortress, 1984.

Freyne, Seán. "Behind the Names: Galileans, Samarians, *Ioudaioi*." In *Galilee through the Centuries: Confluence of Cultures*, edited by Eric M. Meyers, 39–55. Winona Lake, IN: Eisenbrauns, 1999.

———. "Galilean Studies: Old Issues and New Questions." In *Religion, Ethnicity and Identity in Ancient Galilee*, edited by Harold W. Attridge, Dale B. Martin, and Jürgen Zangenberg, 13–29. WUNT 210. Tübingen: Mohr/Siebeck, 2007.

———. *Galilee from Alexander the Great to Hadrian 323 B.C.E. to 135 C.E.* Wilmington, DE: Glazier, 1980.

———. *Galilee, Jesus and the Gospels: Literary Approaches and Historical Investigations*. Philadelphia: Fortress, 1988.

———. "The Geography, Politics, and Economics of Galilee and the Quest for the Historical Jesus." In *Studying the Historical Jesus: Evaluations of the State of Current Research*, edited by Bruce Chilton and Craig A. Evans, 75–121. New Testament Tools and Studies 19. Leiden: Brill, 1994.

———. "Herodian Economics in Galilee: Searching for a Suitable Model." In *Modelling Early Christianity: Social-Scientific Studies of the New Testament in Its Context*, edited by Philip F. Esler, 23–46. London: Routledge, 1995.

———. *Jesus, A Jewish Galilean: A New Reading of the Jesus-Story.* London: T. & T. Clark, 2004.

———. *The Jesus Movement and Its Expansion: Meaning and Mission.* Grand Rapids: Eerdmans, 2014.

———. "Urban–Rural Relations in First-Century Galilee: Some Suggestions from the Literary Sources." In *The Galilee in Late Antiquity*, edited by Lee I. Levine, 75–94. New York: Jewish Theological Seminary of America, 1992.

Fuller, Reginald. *The Foundations of New Testament Christology.* Cambridge, UK: James Clarke, 2002.

Gadamer, Hans-Georg. *Truth and Method.* Translation revised by Joel Weinsheimer and Donald G. Marshall. 2nd revised ed. New York: Crossroad, 2004.

Gaghan, Stephen, dir. *Syriana.* Participant Media, 2005.

Gal, Zvi. *Lower Galilee during the Iron Age.* ASOR Dissertation Series 8. Winona Lake, IN: Eisenbrauns, 1992.

Galtung, Johan. "Religions, Hard and Soft." *Cross Currents* 47 (1997–1998) 437–50.

García Martínez, Florentino. *The Dead Sea Scrolls Translated: The Qumran Texts in English.* Translated by Wilfred G. E. Watson. 2nd ed. Grand Rapids: Eerdmans, 1996.

Geertz, Clifford. "Religion as a Cultural System." In *The Interpretation of Cultures*, 87–125. New York: Basic Books, 1973.

Georgi, Dieter. *Remembering the Poor: The History of Paul's Collection for Jerusalem.* Nashville: Abingdon, 1992.

Gilligan, Carol. *In a Different Voice: Psychological Theory and Women's Development.* Cambridge: Harvard University Press, 1982.

———. *Mapping the Moral Domain: A Contribution of Women's Thinking to Psychological Theory and Education.* Center for the Study of Gender, Education, and Human Development, Harvard University Graduate School of Education. Cambridge: Harvard University Press, 1988.

Goodman, Martin. "The First Jewish Revolt: Social Conflict and the Problem of Debt." *JJS* 33 (1982) 417–27.

———. *State and Society in Roman Galilee, A.D. 132–212.* 2nd ed. Oxford Centre for Postgraduate Hebrew Studies. London: Mitchell, 2000.

Goodspeed, Edgar J. *The Meaning of Ephesians.* Chicago: University of Chicago, 1933.

———. *The New Testament: An American Translation.* Chicago: University of Chicago, 1923.

———. *The Story of the New Testament.* Chicago: University of Chicago, 1918.

Grainger, John D. "'Village Government' in Roman Syria and Arabia." *Levant* 27 (1995) 179–95.

Grant, Elihu. *The Peasantry of Palestine: The Life, Manners and Customs of the Village.* Boston: Pilgrim, 1907.

———. *The People of Palestine: An Enlarged Edition of "The Peasantry of Palestine, Life, Manners and Customs of the Village."* 1921. Reprint, Eugene, OR: Wipf & Stock, 2005.

Grant, Robert M., and David Tracy. *A Short History of the Interpretation of the Bible.* 2nd ed. Minneapolis: Fortress, 1984.

Greene, Kevin. *The Archaeology of the Roman Economy.* Berkeley: University of California Press, 1986.

Gregg, Gary S. *The Middle East: A Cultural Psychology.* New York: Oxford University Press, 2005.

Grondin, Jean. *Introduction to Philosophical Hermeneutics*. Translated by Joel Weinsheimer. Foreword by Hans-Georg Gadamer. Yale Studies in Hermeneutics. New Haven: Yale University Press, 1994.

Halpern, Joel M. *A Serbian Village: Social and Cultural Change in a Yugoslav Community*. Rev. ed. New York: Harper Colophon, 1967.

Hamel, Gildas. *Poverty and Charity in Roman Palestine, First Three Centuries C.E.* Near Eastern Studies 23. Berkeley: University of California Press, 1990.

Hanson, K. C. "The Galilean Fishing Economy and the Jesus Tradition." *BTB* 27 (1997) 99–111.

———. "How Honorable! How Shameful! A Cultural Analysis of Matthew's Makarisms and Reproaches." *Semeia* 68 (1994 [1996]) 81–111.

———. "Jesus and the Social Bandits." In *The Social Setting of Jesus and the Gospels*, edited by Wolfgang Stegemann, Bruce J. Malina, and Gerd Theissen, 283–300. Minneapolis: Fortress, 2002.

———. *Jesus in Galilean Social Context*. Matrix. Eugene, OR: Cascade Books, forthcoming.

———. "The Theodotus Inscription." 2002. https://www.kchanson.com/ANCDOCS/greek/theodotus.html.

Hanson, K. C., and Douglas E. Oakman. *Palestine in the Time of Jesus: Social Structures and Social Conflicts*. 2nd ed. Minneapolis: Fortress, 2008.

Hanson, Richard S. *Tyrian Influence in the Upper Galilee*. Cambridge, MA: ASOR, 1980.

Harnack, Adolf von. *Marcion: The Gospel of the Alien God*. Translated by John E. Steely and Lyle D. Bierma. Durham, NC: Labyrinth, 1990.

Harper, George McLean, Jr. "Village Administration in the Roman Province of Syria." *Yale Classical Studies* 1 (1928) 105–68.

Hasel, Gerhard F. *Old Testament Theology: Basic Issues in the Current Debate*. Grand Rapids: Eerdmans, 1972.

Hauck, Friedrich. "Mamōnas." In *TDNT* 4:388–90.

Heisig, James W. "Symbolism." In *Encyclopedia of Religion*, edited by Mircea Eliade, 14:198–208. 16 vols. New York: Macmillan, 1987.

Hengel, Martin. *Judaism and Hellenism: Studies in Their Encounter in Palestine during the Early Hellenistic Period*. Translated by John Bowden. 2 vols. in 1. Philadelphia: Fortress, 1974.

Herzog, William R., II. *Jesus, Justice, and the Reign of God: A Ministry of Liberation*. Louisville: Westminster John Knox, 2000.

———. *Parables as Subversive Speech: Jesus as Pedagogue of the Oppressed*. Louisville: Westminster John Knox, 1994.

Hezser, Catherine. *Jewish Literacy in Roman Palestine*. Texte und Studien zum Antiken Judentum 81. Tübingen: Mohr/Siebeck, 2001.

———. *The Social Structure of the Rabbinic Movement in Roman Palestine*. Texte und Studien zum Antiken Judentum 66. Tübingen: Mohr/Siebeck, 1997.

Hirschfeld, Yizhar. "Fortified Manor Houses of the Ruling Class in the Herodian Kingdom of Judaea." In *The World of the Herods*, edited by Nikos Kokkinos, 197–226. International Conference The World of the Herods and the Nabataeans Held at the British Museum, 17–19 April 2001. Stuttgart: Steiner, 2007.

Hirschfeld, Yizhar, Gideon Foerster, and Fanny Vitto. "Tiberias." In *The New Encyclopedia of Archaeological Excavations in the Holy Land*, edited by Ephraim Stern, 4:1464–73. 5 vols. New York: Simon & Schuster, 1993, 2008.

Hobsbawm, Eric J. "Peasants and Politics." *JPS* 1 (1973) 3–22.

———. *Primitive Rebels*. New York: Norton, 1959.

Hoehner, Harold W. *Herod Antipas*. SNTSMS 17. Cambridge: Cambridge University Press, 1972.

Hoenig, Sidney B. "The Ancient City-Square: The Forerunner of the Synagogue." In *ANRW* II 19.1, 448–76. Berlin: de Gruyter, 1979.

Hollenbach, Paul W. "The Conversion of Jesus: From Jesus the Baptizer to Jesus the Healer." In *ANRW* II. 25, 196–219. Berlin: de Gruyter, 1982.

Hopkins, David C. "Agriculture." In *The Oxford Encyclopedia of Archaeology in the Near East*, edited by Eric M. Meyers, 1:22–30. 5 vols. Oxford: Oxford University Press, 1997.

Hopkins, Keith. "Rome, Taxes, Rent and Trade." In *The Ancient Economy*, edited by Walter Scheidel and Sitta von Reden, 190–230. New York: Routledge, 2002.

Hornblower, Simon, and Antony Spawforth. *The Oxford Classical Dictionary*. 3rd ed. Oxford: Oxford University Press, 2003.

Horsley, Richard A. "Archaeology and the Villages of Upper Galilee: A Dialogue with Archaeologists." *BASOR* 297 (February 1995) 1–16.

———. *Archaeology, History, and Society in Galilee: The Social Context of Jesus and the Rabbis*. Valley Forge, PA: Trinity, 1996.

———. *Galilee: History, Politics, People*. Valley Forge, PA: Trinity, 1995.

———. *Jesus and Magic: Freeing the Gospel Stories from Modern Misconceptions*. Eugene, OR: Cascade, 2014.

———. *Jesus and the Politics of Roman Palestine*. Columbia: University of South Carolina Press, 2014.

———, ed. *Paul and Empire: Religion and Power in Roman Imperial Society*. Harrisburg, PA: Trinity, 1997.

———, ed. *Paul and Politics: Ekklesia, Israel, Imperium, Interpretation*. Harrisburg, PA: Trinity, 2000.

Horsley, Richard A., and John S. Hanson. *Bandits, Prophets, and Messiahs: Popular Movements at the Time of Jesus*. San Francisco: Harper & Row, 1985.

Hultgren, Arland. *Christ and His Benefits: Christology and Redemption in the New Testament*. Philadelphia: Fortress, 1987.

Humphreys, S. C. "History, Economics, and Anthropology: The Work of Karl Polanyi." *History and Theory* 8 (1969) 165–212.

Hutchins, Robert M. "Universal and Particular." In *Syntopicon*, 957–74. Chicago: Encyclopedia Britannica, 1952.

Ingram, Paul O. *Wrestling with the Ox: A Theology of Religious Experience*. 1997. Reprint, Eugene, OR: Wipf & Stock, 2006.

Jacobson, Arland D. *The First Gospel: An Introduction to Q*. 1992. Reprint, Eugene, OR: Wipf & Stock, 2005.

Jaspers, Karl. *The Origin and Goal of History*. Translated by Michael Bullock. New Haven: Yale University Press, 1953.

Jenkins, Philip. *The Next Christendom: The Coming of Global Christianity*. 3rd ed. Oxford: Oxford University Press, 2011.

———. "The Next Christianity." *The Atlantic* 10 (2002) http://www.theatlantic.com/past/docs/issues/2002/10/jenkins.htm.

Jensen, Morten Hørning. "Herod Antipas in Galilee: Friend or Foe of the Historical Jesus?" *Journal for the Study of the Historical Jesus* 5.1 (2007) 7–32.

——. *Herod Antipas in Galilee: The Literary and Archaeological Sources on the Reign of Herod Antipas and Its Socio-Economic Impact on Galilee*. WUNT 215. Tübingen: Mohr/Siebeck, 2006.

Jeremias, Joachim. *Jerusalem in the Time of Jesus*. Translated by F. H. Cave and C. H. Cave. Philadelphia: Fortress, 1969.

——. *The Parables of Jesus*. Translated by S. H. Hooke. 2nd ed. New York: Scribner, 1972.

Jewitt, Robert. *Paul, the Apostle to America: Cultural Trends and Pauline Scholarship*. Louisville: Westminster John Knox, 1994.

Jonas, Hans. *The Gnostic Religion: The Message of the Alien God and the Beginnings of Christianity*. 2nd ed. Boston: Beacon, 1963.

Jones, A. H. M., J. R. Martindale, and J. Morris. *Prosopography of the Later Roman Empire*. 3 vols. Cambridge: Cambridge University Press, 1971–1992.

Josephus, Flavius. *Josephus*. Translated by St. J. Thackeray, Ralph Marcus, Allen Wikgren, and Louis H. Feldman. LCL. 9 vols. Cambridge: Harvard University Press, 1926–1981.

Juergensmeyer, Mark. *Terror in the Mind of God: The Global Rise of Religious Violence*. Updated ed. Comparative Studies in Religion and Society. Berkeley: University of California Press, 2001.

Kaplan, David, and Robert A. Manners. *Culture Theory*. Foundations of Modern Anthropology. Englewood Cliffs, NJ: Prentice-Hall, 1972.

Kautsky, John H. *The Politics of Aristocratic Empires*. Chapel Hill, NC: University of North Carolina Press, 1982.

Kähler, Martin. *The So-Called Historical Jesus and the Historic, Biblical Christ*. Translated by Carl E. Braaten. Seminar Editions. Philadelphia: Fortress, 1964.

Käsemann, Ernst. "The Problem of the Historical Jesus." In *Essays on New Testament Themes*, 15–47. Translated by W. J. Montague. Studies in Biblical Theology 41. Naperville, IL: Allenson, 1964.

Kearney, Michael. "Peasantry." In *International Encyclopedia of the Social Sciences*, edited by William A. Darity Jr., 6:195–96. 2nd. ed. 9 vols. Detroit: Thomson Gale, 2008.

Kegan, Robert. *In Over Our Heads: The Mental Demands of Modern Life*. Cambridge: Harvard University Press, 1994.

Klausner, Joseph. *Jesus of Nazareth: His Life, Times, and Teaching*. Translated by Herbert Danby. New York: Macmillan, 1925.

Kloppenborg [Verbin], John S. *Conflict and Invention: Literary, Rhetorical and Social Studies on the Sayings Gospel Q*. Valley Forge, PA: Trinity, 1995.

——. "Discursive Practices in the Sayings Gospel Q." In *Synoptic Problems: Collected Essays*, 366–406. WUNT 329. Tübingen: Mohr/Siebeck, 2014.

——. *Excavating Q: The History and Setting of the Sayings Gospel*. Minneapolis: Fortress, 2000.

——. *The Formation of Q: Trajectories in Ancient Wisdom Collections*. Studies in Antiquity and Christianity. Philadelphia: Fortress, 1987.

——. "The Formation of Q and Antique Instructional Genres." *JBL* 105 (1986) 443–62.

——. "The Growth and Impact of Agricultural Tenancy in Jewish Palestine (III BCE–I CE)." *Journal of the Economic and Social History of the Orient* 51 (2008) 33–66.

——. "Literary Convention, Self-Evidence and the Social History of the Q People." *Semeia* 55 (1991) 77–102.

——. *Q Parallels: Synopsis, Critical Notes, and Concordance.* Foundations and Facets. Sonoma, CA: Polebridge, 1988.

——. *Q, The Earliest Gospel: An Introduction to the Original Stories and Sayings of Jesus.* Louisville: Westminster John Knox, 2008.

——. "The Sayings Gospel Q: Literary and Stratigraphic Problems." In *Symbols and Strata: Essays on the Sayings Gospel Q,* edited by R. Uro, 1–66. PFES 65. Helsinki and Göttingen: Finnish Exegetical Society and Vandenhoeck & Ruprecht, 1996.

——. "The Sayings Gospel Q: Recent Opinion on the People behind the Document." *Currents in Research: Biblical Studies* 1 (1993) 9–34.

——. "The Sayings Gospel Q and the Quest of the Historical Jesus." *HTR* 89 (1996) 307–44.

——. *The Shape of Q: Signal Essays on the Sayings Gospel.* Minneapolis: Fortress, 1994.

Kluckhohn, Florence R., and Fred L. Strodtbeck. *Variations in Value Orientations.* Westport, CT: Glenwood, 1961.

Kohlberg, Lawrence. *The Philosophy of Moral Development: Moral Stages and the Idea of Justice.* San Francisco: Harper & Row, 1981.

Lambert, Yves. "Religion in Modernity as a New Axial Age: Secularization or New Religious Forms?" *Sociology of Religion* 60 (1999) 301–33.

Langer, Susanne K. *Philosophy in a New Key: A Study in the Symbolism of Reason, Rite, and Art.* Cambridge: Harvard University Press, 1942.

Larsen, Matthew D. C. *Gospels before the Book.* New York: Oxford University Press, 2018.

LeClerc, Ivor. *Whitehead's Metaphysics: An Introductory Exposition.* New York: Macmillan, 1958.

Lee, Spike, dir. *Malcolm X.* Based on the autobiography of Malcolm X by Malcolm X and Alex Haley. Written by Arnold Perl and Spike Lee. Produced by Spike Lee et al. 1992. 1 DVD. Burbank, CA: Warner Home Video, 2005.

Lenski, Gerhard E. *Power and Privilege: A Theory of Social Stratification.* 2nd ed. Chapel Hill: University of North Carolina, 1984.

Lenski, Gerhard E., and Jean Lenski. *Human Societies: An Introduction to Macrosociology.* 5th ed. New York: McGraw-Hill, 1987.

Levine, Lee I., ed. *The Galilee in Late Antiquity.* New York: Jewish Theological Seminary of America, 1992.

——. "Synagogues." In *The New Encyclopedia of Archaeological Excavations in the Holy Land,* edited by Ephraim Stern, 4:1421–24. 5 vols. New York: Simon & Schuster, 1993, 2008.

Lewis, Naphtali, and Meyer Reinhold, eds. *Roman Civilization.* Vol. 2, *The Empire.* New York: Columbia University, 1955.

Lindbeck, George A. *The Nature of Doctrine: Religion and Theology in a Postliberal Age.* Philadelphia: Westminster, 1984.

Loffreda, Stanislao, and Vassilios Tzaferis. "Capernaum." In *The New Encyclopedia of Archaeological Excavations in the Holy Land,* edited by Ephraim Stern, 1:291–96. 5 vols. New York: Simon & Schuster, 1993, 2008.

Lundeen, Lyman T. *Risk and Rhetoric in Religion: Whitehead's Theory of Language and the Discourse of Faith.* Philadelphia: Fortress, 1972.

Luther, Martin. "Theses for the Heidelberg Disputation." In *Martin Luther: Selections from His Writings,* edited by John Dillenberger, 500–503. Garden City, NY: Doubleday, 1961.

Mack, Burton L. *The Lost Gospel: The Book of Q and Christian Origins*. San Francisco: HarperSanFrancisco, 1993.

———. *A Myth of Innocence: Mark and Christian Origins*. Minneapolis: Fortress, 1988.

MacMullen, Ramsay. "Market-Days in the Roman Empire." *Phoenix* 24 (1970) 333–41.

———. *Roman Social Relations*. New Haven: Yale University Press, 1974.

Magan, Yitzhak. "Samaritan Synagogues." In *The New Encyclopedia of Archaeological Excavations in the Holy Land*, edited by Ephraim Stern, 4:1424–27. 5 vols. New York: Simon & Schuster, 1993, 2008.

———. *The Stone Vessel Industry in the Second Temple Period*. Jerusalem: Israel Exploration Society, 2002.

Magness, Jodi. *Stone and Dung, Oil and Spit: Jewish Daily Life in the Time of Jesus*. Grand Rapids: Eerdmans, 2011.

Malina, Bruce J. *Christian Origins and Cultural Anthropology: Practical Models for Biblical Interpretation*. 1986. Reprint, Eugene, OR: Wipf & Stock, 2010.

———. "Interpretation: Reading, Abduction, Metaphor." In *The Bible and the Politics of Exegesis: Essays in Honor of Norman K. Gottwald on His Sixty-Fifth Birthday*, edited by David Jobling, Peggy L. Day, and Gerald T. Sheppard, 253–66. Cleveland, OH: Pilgrim, 1991.

———. "Limited Good and the Social World of Early Christianity." *BTB* 8 (1978) 162–76.

———. *The New Testament World: Insights from Cultural Anthropology*. 1st ed. Atlanta: John Knox, 1981.

———. *The New Testament World: Insights from Cultural Anthropology*. Rev. ed. Louisville: Westminster John Knox, 1993.

———. *The New Testament World: Insights from Cultural Anthropology*. 3rd ed. Louisville: Westminster John Knox, 2001.

———. "Patron and Client: The Analogy behind Synoptic Theology." *Forum* 4.1 (1988) 1–32. Reprinted in *The Social World of Jesus and the Gospels*, 143–75.

———. *The Social Gospel of Jesus: The Kingdom of God in Mediterranean Perspective*. Minneapolis: Fortress, 2001.

———. *The Social World of Jesus and the Gospels*. London: Routledge, 1996.

———. "Wealth and Poverty in the New Testament and Its World." *Interpretation* 41 (1987) 354–67.

Malina, Bruce J., and Richard L. Rohrbaugh. *Social-Science Commentary on the Synoptic Gospels*. 1st ed. Minneapolis: Fortress, 1992.

———. *Social-Science Commentary on the Synoptic Gospels*. 2nd ed. Minneapolis: Fortress, 2003.

Malina, Bruce J., and Chris Seeman. "Envy." In *Handbook of Biblical Social Values*, edited by John J. Pilch and Bruce J. Malina, 51–54. Matrix 10. 3rd ed. Eugene, OR: Cascade Books, 2016.

Marx, Karl. "The Eighteenth Brumaire of Louis Bonaparte." In *Peasants and Peasant Societies: Selected Readings*, edited by Teodor Shanin, 229–37. Harmondsworth, UK: Penguin, 1971.

Mason, Steve. "Jews, Judaeans, Judaizing, Judaism: Problems of Categorization in Ancient History." *JSJ* 38 (2007) 457–512.

Mattila, Sharon Lea. "Jesus and the 'Middle Peasants?' Problematizing a Social-Scientific Concept." *CBQ* 72 (2010) 291–313.

———. "Revisiting Jesus' Capernaum: A Village of Only Subsistence-Level Fishers and Farmers?" In *The Galilean Economy in the Time of Jesus*, edited by David A. Fiensy and Ralph K. Hawkins, 75–138. Early Christianity and Its Literature 11. Atlanta: Society of Biblical Literature, 2013.

McCown, Chester C. "*Ho Tektōn.*" In *Studies in Early Christianity*, edited by Shirley Jackson Case, 173–89. New York: The Century, 1928.

McFague, Sallie. *Metaphorical Theology: Models of God in Religious Language*. Philadelphia: Fortress, 1982.

McKenzie, John L. *A Theology of the Old Testament*. Garden City, NY: Doubleday, 1974.

McRobbie, Kenneth. *Humanity, Society and Commitment: On Karl Polanyi*. Critical Perspectives on Historic Issues 4. Montréal: Black Rose, 1994.

Meeks, Wayne A. *The First Urban Christians: The Social World of the Apostle Paul*. New Haven: Yale University Press, 1983.

———. "The Image of the Androgyne: Some Uses of a Symbol in Earliest Christianity." *History of Religions* 13 (1974) 165–208.

———. "In One Body: The Unity of Humankind in Colossians and Ephesians." In *God's Christ and His People: Studies in Honour of Nils Alstrup Dahl*, 209–21. Oslo: Universitetsforlaget, 1977.

Meier, John P. *A Marginal Jew: Rethinking the Historical Jesus*. 5 vols. New York: Doubleday; New Haven: Yale University Press, 1991–2016.

Meyers, Carol. "Temple, Jerusalem." In *ABD* 6:350–69.

Meyers, Carol L., and Eric M. Meyers. "Sepphoris." In *Oxford Encyclopedia of Archaeology in the Near East*, edited by Eric M. Meyers, 4:527–36. 5 vols. Oxford: Oxford University Press, 1997.

Meyers, Eric M. "An Archaeological Response to a New Testament Scholar." *BASOR* 297 (February 1995) 17–26.

———, ed. *Oxford Encyclopedia of Archaeology in the Near East*. 5 vols. Oxford: Oxford Uni-versity Press, 1997.

———. "Roman Sepphoris in Light of New Archaeological Evidence and Recent Research." In *The Galilee in Late Antiquity*, edited by Lee I. Levine, 321–38. New York: Jewish Theological Seminary of America, 1992.

———. "Sepphoris, the Ornament of All Galilee." *BA* 49 (1986) 4–19.

Meyers, Eric M., and R. Martin-Nagy, eds. *Sepphoris in Galilee: Crosscurrents of Culture*. Raleigh: North Carolina Museum of Modern Art/Eisenbrauns, 1997.

Millett, Paul C. "Monopolies." In *OCD*, 994.

Mintz, Sidney W. "A Note on the Definition of Peasantries." *JPS* 1 (1973) 91–106.

Moore, Barrington. *Social Origins of Dictatorship and Democracy: Lord and Peasant in the Making of the Modern World*. Boston: Beacon, 1966.

Morgan, Robert, and John Barton. *Biblical Interpretation*. Oxford Bible Series. Oxford: Oxford University Press, 1988.

Morley, Neville. "The Early Roman Empire: Distribution." In *The Cambridge Economic History of the Greco-Roman World*, edited by Walter Scheidel, Ian Morris, and Richard Saller, 570–91. Cambridge: Cambridge University Press, 2007.

———. *Theories, Models and Concepts in Ancient History*. Approaching the Ancient World. London: Routledge, 2004.

———. *Trade in Classical Antiquity*. Cambridge, UK: Cambridge University Press, 2007.

Morris, Brian. *Anthropological Studies of Religion: An Introduction*. Cambridge: Cambridge University Press, 1987.

Moxnes, Halvor. "The Construction of Galilee as a Place for the Historical Jesus." *BTB* 31 (2001) 26–37, 64–77.

Murdock, George P. "Review of Wittfogel's *Oriental Despotism*." *American Anthropologist* n.s. 59 (1957) 545–47.

Murphy-O'Connor, Jerome. "Christological Anthropology in Phil, II, 6–11." *RB* 83 (1976) 25–50.

Myers, Ched. *Binding the Strong Man: A Political Reading of Mark's Story of Jesus*. Maryknoll, NY: Orbis, 1988.

Nasr, Seyyed Hossein, editor-in-chief. *The Study Quran: A New Translation and Commentary*. San Francisco: HarperOne, 2015.

Nestle, Eberhard. "Mammon." In *Encyclopaedia Biblica*, edited by T. K. Cheyne and J. Sutherland Black, 3:2912–15. 4 vols. New York: Macmillan, 1913.

Netzer, Ehud, and Zev Weiss. *Zippori*. Jerusalem: The Israel Exploration Society, 1994.

Neyrey, Jerome H. "Bewitched in Galatia: Paul in Social Science Perspective." *CBQ* 50 (1988) 72–100.

———. *Christ Is Community: The Christologies of the New Testament*. Good News Studies 13. Wilmington, DE: Glazier, 1985.

———. "Limited Good." In *Handbook of Biblical Social Values*, edited by John J. Pilch and Bruce J. Malina, 103–6. Matrix 10. 3rd ed. Eugene, OR: Cascade Books, 2016.

———. "'My Lord and My God': The Divinity of Jesus in John's Gospel." *SBLSP* 25 (1986) 152–71.

———. *Render to God: New Testament Understandings of the Divine*. Minneapolis: Fortress, 2004.

Neyrey, Jerome H., and Anselm C. Hagedorn. "'It Was Out of Envy That They Handed Jesus Over' (Mark 15:10): The Anatomy of Envy and the Gospel of Mark." *JSNT* 69 (1998) 15–56.

Neyrey, Jerome H., and Richard L. Rohrbaugh. "'He Must Increase, I Must Decrease' (John 3:30): A Cultural and Social Interpretation." *CBQ* 63 (2001) 464–83.

Nickelsburg, George W. E. *1 Enoch 1: A Commentary on the Book of 1 Enoch, Chapters 1—36; 81—108*. Hermeneia. Minneapolis: Fortress, 2001.

———. "Enoch, First Book of." In *ABD* 2:508–16.

———. "Enoch, Levi, and Peter: Recipients of Revelation in Upper Galilee." *JBL* 100 (1981) 575–600.

———. "Son of Man." In *ABD* 6:137–50.

Niebuhr, H. Richard. *Christ and Culture*. 1951. Reprint, San Francisco: HarperSanFrancisco, 2001.

Nord, Warren A. *Religion and American Education: Rethinking a National Dilemma*. Chapel Hill: University of North Carolina Press, 1995.

North, Douglass C. *Structure and Change in Economic History*. New York: Norton, 1981.

Nun, Mendel. *Ancient Anchorages and Harbours Around the Sea of Galilee*. Kibbutz Ein Gev, Israel: Kinnereth Sailing Co., 1988.

———. *The Sea of Galilee and Its Fishermen in the New Testament*. Kibbutz Ein Gev, Israel: Kinnereth Sailing Co., 1989.

Nussbaum, Martha C. *Creating Capabilities: The Human Development Approach*. Cambridge: Belknap Press of Harvard University Press, 2011.

Oakman, Douglas E. "'All the Surrounding Country': The Countryside in Luke-Acts." In *Jesus and the Peasants*, 132–63.

———. "The Ancient Economy and St. John's Apocalypse." In *Jesus and the Peasants*, 70–83.

———. "Batteries of Power: Coinage in the Judean Temple System." In *In Other Words: Essays on Social Science Methods and the New Testament in Honor of Jerome H. Neyrey*, edited by Anselm C. Hagedorn, Zeba A. Crook, and Eric Stewart, 171–85. Sheffield: Sheffield Phoenix, 2007.

———. "Begrenzte Güter in der Biblischen Welt: Kulturelle, Soziale und Technologische Perspektiven." In *Alte Texte in Neuen Kontexten: Wo Steht die Sozialwissenschaftliche Bibelexegese?* edited by Richard E. DeMaris and Wolfgang Stegemann, 301–14. Translated by Anselm Hagedorn. Stuttgart: Kohlhammer, 2014.

———. "The Economics of Palestine." In *Jesus and the Peasants*, 98–107.

———. *Jesus and the Economic Questions of His Day*. Studies in the Bible and Early Christianity 8. Lewiston: Mellen, 1986.

———. *Jesus and the Peasants*. Matrix 4. Eugene, OR: Cascade Books, 2008.[1]

———. *Jesus, Debt, and the Lord's Prayer*. Foreword by K. C. Hanson. Eugene, OR: Cascade, 2014.

———. "Jesus, Q, and Ancient Literacy in Social Perspective." In *Jesus and the Peasants*, 298–308.

———. "Jesus the Tax Resister." In *Jesus and the Peasants*, 280–97; also *Jesus, Debt, and the Lord's Prayer*, chapter 4.

———. "The Lord's Prayer in Social Perspective." In *Jesus and the Peasants*, 199–242; also *Jesus, Debt, and the Lord's Prayer*, chapter 3.

———. "Models and Archaeology in the Social Interpretation of Jesus." In *Jesus and the Peasants*, 245–79.

———. *The Political Aims of Jesus: Peasant Politics and Herodian Galilee*. Minneapolis: Fortress, 2012.

Oxford English Dictionary. *The Compact Edition of the Oxford English Dictionary*. Complete text reproduced micrographically. 2 vols. Glasgow: Oxford University Press, 1971.

Ogden, C. K., and I. A. Richards. *The Meaning of Meaning*. New York: Harcourt, Brace, 1923.

Overman, J. Andrew. "Debate: Was the Galilean Economy Oppressive or Prosperous? A. Late Second Temple Galilee: A Picture of Relative Economic Health." In *Galilee in the Late Second Temple and Mishnaic Periods*, edited by David A. Fiensy and James Riley Strange. Vol. 1, *Life, Culture, and Society*, 357–65. Minneapolis: Fortress, 2014.

Palmer, Richard E. *Hermeneutics: Interpretation Theory in Schleiermacher, Dilthey, Heidegger, and Gadamer*. Evanston, IL: Northwestern University Press, 1969.

Parkin, Tim G. *Demography and Roman Society*. Baltimore: Johns Hopkins University Press, 1992.

Parks, Sharon Daloz. *Big Questions, Worthy Dreams: Mentoring Young Adults in Their Search for Meaning, Purpose, and Faith*. San Francisco: Josey-Bass, 2000.

Parsons, Talcott. "A Paradigm of the Human Condition." In *Action Theory and the Human Condition*, 352–433. New York: Free Press, 1978.

———. *The System of Modern Societies*. Englewood Cliffs, NJ: Prentice-Hall, 1971.

Patterson, Stephen J. "The Gospel of Thomas and the Synoptic Tradition: A Forschungsbericht and Critique." *Forum* 8.1–2 (1992) 45–97.

---

1. See Acknowledgments for information on original publication of Oakman chapters in this volume.

———. "Wisdom in Q and *Thomas*." In *In Search of Wisdom: Essays in Memory of John G. Gammie*, edited by Leo G. Perdue et al., 187–221. Louisville: Westminster John Knox, 1993.

———. "The View from across the Euphrates." *HTR* 104 (2011) 411–31.

Pilch, John J., ed. *Social Scientific Models for Interpreting the Bible: Essays by the Context Group in Honor of Bruce J. Malina*. Biblical Interpretation Series 53. Leiden: Brill, 2001.

Pilch, John J., and Bruce J. Malina, eds. *Handbook of Biblical Social Values*. 3rd ed. Matrix 10. Eugene, OR: Cascade Books, 2016.

Piper, Ronald A. *The Gospel behind the Gospels: Current Studies on Q*. NovTSup 75. Leiden: Brill, 1995.

———. "Matthew 7:7–11 Par. Luke 11:9–13: Evidence of Design and Argument in the Collection of Jesus' Sayings." In *The Shape of Q: Signal Essays on the Sayings Gospel*, edited by John S. Kloppenborg, 131–37. Minneapolis: Fortress, 1994.

———. "Satan, Demons and the Absence of Exorcisms in the Fourth Gospel." In *Christology, Controversy, and Community: New Testament Essays in Honour of David R. Catchpole*, ed. David G. Horrell and Christopher M. Tucket, 253–78. NovTSup 99. Leiden: Brill, 2000.

———. "Wealth, Poverty, and Subsistence in Q." In *From Quest to Q: Festschrift James M. Robinson*, edited by Jon Ma. Asgeirsson, Kristin de Troyer, and Marvin W. Meyer, 219–64. BETL 146. Leuven: Leuven University Press, 2000.

———. *Wisdom in the Q-Tradition: The Aphoristic Teaching of Jesus*. SNTSMS 61. Cambridge: Cambridge University Press, 1989.

Plato. *Republic*. Translated by G. M. A. Grube. Edited by C. D. C. Reeve. Indianapolis: Hackett, 1992.

Plattner, Stuart, ed. *Economic Anthropology*. Stanford: Stanford University Press, 1989.

Polanyi, Karl. "Aristotle Discovers the Economy." In *Trade and Market in the Early Empires: Economies in History and Theory*, edited by Karl Polanyi, Conrad M. Arensberg, and Harry W. Pearson, 64–93. Glencoe, IL: Free Press, 1957.

———. *The Great Transformation: The Political and Economic Origins of Our Time*. 2nd ed. Boston: Beacon, 2001.

———. *The Livelihood of Man*. Edited by Harry W. Pearson. Studies in Social Discontinuity. New York: Academic Press, 1977.

Polanyi, Karl, Conrad Arensberg, and Harry W. Pearson, eds. *Trade and Market in the Early Empires: Economies in History and Theory*. Glencoe, IL: Free Press, 1957.

Priest, John. "The Testament of Moses." In *OTP* 1:919–34.

Randerson, James. "World's Richest 1 percent Own 40 Percent of All Wealth, UN Report Discovers." *The Guardian* (6 December 2006) http://www.guardian.co.uk/money/2006/dec/06/business.internationalnews.

Rappaport, Roy A. *Ritual and Religion in the Making of Humanity*. Cambridge Studies in Social and Cultural Anthropology. Cambridge: Cambridge University Press, 1999.

Rasmussen, Larry L. *Earth Community, Earth Ethics*. Maryknoll, NY: Orbis, 1998.

Rathbone, Dominic W. "Roman Egypt." In *The Cambridge Economic History of the Greco-Roman World*, edited by Walter Scheidel, Ian Morris, and Richard Saller, 698–719. Cambridge: Cambridge University Press, 2007.

Räisänen, Heikki. "Attacking the Book, not the People: Marcion and the Jewish Roots of Christianity." In *Marcion, Muhammad and the Mahatma*, 64–80.

———. *Marcion, Muhammad and the Mahatma: Exegetical Perspectives on the Encounter of Cultures and Faiths*. The Edward Cadbury Lectures at the University of Birmingham 1995/1996. London: SCM, 1997.

Reagan, Ronald. "Remarks at a Meeting with Reagan–Bush Campaign Leadership Groups." In *The National Archives and Records Administration: Ronald Reagan Presidential Library & Museum* (October 1984). https://www.reaganlibrary.gov/research/speeches/103084b.

Redfield, Robert. *The Little Community and Peasant Society and Culture*. Chicago: Phoenix, 1960.

———. *Tepoztlán, a Mexican Village: A Study of Folk Life*. University of Chicago Publications in Anthropology. Ethnological Series. Chicago: University of Chicago Press, 1930.

Reed, Jonathan L. *Archaeology and the Galilean Jesus: A Re-Examination of the Evidence*. Harrisburg, PA: Trinity, 2000.

———. "Galilean Archaeology and the Historical Jesus." In *Jesus Then and Now: Images of Jesus in History and Christology*, edited by Marvin Meyer and Charles Hughes, 113–29. Harrisburg, PA: Trinity, 2001.

———. "Mortality, Morbidity, and Economics in Jesus' Galilee." In *Galilee in the Late Second Temple and Mishnaic Periods*. Vol. 1, *Life, Culture, and Society*, edited by David A. Fiensy and James Riley Strange, 242–52. Minneapolis: Fortress, 2014.

———. "The Social Map of Q." In *Conflict and Invention: Literary, Rhetorical and Social Studies on the Sayings Gospel Q*, edited by John S. Kloppenborg, 17–36. Valley Forge, PA: Trinity, 1995.

Reventlow, Henning Graf. "Theology (Biblical), History of." In *ABD* 6:483–505.

Riesner, Rainer. "Synagogues in Jerusalem." In *The Book of Acts in Its First-Century Setting*, edited by Richard Bauckham, 179–211. Grand Rapids: Eerdmans, 1995.

Robinson, James M. "The Jesus of Q as Liberation Theologian." In *The Gospel behind the Gospels: Current Studies on Q*, edited by Ronald A. Piper, 259–74. NovTSup 75. Leiden: Brill, 1995.

———. "*Logoi Sophon*: On the Gattung of Q." In *Trajectories through Early Christianity*, edited by James M. Robinson and Helmut Koester, 71–113. 1971. Reprint, Eugene, OR: Wipf & Stock, 2006.

———, gen. ed. *The Nag Hammadi Library*. Rev. ed. San Francisco: Harper & Row, 1988.

Robinson, James M., Paul Hoffmann, and John S. Kloppenborg, eds. *The Critical Edition of Q: Synopsis Including the Gospels of Matthew and Luke, Mark and Thomas with English, German, and French Translations of Q and Thomas*. Hermeneia Supplement. Minneapolis: Fortress, 2000.

———, eds. *The Sayings Gospel Q in Greek and English with Parallels from the Gospels of Mark and Thomas*. Minneapolis: Fortress, 2002.

Rogerson, John W. *An Introduction to the Bible*. Rev. ed. London: Equinox, 2005.

———. *A Theology of the Old Testament: Cultural Memory, Communication, and Being Human*. Minneapolis: Fortress, 2009.

Rogerson, John W., Christopher Rowland, and Barnabas Lindars. *The Study and Use of the Bible*. The History of Christian Theology 2. Grand Rapids: Eerdmans, 1988.

Rohden, Paul von, et al. *Prosopographia Imperii Romani: Saec. I. II. III.* 2nd ed. 8 vols. Akademie der Wissenschaften der DDR, 1933–2015. Searchable version http://pir.bbaw.de.

Rohrbaugh, Richard L. *The Biblical Interpreter: An Agrarian Bible in an Industrial Age.* 1978. Reprint, Eugene, OR: Wipf & Stock, 2018.

———. "Models and Muddles: Discussions of the Social Facets Seminar." *Forum* 3.2 (1987) 22–33.

———. *The New Testament in Cross-Cultural Perspective.* Matrix 1. Eugene, OR: Cascade Books, 2007.

———. "A Peasant Reading of the Parable of the Talents/Pounds: A Text of Terror?" In *The New Testament in Cross-Cultural Perspective*, 109–23.

Ronen, Avraham, Zvi Gal, and Mordechai Aviam. "Galilee." In *The New Encyclopedia of Archaeological Excavations in the Holy Land*, edited by Ephraim Stern, 2:449–58. 5 vols. New York: Simon & Schuster, 1993, 2008.

Rostovtzeff, Michael. *Social and Economic History of the Hellenistic World.* 3 vols. Oxford: Clarendon, 1941.

———. *The Social and Economic History of the Roman Empire.* 2 vols. Oxford: Clarendon, 1957.

Safrai, Ze'ev. *The Economy of Roman Palestine.* London: Routledge, 1994.

Said, Edward W. *Orientalism.* New York: Vintage, 1979.

Saldarini, Anthony J. *Jesus and Passover.* New York: Paulist, 1984.

———. *Pharisees, Scribes and Sadducees: A Sociological Approach.* Wilmington, DE: Glazier, 1988.

Sandel, Michael J. "What Isn't for Sale." *The Atlantic* 1 (April 2012) http://www.theatlantic.com/magazine/archive/2012/04/what-isnt-for-sale/308902/.

———. *What Money Can't Buy: The Moral Limits of Markets.* New York: Farrar, Straus & Giroux, 2012.

Sanders, E. P. *Jesus and Judaism.* Philadelphia: Fortress, 1985.

Sanders, Irwin T. *Rural Society.* Foundations of Modern Sociology Series. Englewood Cliffs, NJ: Prentice-Hall, 1977.

Schaberg, Jane. *The Illegitimacy of Jesus: A Feminist Theological Interpretation of the Infancy Narratives.* San Francisco: Harper & Row, 1987.

Scheidel, Walter. "Demography." In *The Cambridge Economic History of the Greco-Roman World*, edited by Walter Scheidel, Ian Morris, and Richard Saller, 38–86. Cambridge: Cambridge University Press, 2007.

———. "Emperors, Aristocrats, and the Grim Reaper: Towards a Demographic Profile of the Roman Élite." *Classical Quarterly* n.s. 49 (1999) 254–81.

Schneider, Helmuth. "Technology." In *The Cambridge Economic History of the Greco-Roman World*, edited by Walter Scheidel, Ian Morris, and Richard Saller, 144–71. Cambridge: Cambridge University Press, 2007.

Schneider, Jane. "Of Vigilance and Virgins: Honor, Shame and Access to Resources in Mediterranean Societies." *Ethnology* 10 (1971) 1–24.

Schürer, Emil. *The History of the Jewish People in the Age of Jesus Christ (175 B.C.–A.D. 135).* A New English Version. Edited by Geza Vermes, Fergus Millar, and Matthew Black. 4 vols. Edinburgh: T. & T. Clark, 1973–1987.

Scott, Bernard Brandon. *Hear Then the Parable: A Commentary on the Parables of Jesus.* Minneapolis: Fortress, 1989.

Scott, James C. *Domination and the Arts of Resistance: Hidden Transcripts.* New Haven: Yale University Press, 1990.

———. *The Moral Economy of the Peasant: Rebellion and Subsistence in Southeast Asia.* New Haven: Yale University Press, 1976.

Scroggs, Robin. *Paul for a New Day*. 1978. Reprint, Eugene, OR: Wipf & Stock, 2002.

Sen, Amartya. *Development as Freedom*. New York: Anchor, 1999.

Shanin, Teodor, ed. *Peasants and Peasant Societies: Selected Readings*. Harmondsworth, UK: Penguin, 1971.

Shelton, Jo-Ann. *As the Romans Did: A Source Book in Roman Social History*. New York: Oxford University Press, 1998.

Sheppard, Gerald T. "Childs, Brevard." In *Historical Handbook of Major Biblical Interpreters*, edited by Donald K. McKim, 575–84. Downers Grove, IL: InterVarsity, 1998.

Shermer, Michael. *The Mind of the Market: How Biology and Psychology Shape Our Economic Lives*. New York: Holt Paperback, 2007.

Shroder, J. F., Jr., and M. Inbar. "Geologic and Geographic Background to the Bethsaida Excavations." In *Bethsaida: A City by the North Shore of the Sea of Galilee*, edited by Rami Arav and Richard A. Freund, 1:65–98. 4 vols. Kirksville, MO: Truman University Press, 1995–2009.

Sidebotham, Steven E. "Trade and Commerce (Roman)." In *ABD* 6:629–33.

Sjøberg, Gideon. *The Preindustrial City: Past and Present*. New York: Free Press, 1960.

Skinner, Quentin. *The Return of Grand Theory in the Human Sciences*. Cambridge: Cambridge University Press, 1985.

Smith, Dan. *The Penguin State of the World Atlas*. 8th ed. New York: Penguin, 2008.

Smith, Daniel A. "Discussion of the Books of Sarah Rollens, *Framing Social Criticism in the Jesus Movement* and of Giovanni Bazzana, *Kingdom of Bureaucracy: The Political Theology of Village Scribes in the Sayings Gospel Q*." *Annali Di Storia Dell'esegesi* 34,1 (2017) 229–69.

Smith, Robert H. *Easter Gospels: The Resurrection of Jesus according to the Four Evangelists*. Minneapolis: Augsburg, 1983.

Snell, Daniel C. "Trade and Commerce (ANE)." In *ABD* 6:625–29.

Sombart, Werner. "Der Moderne Kapitalismus." In Sorokin, et al. *A Systematic Source Book in Rural Sociology*, 1:170–84.

Sorokin, Pitirim Aledsandrovich, Carle C. Zimmerman, and Charles Josiah Galpin, eds. *A Systematic Source Book in Rural Sociology*. 3 vols. New York: Russell & Russell, 1930–1932.

Spielberg, Steven, dir. *Munich*. Written by Tony Kushner et al. Produced by Dreamworks Pictures, Universal Pictures, 2005. 2 DVDs (collector's set). Universal City, CA: Universal Studios Home Entertainment, 2006.

Stegemann, Ekkehard, and Wolfgang Stegemann. *The Jesus Movement: A Social History of Its First Century*. Translated by O. C. Dean Jr. Minneapolis: Fortress, 1999.

Stendahl, Krister. "Biblical Theology, Contemporary." In *IDB*, 1:418–32.

———. *The School of St. Matthew: And Its Use of the Old Testament*. 2nd ed. Philadelphia: Fortress, 1968.

Stepansky, Yosef, Yizhar Hirschfeld, and Oren Gutfeld. "Tiberias." In *The New Encyclopedia of Archaeological Excavations in the Holy Land: Supplementary Volume*, edited by Ephraim Stern, 5:2048–54. 5 vols. New York: Simon & Schuster, 1993, 2008.

Stern, Ephraim, ed. *The New Encyclopedia of Archaeological Excavations in the Holy Land*. 5 vols. New York: Simon & Schuster, 1993, 2008.

Stewart, Eric C. *Gathered Around Jesus: An Alternative Spatial Practice in the Gospel of Mark*. Matrix 6. Eugene, OR: Cascade Books, 2009.

———. "Mark and Space in Recent Discussion." In *Gathered Around Jesus: An Alternative Spatial Practice in the Gospel of Mark*, 1–29.

Strange, James F. "The Galilean Road System." In *Galilee in the Late Second Temple and Mishnaic Periods*. Vol. 1, *Life, Culture, and Society*, edited by David A. Fiensy and James Riley Strange, 263–71. Minneapolis: Fortress, 2014.

Strange, James F., Dennis Groh, and Thomas Longstaff. "Excavations at Sepphoris: The Location and Identification of Shikhin, Part 1." *IEJ* 44 (1994) 216–27.

———. "Excavations at Sepphoris: The Location and Identification of Shikhin, Part 2." *IEJ* 45 (1995) 171–87.

Strange, James F., and Eric M. Meyers. *Archaeology, the Rabbis, and Early Christianity*. Nashville: Abingdon, 1981.

Strickert, Fred. *Philip's City*. Collegeville, MN: Glazier, 2011.

Stuhlmacher, Peter. *Historical Criticism and Theological Interpretation of Scripture: Toward a Hermeneutics of Consent*. Philadelphia: Fortress, 1977.

Suetonius (Gaius Suetonius Tranquillus). *The Lives of the Twelve Caesars*. Translated by Joseph Gavorse. New York: Modern Library, 1931.

Suter, David W. "Enoch in Sheol: Updating the Dating of the Book of Parables." In *Enoch and the Messiah Son of Man: Revisiting the Book of Parables*, edited by Gabriele Boccaccini, 415–43. Grand Rapids: Eerdmans, 2007.

———. "Why Galilee? Galilean Regionalism in the Interpretation of 1 Enoch 6—16." *Henoch* 25 (2003) 167–212.

Syon, Danny. *Small Change in Hellenistic-Roman Galilee*. Numismatic Studies and Researches 11. Jerusalem: Israel Numismatic Society, 2015.

Tacitus, Cornelius. *Dialogus, Agricola, Germania*. Translated by William Peterson and Maurice Hutton. LCL. 4 vols. New York: Macmillan, 1914.

Tappert, Theodore G. *The Book of Concord: The Confessions of the Evangelical Lutheran Church*. Philadelphia: Fortress, 1959.

Tawney, R. H. *Religion and the Rise of Capitalism*. Holland Memorial Lectures 1922. New York: Mentor, 1954.

Taylor, Mark C. *Critical Terms for Religious Studies*. Chicago: University of Chicago Press, 1998.

Tcherikover, Victor. "Palestine under the Ptolemies (A Contribution to the Study of the Zenon Papyri)." *Mizraim: Journal of Papyrology, Egyptology, History of Ancient Laws, and Their Relations to the Civilizations of Bible Lands* 4–5 (1937) 1–90.

Tertullian (Quintus Septimius Florens Tertullianus). *Adversus Marcionem*. Translated by Ernest Evans. Oxford: Clarendon, 1972.

Theissen, Gerd. *Biblical Faith: An Evolutionary Perspective*. Translated by John Bowden. Philadelphia: Fortress, 1985.

———. *A Critical Faith: A Case for Religion*. Translated by John Bowden. Philadelphia: Fortress, 1979.

———. *The Gospels in Context: Social and Political History in the Synoptic Tradition*. Translated by Linda M. Maloney. Minneapolis: Fortress, 1991.

Theissen, Gerd, and Annette Merz. *The Historical Jesus: A Comprehensive Guide*. Translated by John Bowden. Minneapolis: Fortress, 1998.

Theophrastus. *The Characters of Theophrastus; Herodes, Cercidas, and the Greek Choliambic Poets (Except Callimachus and Babrius)*. Translated by J. M. Edmonds. LCL. Cambridge: Harvard University Press, 1929.

Thorner, Daniel. "Peasantry." In *International Encyclopedia of the Social Sciences*, edited by David L. Sills, 2:503–11. 17 vols. New York: Macmillan, 1968.

Tillich, Paul. *The Dynamics of Faith*. New York: Harper Torchbooks, 1957.

———. *The Future of Religions*. Edited by J. C. Brauer. New York: Harper & Row, 1966.

———. "The Permanent Significance of the Catholic Church for Protestantism." *Protestant Digest* 3 (February–March 1941) 23–31.

———. *The Protestant Era.* Translated by James Luther Adams. Chicago: Phoenix, 1957.

———. "The Protestant Principle and the Proletarian Situation." In *The Protestant Era*, 161–81.

———. "The Religious Symbol." *Daedalus* 87 (1958) 3–21.

———. *The Socialist Decision.* Translated by Franklin Sherman. 1977. Reprint, Eugene, OR: Wipf & Stock, 2012.

———. *Systematic Theology.* 3 vols. Chicago: University of Chicago Press, 1951–1963.

Toorn, Karel van der. *Scribal Culture and the Making of the Hebrew Bible.* Cambridge: Harvard University Press, 2007.

Torvend, Samuel. *Luther and the Hungry Poor: Gathered Fragments.* 2008. Reprint, Eugene, OR: Wipf & Stock, 2018.

Toulmin, Stephen E. *Cosmopolis: The Hidden Agenda of Modernity.* New York: Free Press, 1990.

Toynbee, Arnold J. "Review of Wittfogel's *Oriental Despotism.*" *American Political Science Review* 52 (1958) 195–98.

Troeltsch, Ernst. *The Social Teaching of the Christian Churches.* 2 vols. Translated by Olive Wyon. New York: Macmillan, 1931.

Tuckett, Christopher M. *Q and the History of Early Christianity: Studies in Q.* Peabody, MA: Hendrickson, 1996.

Turner, Bryan S. "Outline of a Theory of Orientalism." In *Readings in Orientalism*, Vol. 1, *Orientalism: Early Sources*, edited by Bryan S. Turner, 1–31. London: Routledge, 2000.

———. *Marx and the End of Orientalism.* Controversies in Sociology 70. Boston: Allen & Unwin, 1979.

Turner, Victor Witter. *Dramas, Fields, and Metaphors Symbolic Action in Human Society.* Ithaca, NY: Cornell University Press, 1974.

———. *The Ritual Process Structure and Anti-Structure.* Lewis Henry Morgan Lectures. London: Routledge and Kegan Paul, 1969.

Udoh, Fabian. "Taxation and Other Sources of Government Income in the Galilee of Herod and Antipas." In *Galilee in the Late Second Temple and Mishnaic Periods.* Vol. 1, *Life, Culture, and Society*, edited by David A. Fiensy and James Riley Strange, 366–87. Minneapolis: Fortress, 2014.

Ulmer, Rivka. *The Evil Eye in the Bible and in Rabbinic Literature.* Hoboken, NJ: Ktav, 1994.

Van Aarde, Andries. *Fatherless in Galilee: Jesus as a Child of God.* Harrisburg, PA: Trinity, 2001.

Van der Spek, Robartus J. "The Hellenistic Near East." In *The Cambridge Economic History of the Greco-Roman World*, edited by Walter Scheidel, Ian Morris, and Richard Saller, 409–33. Cambridge: Cambridge University Press, 2007.

Van Leeuwen, Bas, Peter Földvari, and Reinhard Pirngruber. "Markets in Pre-Industrial Societies: Storage in Hellenistic Babylonia in the English Mirror." *CGEH Working Paper Series No. 0003 1.* Utrecht University, Centre for Global Economic History (January 2011). http://www.cgeh.nl/working-paper-series.

Varro, Marcus Terentius. *Marcus Porcius Cato, On Agriculture; Marcus Terentius Varro, On Agriculture.* Translated by William Davis Hooper and Harrison Boyd Ash. Rev. ed. LCL. Cambridge: Harvard University Press, 1935.

Venturi, Franco. "Oriental Despotism." *Journal of the History of Ideas* 24 (1963) 133–42.

Wachsmann, Shelley. *The Sea of Galilee Boat: An Extraordinary 2000 Year Old Discovery.* Cambridge, MA: Perseus, 2000.

Waetjen, Herman C. *A Reordering of Power: A Socio-Political Reading of Mark's Gospel.* 1989. Reprint, Eugene, OR: Wipf & Stock, 2014.

Weber, Max. *Economy and Society: An Outline of Interpretive Sociology,* edited by Günther Roth and Claus Wittich. 2 vols. Berkeley: University of California Press, 1978.

———. "Peasant Religion and Its Ideological Glorification." In *Economy and Society,* 468–72.

———. "Religious Rejections of the World and Their Directions." In *From Max Weber: Essays in Sociology,* edited by Hans Heinrich Gerth and C. Wright Mills, 323–59. New York: Oxford University Press, 1958.

———. *The Sociology of Religion.* Translated by Ephraim Fischoff. Introduction by Talcott Parsons. Boston: Beacon, 1963.

———. "The Social Psychology of the World Religions." In *From Max Weber: Essays in Sociology,* edited by Hans Heinrich Gerth and C. Wright Mills, 267–301. New York: Oxford University Press, 1958.

Weiss, Zeev. "Sepphoris." In *The New Encyclopedia of Archaeological Excavations in the Holy Land,* edited by Ephraim Stern, 4:1324–28. New York: Simon & Schuster, 1993, 2008.

Wellhausen, Julius. *Einleitung in die Drei Ersten Evangelien.* Berlin: Reimer, 1905.

Werner, Heinz. *Comparative Psychology of Mental Development.* Rev. ed. New York: International Universities Press, 1957.

Werner, Heinz, and Bernard Kaplan. "The Developmental Approach to Cognition: Its Relevance to the Psychological Interpretation of Anthropological and Ethnolinguistic Data." *American Anthropologist* 58 (1956) 866–80.

———. *Symbol Formation: An Organismic-Developmental Approach to Language and the Expression of Thought.* New York: Wiley, 1963.

White, K. D. *Greek and Roman Technology.* Aspects of Greek and Roman Life. Ithaca, NY: Cornell University Press, 1984.

Wilson, Carol G. *For I Was Hungry and You Gave Me Food: Pragmatics of Food Access in the Gospel of Matthew.* Eugene, OR: Pickwick Publications, 2014.

Wilson, Stephen G. "Voluntary Associations: An Overview." In *Voluntary Associations in the Greco-Roman World,* edited by John S. Kloppenborg and Stephen G. Wilson, 1–15. New York: Routledge, 1996.

Wink, Walter. *The Human Being: Jesus and the Enigma of the Son of Man.* Minneapolis: Fortress, 2001.

Wittfogel, Karl A. *Oriental Despotism: A Comparative Study of Total Power.* New Haven: Yale University Press, 1957.

———. "Results and Problems of the Study of Oriental Despotism." *Journal of Asian Studies* 28 (1969) 357–65.

Wolf, Eric R. *Peasants.* Foundations of Modern Anthropology Series. Englewood Cliffs, NJ: Prentice-Hall, 1966.

———. *Peasant Wars of the Twentieth Century.* New York: Harper Torchbooks, 1969.

Wuellner, Wilhelm H. *The Meaning of "Fishers of Men."* New Testament Library. Philadelphia: Westminster, 1967.

Wuthnow, Robert. *God and Mammon in America.* New York: Simon & Schuster, 1998.

Yoder, John Howard. *The Politics of Jesus: Vicit Agnus Noster.* Grand Rapids: Eerdmans, 1972.

Youtie, Herbert C. "*Hypographeus:* The Social Impact of Illiteracy in Graeco-Roman Egypt." *Zeitschrift für Papyrologie und Epigraphik* 17 (1975) 201–21.

Zahavy, Tzvee. *Studies in Jewish Prayer.* Studies in Judaism. Lanham, NY: University Press of America, 1990.

Index of Ancient Documents

HEBREW BIBLE

Index of Subjects

Malaria, 63, 188

Malina, Bruce, J., 18–19, 23–24, 28, 31, 90

Malinowski, Bronislaw, 192n24, 193

Mammon, 3–7, 13–17, 29, 36, 40, 53, 72, 87, 93–94, 142, 145, 199, 203

Marcion, 148–49, 155

Markets, 43, 46n23, 107, 143–47, 196
Galilee, 39–40, 57, 71, 79
local, 40, 48–49, 60, 74, 76–77, 139

Marx, Karl, 27, 42–43, 46, 54, 121, 193n30

McFague, Sallie
metaphorical theology, 195, 197

Mediterranean culture, 18–19, 20
core values, 23, 28–31, 56, 66, 123, 133, 201
honor and shame, 19, 123, 133, 177
Roman imperial Mediterranean, 25, 74, 81

Miqva'oth, 81–82

Mintz, Sidney, 43, 54–55

Models, see also History
cross-cultural understanding, 19, 176
homomorphic, isomorphic, 56n47, 70
necessity of models, 53n36

Money
bronze or copper (token), 39–40, 49, 57–58, 74, 77
coin profiles, 58–59
imperial, 8, 11, 58, 60, 77
political function, 29, 125
silver, 8, 29, 40, 49, 58, 71, 74, 77

Moses, 68n24

Nehemiah, 125
food ration, 138

Oakman, Douglas E.
Philippians Christ Hymn translation, 170–71

Parsons, Talcott
human condition, 156–57, 193

Passover, 12, 14–15, 29, 84–85, 88, 108, 111, 113–14, 126–27, 185

Patronage politics, 35, 49, 52, 56–58, 67, 83, 85–86
Galilee, 72–73, 87
Herod the Great, 69

Paul
assemblies (ekklēsiai), 88, 124–25, 128, 130
Greco-Roman pluralism, 166, 173–74

Peasant, see also Agriculture, Economy
anthropology, 18–19, 26, 43, 195
core values, 47–49, 52–53
criticism, 54–56
definition, 43, 46, 54–55
modern farmer, 48–49, 60
multidimensional concept, 56
peasant society, 22–23, 51
religion, 24
resistance, 8–9, 11, 15, 110
revolt, 9, 53, 72, 76
writing, 10, 27, 89–91, 105, 108

Pharisees, 9, 69, 77, 83–84, 88, 95, 100–101, 108–9, 113–15, 129, 189

Philippians Christ Hymn, 168–69, 172–73, 188

Polanyi, Karl, 15, 45–46, 119, 122–23, 143–44, 146

Political economy, see Economy

Politics, see Patronage politics

Population, 34, 36–37, 51, 55, 59n58, 136
Galilee, 51n34, 63, 75–76
global population and wealth in 2006, 145
Sepphoris and Tiberias, 51n34

Priests, see Temple in Jerusalem

Production
agrarian, 8, 19–22, 25–28, 34–38, 42, 45, 47–53, 55–59, 69–71, 74–77, 87, 128, 135, 141–42

CPSIA information can be obtained
at www.ICGtesting.com
Printed in the USA
FSHW011217250221
78927FS

9 781725 286641